IMAGES
of America

FOUNTAIN

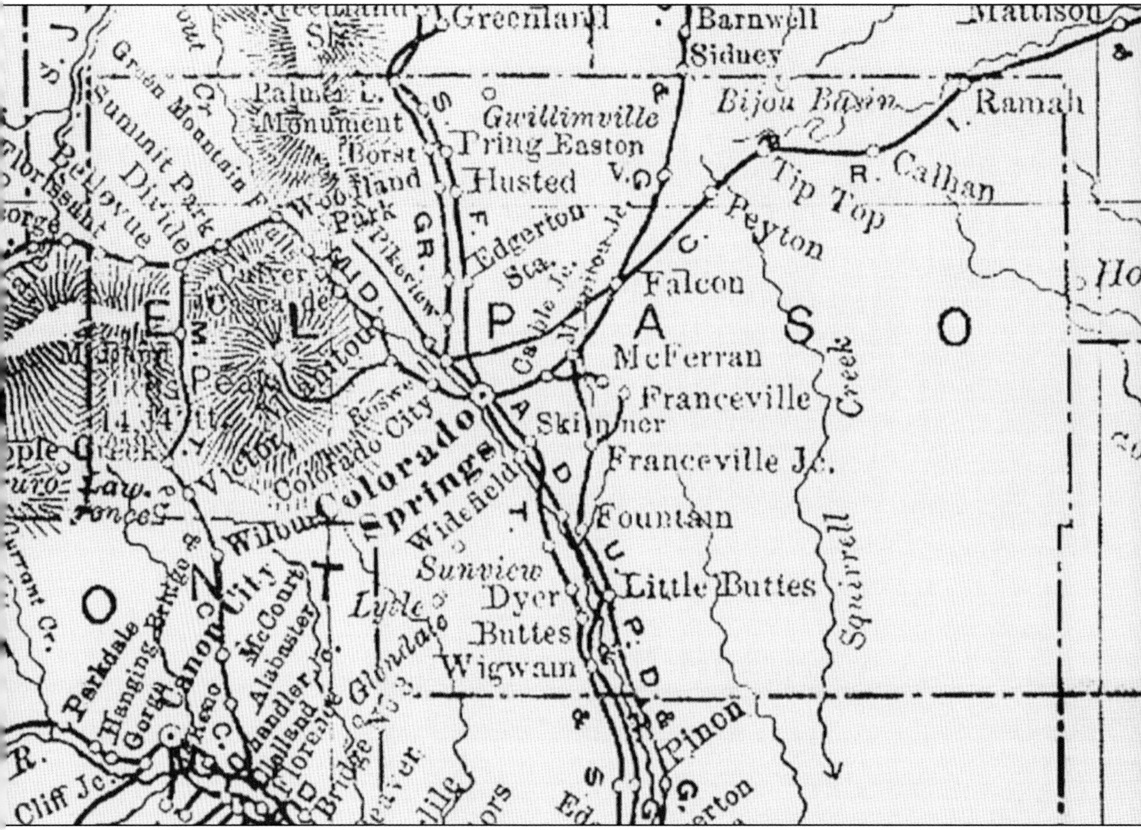

This 1896 map of El Paso County is helpful when looking for places mentioned in this pictorial history. Fountain is in the lower central portion of the county, with Lytle, Buttes, and Wigwam all to the south and west. To the northeast is Franceville. Widefield, Colorado Springs, Colorado City, Manitou, and Pikes Peak are all to the northwest. (ML.)

On the Cover: Everyone from near and far is welcome to attend Fountain's fall festival. In the 1920s, this event featured several types of foot races along Main Street. Today, the Fountain Fall Festival is held on Labor Day, and Fountain continues to welcome people from all around to enjoy the parade, festivities, and food. (NT.)

IMAGES
of America

FOUNTAIN

Angela Thaden Hahn

ARCADIA
PUBLISHING

ISBN 978-0-7385-9503-0

Published by Arcadia Publishing
Charleston, South Carolina

Printed in the United States of America

Library of Congress Control Number: 2012939528

For all general information, please contact Arcadia Publishing:
Telephone 843-853-2070
Fax 843-853-0044
E-mail sales@arcadiapublishing.com
For customer service and orders:
Toll-Free 1-888-313-2665

Visit us on the Internet at www.arcadiapublishing.com

To my husband and best friend, Michael, for his selfless encouragement and support

Contents

FOREWORD

Even if you are not a Fountain resident, you'll enjoy these photographs of life in small-town Colorado! Extensively researched with never-before-published photographs gathered from a wide range of local sources and families, this book portrays the charm of local life.

From its beginning during the Colorado Gold Rush, through the heyday of ranchers and the railroad and now as a bedroom community of Fort Carson, Fountain is one of the oldest towns in Colorado. It has a rich and colorful past that few are aware of. This book shares some of its stories, struggles, and triumphs through the use of photographs that have been collected from the Fountain Valley Historical Society and Museum, longtime residents, and regional archives.

The staff of the Fountain Library and the Fountain Museum welcomes you to stop by and learn more about the Fountain!

Pamela J. Owens
Librarian, Fountain Library

Acknowledgments

Much gratitude goes out to the ladies of the Fountain Valley Historical Society and Museum, who welcomed this project.

Special, heartfelt thanks go to fellow historians Pam, Pat, and Elaine. All three provided historical material and offered continual encouragement. Also, Pam, along with my mother, Nancy, helped me edit the text.

Professional images of Fountain and its environs are rare, and personally owned cameras were not common; therefore, this publication relies heavily on amateur photographs in the possession of a few generous longtime residents whose histories with Fountain go back generations. Many of the pictures published here are familiar, but quite a few have not been shared until now. Information for the images was obtained from the owners of the photographs, censuses, maps, oral histories, general encyclopedias, and news articles.

This volume is not meant to replace but rather sit alongside the few previously published histories of Fountain.

The collection of images in this volume appear courtesy of Ann Hanna (AH); Angela Thaden Hahn (ATH); Ben Arellano (BA); Betty Powell (BP); Special Collections, Tutt Library, Colorado College, Colorado Springs, Colorado (CC); Dorothy Christian Boyd (DB); Donna Whalen Koop (DK); Elsie Masters (EM); El Paso County Courthouse (EPC); 4th Infantry Division Fort Carson Museum (FCM); Fountain-Fort Carson School District No. 8 (FFCSD); Florence Wallace Paradise and Peggy Wallace King (FPPK); Fountain Valley Historical Society and Museum (FVM); El Paso County and Fountain Valley Advertiser and News (FVN); Bureau of Land Management Government Land Office Records (GLO); Jim Chancellor (JC); Jay Frost, photographs by Myron Wood (JF); Kathy Duran (KD); Leroy Turner (LT); Mary Seymour Baker (MB); Mildred Chenoweth (MC); Memoriallibrary.com (ML); Meridee Dunn (MD); Moises Martinez (MM); Nancy Bright Thaden (NBT); Neva Torbit (NT); Colorado Springs Pioneers Museum (PM); Special Collections, Pikes Peak Library District, photographs by Andrew Gulliford (PPLD); Richard Williams (RW); and Wendy Sample Speckman (WS).

INTRODUCTION

This pictorial history of Fountain is arranged chronologically and divided into the town's natural phases. Chapter one begins with settlement in a valley void of anything but its indigenous people, the river, and passersby. Chapter two covers the farmers and ranchers who turned the valley into an agricultural paradise. Following in chapter three are the railroads that surged through town, changing the look and sound of the landscape and bringing more people from the East. The village prospered and flourished, and featured in chapter four is the oldest part of town, bounded roughly by Fountain Street on the west, Wellington Street on the north, the Denver & Rio Grande Railroad on the east, and Indiana Avenue on the south. Finally, the last phase in Fountain's history is summed up in chapter five with various definitions of the word *community*.

The town of Fountain was founded near where Jimmy Camp Creek meets Fountain Creek in a long, lazy valley. The closest towns were Pueblo to the south and Colorado City to the northwest. Pikes Peak, snowcapped much of the year, looms above the mountains on the western horizon.

The river in this valley has long been a companion to the road beside it. Known as the Cherokee Trail, it was traversed by nomadic Indians, French fur trappers, Spanish and American explorers, burly freighters, gold and silver miners, lurching stagecoaches, Army soldiers, and hopeful homesteaders. Additionally, the First Colorado Volunteers marched through here on their way to New Mexico during the Civil War.

By 1862, Rhode Island native Thomas Owen found some well-watered acreage to his liking near the confluence of the Fontaine qui Bouille and a creek named the Little Fontaine qui Bouille. Known by everyone as "Tom," he had passed through this spot a time before and made a mental note of its tree-lined river, location to the main road, and farming potential. Within a year, he had staked his claim in the valley and was quite possibly the first settler of Fountain's environs.

Mathias and Barbara Lock left the gold fields near Denver to try their luck in California. Upon entering the beautiful valley and seeing its agrarian potential, they decided to acquire gold here in the form of grain. A miller by trade, Lock put his millstones to use as soon as his first crop came in.

Amos and Mary Terrell homesteaded on Jimmy Camp Creek with her brothers Isaac and Henry Hutchin nearby. The Cherokee Trail was frequently used by travelers on horse, wagon, and stagecoach seeking to hook up with major roads at Denver and Pueblo, and they often stopped at the Terrells' place to rest, freshen up, and enjoy a hot meal. Seeing an opportunity, Amos Terrell built a stage station here and another three miles north on the road that branched off to Colorado City; thus began the settlement of Terrellville on the banks of the Fontaine qui Bouille.

The few pioneers trickling into this region faced many dangers. For instance, about 14 miles to the west on the Little Fontaine qui Bouille, the Espinosa bandits murdered Henry Harkins at his sawmill in 1863. He is buried near that spot in Dead Man's Canyon. Though the havoc they wreaked claimed victims west of the Fountain Valley, one of their brief captives, Eugenia Lucero, later lived in Fountain.

Determined pioneers were well aware of the stories of bloody massacres perpetrated by Indians, especially in the Southwest. Isolated reports of murders came out of the north near Colorado City until about 1868; therefore, whenever the warning went out of an uprising nearby, the settlers retreated to one of four forts in the valley. These were terrifying times until they learned that the Ute Indians were friendly and meant no harm; they were more curious than dangerous. Eventually, many of those early settlers befriended the Utes and welcomed them as guests into their homes.

Land in the valley held a lot of potential if the farmers could just get water to it, so began the work of digging ditches from the river to the farms in order to irrigate for crop growing. Eventually, this portion of the valley became laced with ditches, some several miles long, carrying life-giving water to the dry land. For 100 years, these farmers provided food for the cities at each end of the valley. At first, farmers grew bluestem hay, Mexican beans, apples, and cherries, but many of them switched to sugar beets in the 1920s and 1930s. By the 1960s, sugar production had gone to other countries, and farmers switched to corn and alfalfa.

With the 1871 announcement of the coming Denver & Rio Grande Railroad, many towns, including Fountain, were platted in its path. Terrell and Isaac Hutchin immediately sold off portions of their land for town lots. Farmers and ranchers were attracted to the outlying area for its close proximity to the depot, and merchants set up businesses in the new town, seeing the opportunity to meet the needs of these growers. Interestingly, the names of the eastbound and westbound streets in town identify the eastern states from which many early residents originated.

The Denver & Rio Grande arrived on the east side of town in 1872, and the Santa Fe reached the west side in 1887. Men from the East and the Southwest came to work on the railroad, bringing their families. The railroad provided plenty of steady work and a means of transportation for people seeking to relocate in the West.

It was hoped that Fountain would become a major rail hub in the valley, but that hope was dashed after an 1888 train explosion greatly damaged the town. The opportunity then fell into the lap of Colorado Springs, situated just up the road.

Nevertheless, Fountain steadily grew in all the typical ways: population increased as new additions were built onto the original town, making more residential lots available. While constructing a house on North El Paso Street in 1899, carpenter John Spicer penciled his confession to a murder he committed in 1893 on the back of a piece of molding. Discovered in 1986, long after Spicer had died, the confession was a surprise to Fountain residents, but not so much so to his daughter, the only person left among his family and acquaintances.

Meanwhile, cattle drives passed through on their way to Cheyenne every spring for 20 years on the Goodnight-Loving Trail, which closely followed the old Cherokee Trail up Jimmy Camp Creek. Cowboys came into town on Saturday nights to shoot off their guns and ride their horses on the board sidewalks, lending to a hint of lawlessness. The town incorporated in 1903, bringing with it a town marshal, as well as a new school building, a mayor, and other officials to oversee the town's law enforcement, water supply, electric and phone services, and other improvements.

An influx of farmers and miners of Mexican ancestry from southern Colorado and New Mexico arrived in the 1920s, adding a certain flavor to the town, and this decade saw Fountain flourish and prosper; however, the Depression of the 1930s and the war in the 1940s reduced everyone to the same economic class, and all became equals as they endeavored to come out of hard times. Coal for cooking was picked up along the railroad tracks or hauled by wagon from the Franceville Mine, which was about 15 miles away. The mine also became a source of employment for some of Fountain's men. Other intuitive entrepreneurs started their own businesses in areas where people were willing to spend their money. Various cafés and filling stations sprung up, and Chancellor's pottery factory and trailer park provided for both need and whimsy. Camp Carson became Fountain's new neighbor to the west in 1942, dismantling the ranches in its swathe but bringing much-needed jobs to the Depression-weary residents of Fountain. Uniformed soldiers coming to town by train or bus became a common sight as they trickled money into Fountain's economy. Widefield, located just a few miles north, was joined by the new suburb of Security, and the population in the Fountain Valley increased with active-duty and retired servicemen. Gradually, nearby farms sold out to increasing housing developments. All the while, Fountain continued its relationship with ranching communities to the east and south, namely Squirrel Creek, Hanover, Buttes, and Wigwam.

People who can remember say Fountain was a great place to live and grow up. In this small town, everyone knew everyone else's names. Children's outdoor games overflowed into the yards next door, but the neighbors did not mind. Children walked down the street and around the corner with a dime to the drugstore for candy, small toys, and ice cream cones, and their parents were not afraid. Westerns and cartoons were shown upstairs at the Woodmen Hall on Saturdays for a quarter. The alfalfa fields were so close to town, the sweet smell of freshly mowed hay filled the air. Yards were lush with shade trees, flowers, and victory gardens, and the smell of Mama's home cooking drifted on the breezes. People from the outlying farms still rode their horses into town because Fountain had most everything they needed. A 17¢ Trailways bus trip into Colorado Springs once a month took care of the rest of one's needs or wants. With the help of those who have grown old here and remember when people had time for each other, Fountain's sense of community survives.

Businesses came and went until the town almost dried up in the 1970s. Without revenue, it could not keep up with modern improvements to roads, housing, and utilities. Increased taxes helped rejuvenate the town but not without some urban renewal, in which many of the old structures condemned as unfit were destroyed to make way for modern buildings. Much of Fountain's structural history was taken down with a bulldozer. Realizing the damage done, today's historians and activists work to preserve what is left in order to tell Fountain's rich history.

All who live in the valley know that Fountain is closely associated with Security-Widefield, located a few miles north. Reluctantly, they will not be included in detail in this publication. For this book's purposes, areas outside of Fountain are limited to Mesa Road on the north, Hanover to the east, Buttes and Wigwam to the south, and the eastern portions of Fort Carson on the west. There are quite a few Fountainites and valley dwellers that are descendents of the area's early inhabitants, and it would be impossible to acknowledge all of the early families here. Mention of any early families other than those appearing in this introduction are limited to and determined by the photographs acquired for this work.

One

Resting by the Bubbling Fountain

Long before white men ever set foot in the Pikes Peak region, the Ute Indians frequented the south-flowing river in the long valley lying between two mesas. They came down out of the mountains through the pass west of here to spend the winter camping in the bottomlands near the water's edge.

The presence of French fur trappers in the region is evidenced in the river's original name, the Fontaine qui Bouille. As it came out of the pass, the river must have looked like a bubbling fountain to the trappers

Later, Lt. Zebulon Pike, who was sent to explore this southern region of the newly acquired Louisiana Purchase, is said to have set off in November 1806 from the vicinity of where the Little Fontaine qui Bouille meets the main river to scale the tallest mountain he could see to the west. He did not succeed and turned his ill-equipped men back to the river. He might wince to see so many thousands of people ascending yearly to the top of the mountain that now bears his name.

Settlers began to arrive in the early 1860s. Oliver Cotten and Joseph Robinson claimed homesteads near the cone-shaped hills on the east side of the river; this place would later be called Little Buttes. Thomas Owen staked a claim on the Little Fontaine qui Bouille, west of where it joins the river. Shortly thereafter, a covered wagon heading south on the old Cherokee Road stopped to rest at Owen's unfinished cabin, where he offered to share his fire and the shelter of three walls. During the course of their visit, he convinced the young couple in the wagon, Mathias and Barbara Lock, to homestead in the fertile valley. They chose a place on high ground along the river about two miles north of Owen. Quakers Amos and Mary Terrell headed west at the start of the Civil War to avoid conscription into the military. They homesteaded on the banks of Jimmy Camp Creek, near where it joins the river that later became known as Fountain Creek.

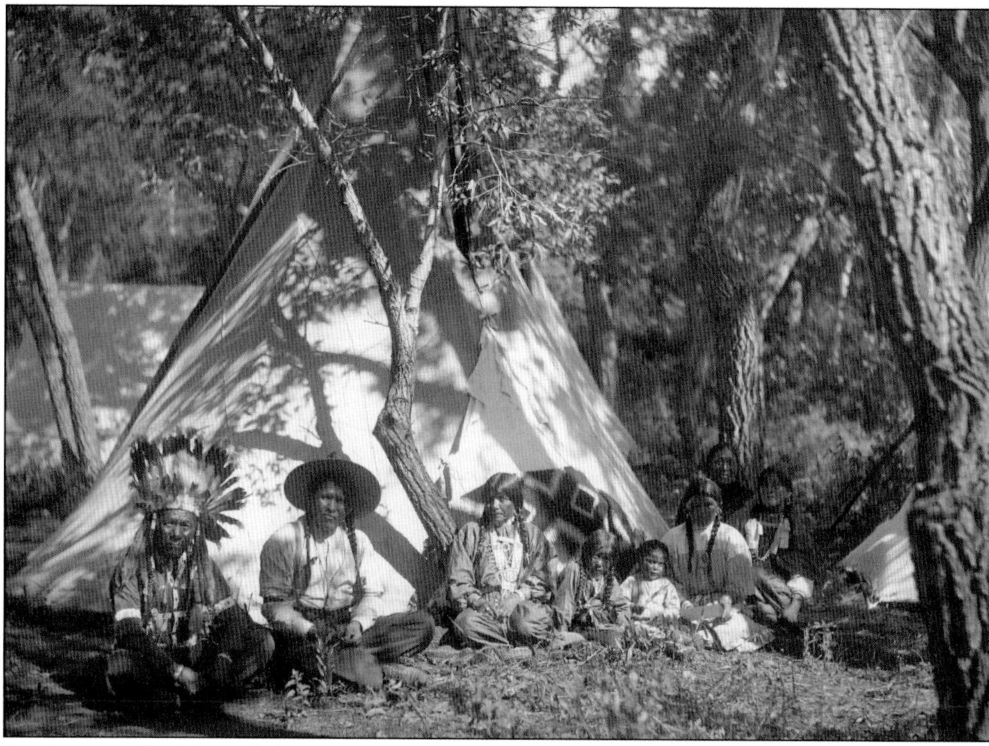

Roads naturally followed the water sources, as did the Cherokee Trail, which paralleled its way along much of the Fontaine qui Bouille. Ute Indians, who historically dwelled along rivers, came down from the mountains during the winter to camp among the giant cottonwood trees and thick willows lining the river's sandy banks. (PM.)

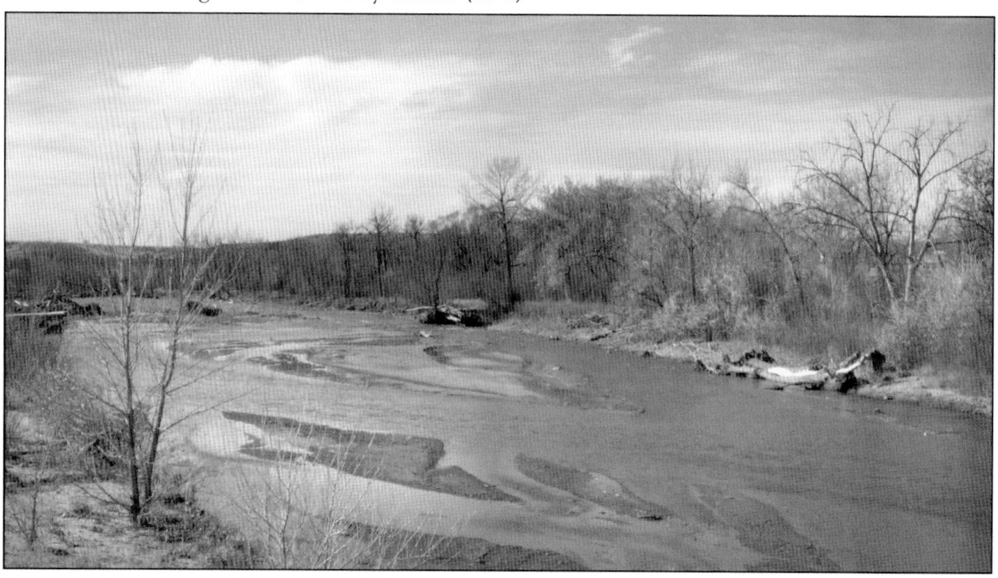

Fountain Creek, seen here in the fall season, originates in the mountains above Manitou and was first named the Fontaine qui Bouille, which is French for "the fountain that boils." In times of spring runoff or flooding, the river does indeed seem to boil as it churns away the banks and rips huge trees out by the roots. (ATH.)

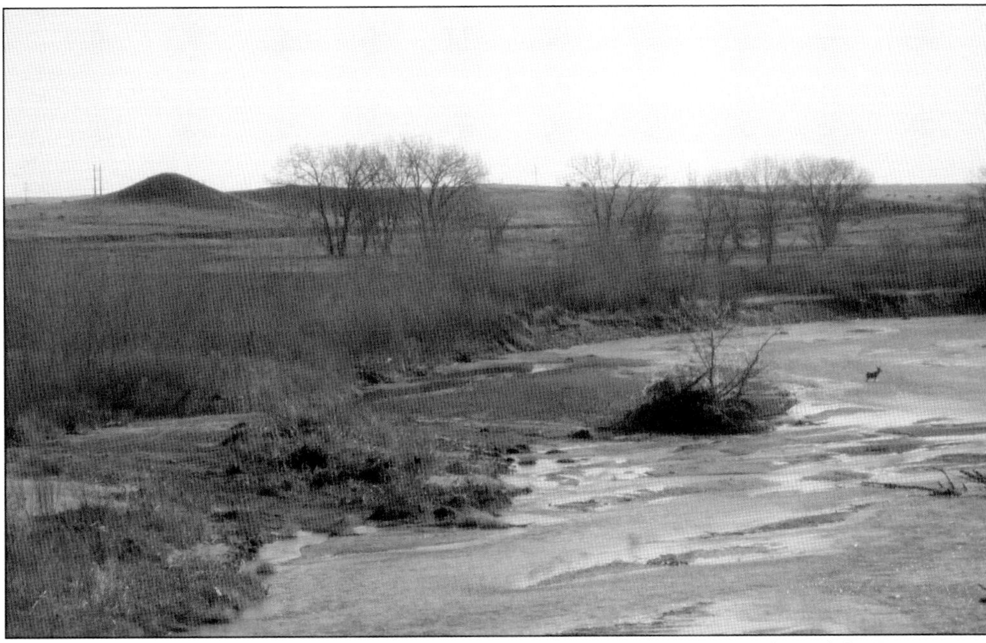

A few miles downstream of Fountain, the river provides water for the ranches of the Buttes area, named for the geologic formations known as Tepee Buttes. One of these buttes can be seen on the left horizon in this picture. Some historians believe it was from this area that Lt. Zebulon Pike set off in an attempt to climb the highest peak to the west. (ATH.)

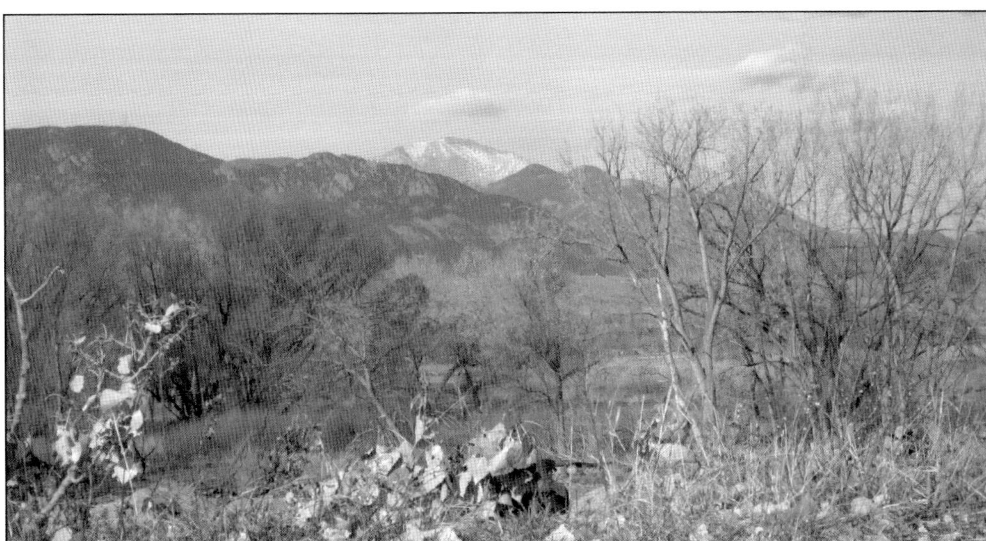

Pikes Peak, named for explorer Lt. Zebulon Pike, has always been a significant landmark in the Pikes Peak region and can be seen from the Fountain Valley and a far distance beyond. In the summer, Fountain Creek looks like a ribbon of green lying loosely across the dry plains as it flows through the valley on its way to the Arkansas River. (ATH.)

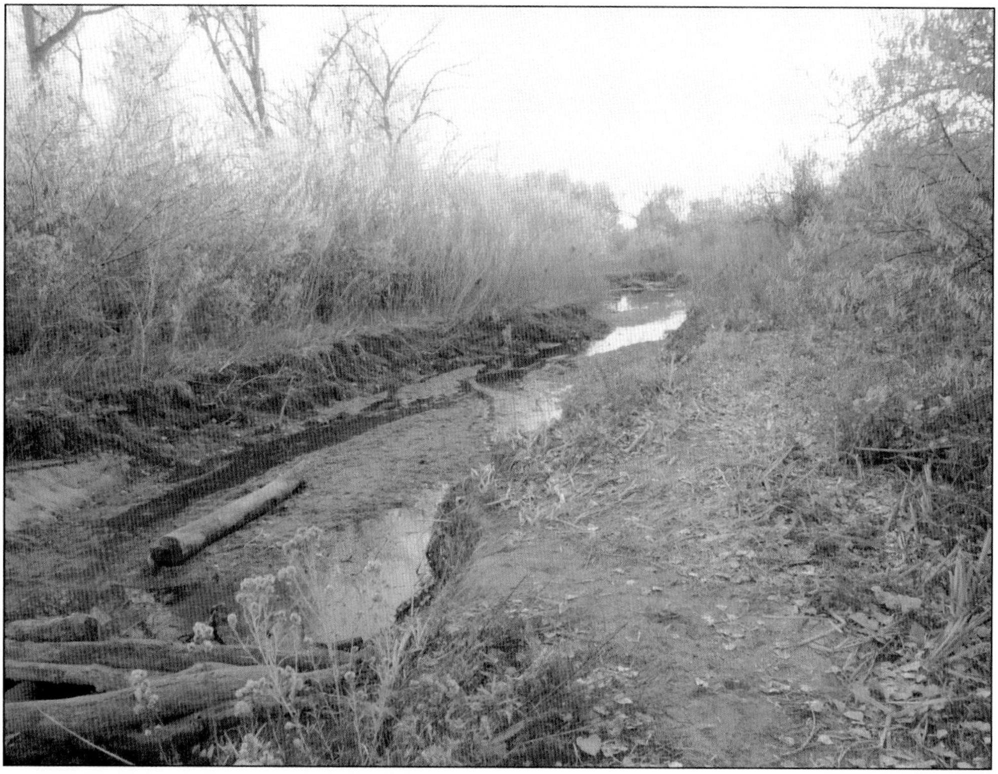

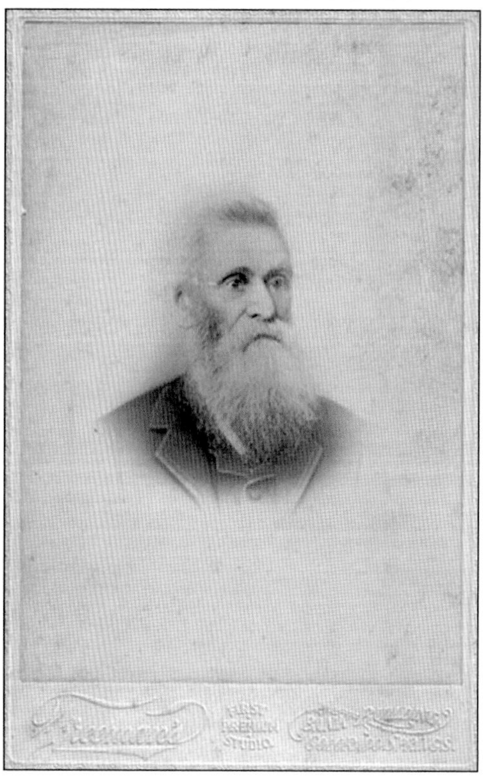

The availability of water was an essential requirement when settlers chose their homesteads. It was on the banks of Jimmy Camp Creek, known locally as Sand Creek, that Amos and Mary Terrell built their home in the early 1860s. Some call it the first house in the county, but that is difficult to confirm since Mathias and Barbara Lock and Thomas Owen were constructing homes at the same time. (ATH.)

Isaac Hutchin made his home near the Fontaine qui Bouille and Jimmy Camp Creek in the early 1860s. He lived near his sister and brother-in-law, Mary and Amos Terrell, and his brother Henry Hutchin, who later died from injuries received in an 1888 train explosion that occurred in Fountain. (MD.)

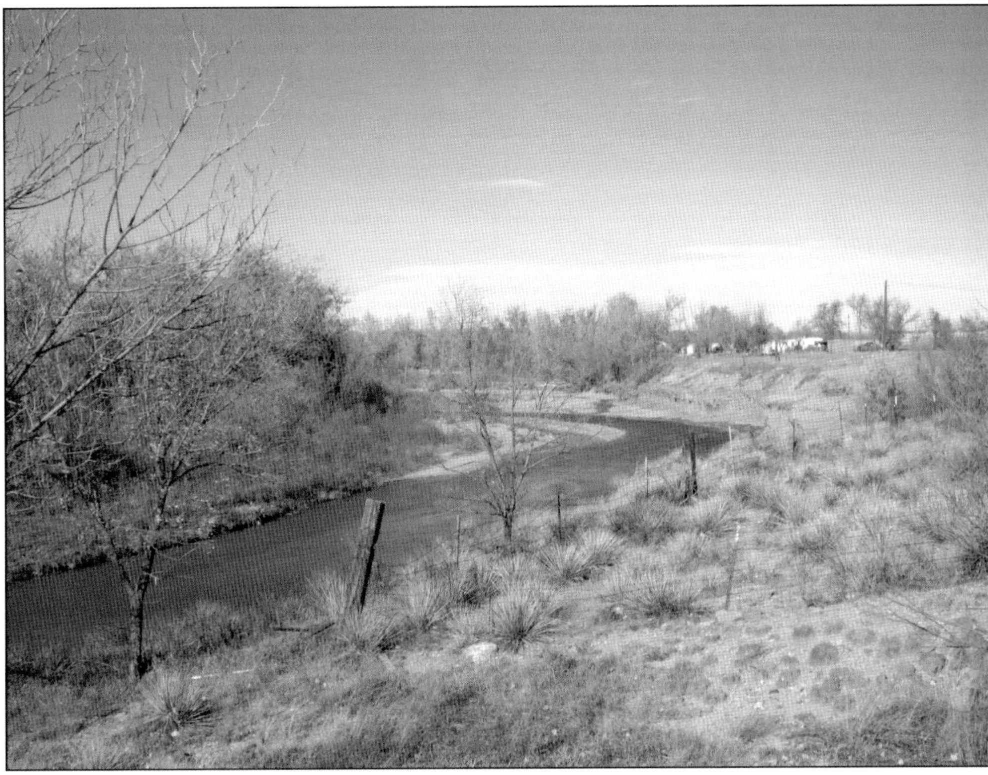

While on their way to California, Mathias and Barbara Lock decided to settle on this high bank along the Fontaine qui Bouille, south of what would later become the town of Fountain. Thomas Owen, who was constructing a cabin farther downstream, became a fast and true lifetime friend. The Lock grain mill, built lower on the water's edge, washed away with one of Fountain Creek's destructive floods. (ATH.)

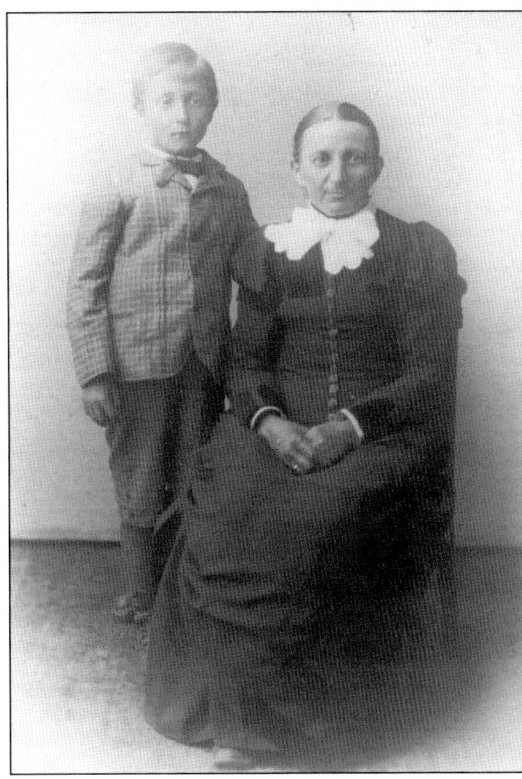

Barbara Lock, posing here next to a son or grandson, was a remarkable pioneer woman. After leaving Germany with her parents and crossing the ocean, they eventually arrived in Illinois where she later married fellow German Mathias Lock. While passing through the fertile valley, they decided to settle south of the future town of Fountain. During her husband's frequent absences, the Lock ranch flourished under her management. (FVM.)

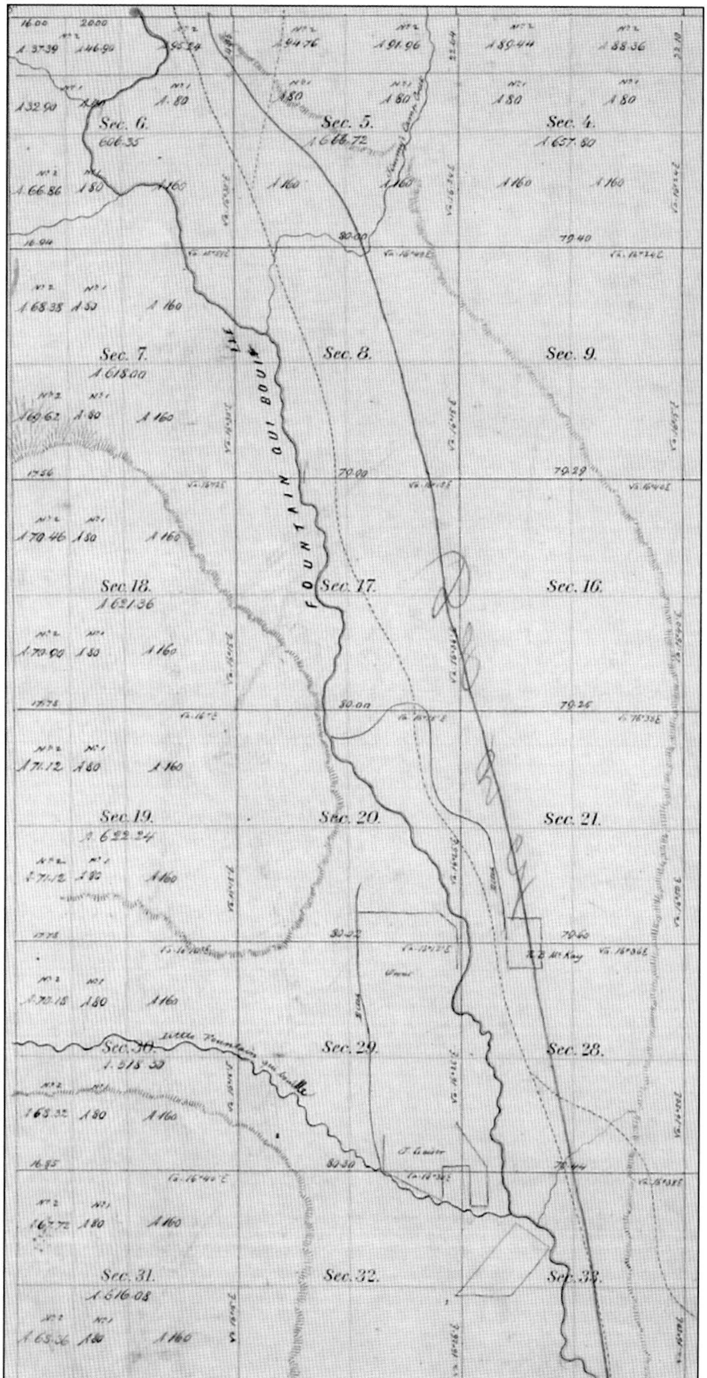

In 1862, there were few settlers in this portion of the valley. Thomas Owns [sic] homesteaded section No. 29 near the Little Fontaine qui Bouille. He had only two neighbors. Irrigation ditches and stage routes are marked with the Denver & Rio Grande line, penciled in 10 years later. After this map was charted, Amos Terrell homesteaded in sections No. 5 and 8, and the Locks homesteaded in section No. 17. (GLO.)

Two

HOMESTEADING ON THE RANGE

Tom Owen spent his time between his properties in Aspen and on Fountain Creek; however, the Locks built up quite a prosperous ranch about a mile south of Fountain.

From the mid-1860s into the early 1870s, settlers worried about Indian attacks. Whenever Indians were seen in the region, the settlers took the precaution of sending the women and children to fortified homes, which they commonly referred to as forts; nevertheless, there never were any attacks in the Fountain Valley, and the settlers learned that the Utes, who were often seen in the valley, were friendly. Eventually, farms and ranches dotted the Denver-to-Pueblo Road that meandered through the valley, while other settlers homesteaded on the adjoining mesas.

With the help of hand-dug ditches, area farms received the water necessary for food production. The change from horse-drawn implements to steam- and gasoline-powered machinery turned the valley into a major farming community. Colorado Springs and Pueblo provided a ready market for the valley's hay, corn, sugar beets, cherries, asparagus, milk, poultry, and beef.

The terms *farm* and *ranch* are used interchangeably to describe the properties in and around the valley. Basically, the difference between the two is that the first grows crops and the latter breeds animals. However, the term *ranch* is commonly used in the southwest to refer to both operations. Likewise, homesites were frequently identified by the word *place*, preceded by the name of the prior owner or sometimes the first owner. In order to avoid confusion, this local terminology must be considered when reading about the rural acreages surrounding Fountain.

It is also helpful to know that the section of the Denver-to-Pueblo Road that connected Fountain to Buttes was bypassed in the early 1930s by the new Highway 85 and then became known as the Old Pueblo Road.

The land south and west of Fountain was more useful for ranching. Cattle ranches west of town were eventually bought from the owners to create a large military installation, and those in the Buttes area southeast of town remain the last cattle-breeding holdouts of the Fountain Valley.

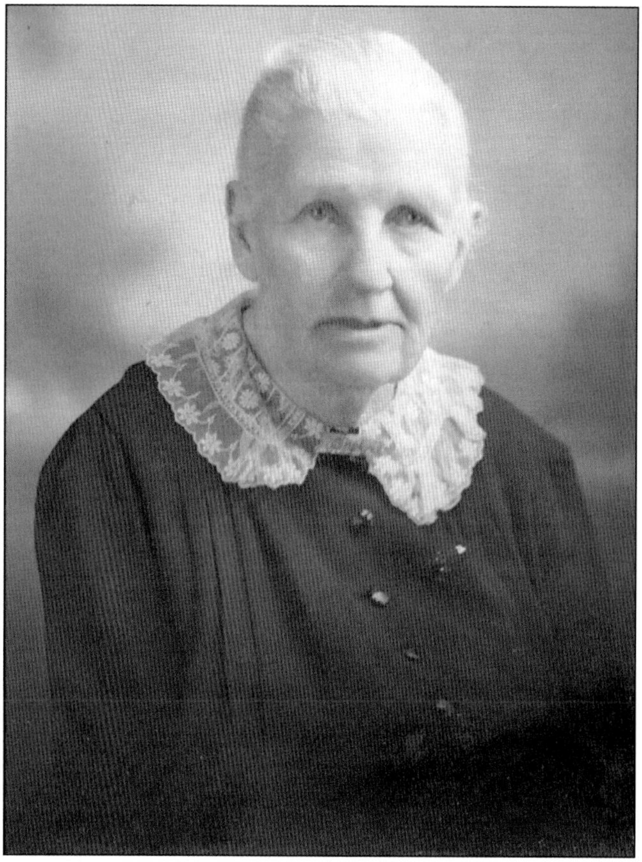

Irene Benedict is considered to be the first white baby born in El Paso County. She was delivered in her family's covered wagon in 1861 in the hills southwest of Fountain. The family had recently arrived from Wisconsin. When the baby's mother died a few weeks later, her father, Henry Morse, gave the infant to the Joseph Robinson family, who lived in the Buttes area. (FVM.)

Indians of the Ute tribe were friendly. They were a familiar sight as they rode past settlers' homes, sometimes peering in the windows. Often, the Indians stopped to visit and especially enjoyed sampling fresh biscuits. (PM.)

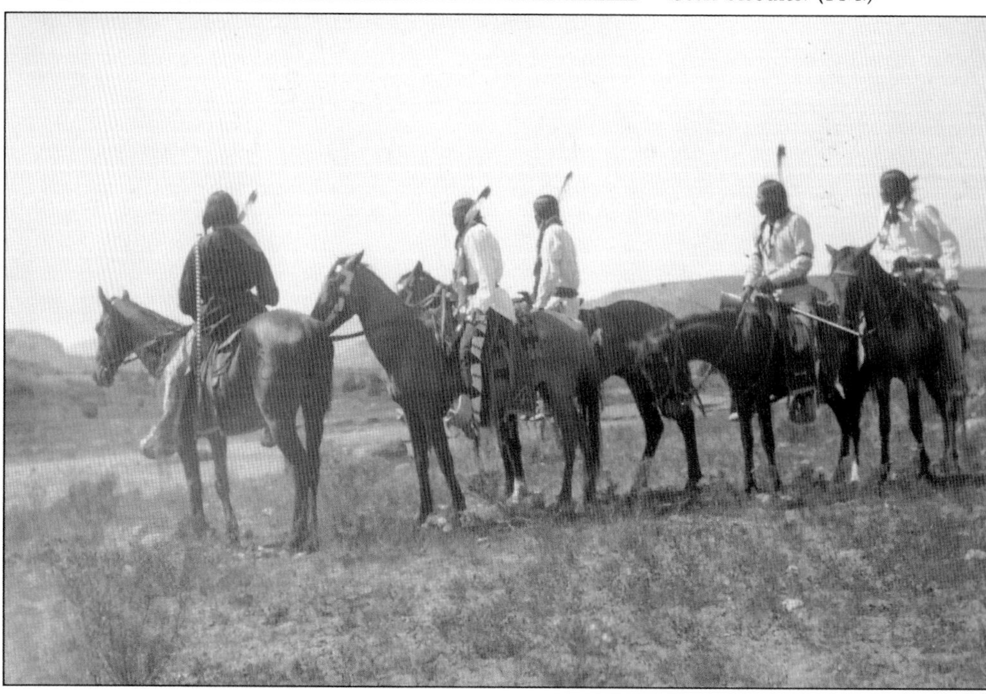

Remodeling began around 1950 on this 1885 structure that served as the second home of Fountain pioneers Mathias and Barbara Lock. The walls were built of an early form of concrete commonly referred to as grout by early homesteaders in this region. This solution was a mixture of sand, cementitious material, rocks, and water. Homes made of grout compared favorably to those made of sod and adobe. (BP.)

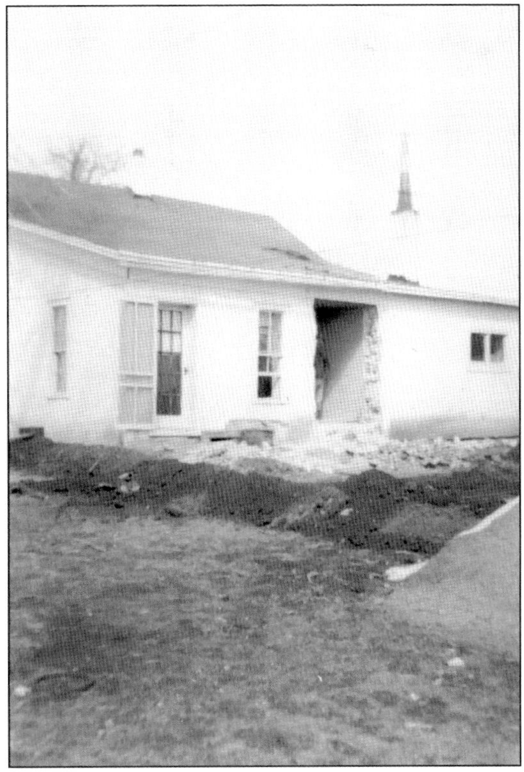

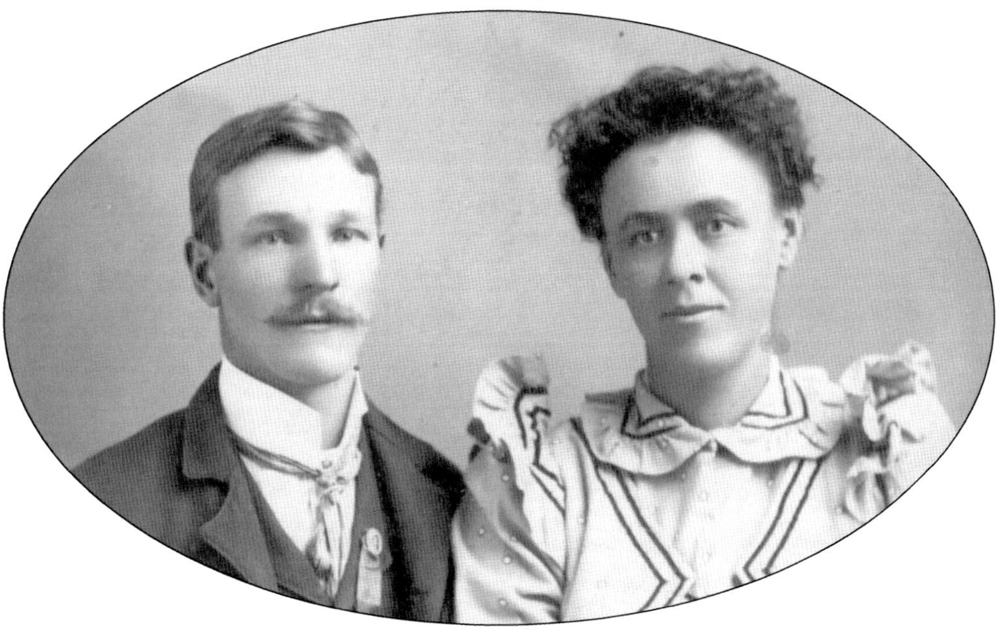

Henry Williams, pictured here, arrived in Colorado with his family when he was a young child and later married Tena Lock, also pictured, from a nearby ranch in about 1896. Together, they worked the Lock ranch, established by Lock's parents, Mathias and Barbara Lock. Under the Williamses' care, the ranch produced sizeable amounts of hay from its natural meadows and fruit from its orchards. (RW.)

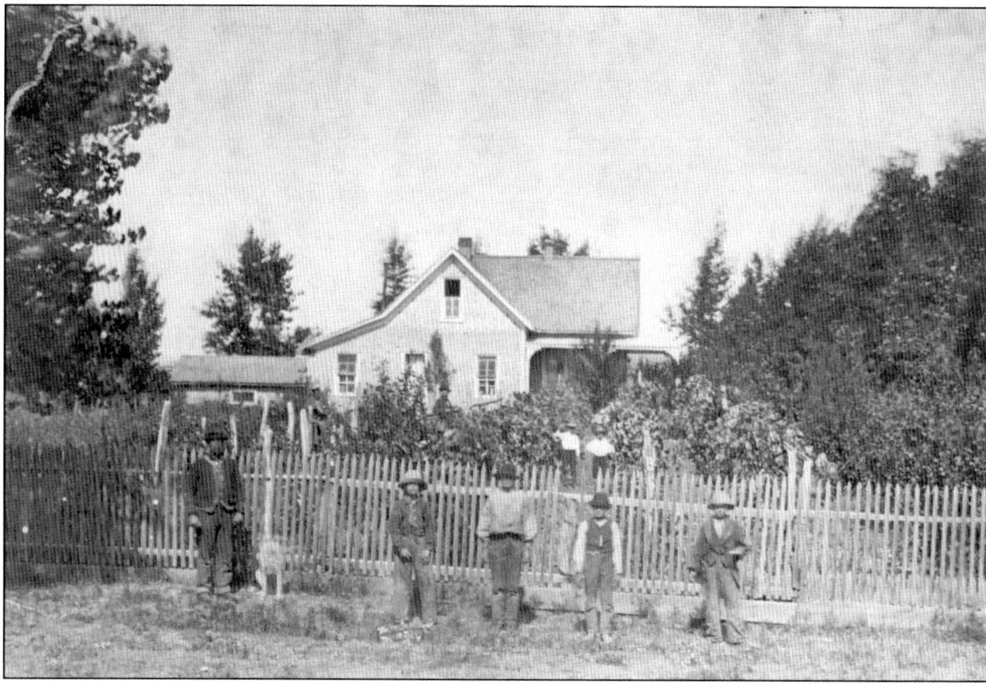

Men and boys stand alongside of the Orin Loomis place in 1888. The entire yard is filled with a vegetable garden. Loomis sold hay and grain from the corner of Race Street and Iowa Avenue, but records show he also owned land about 1.5 miles southeast of town. (FVM.)

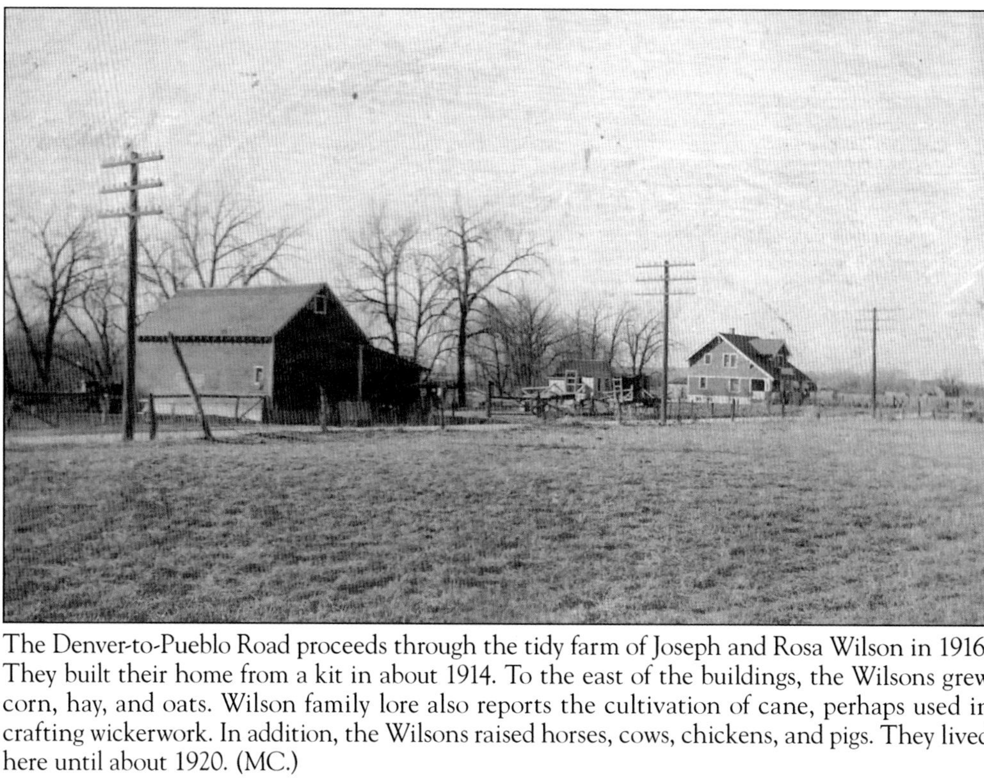

The Denver-to-Pueblo Road proceeds through the tidy farm of Joseph and Rosa Wilson in 1916. They built their home from a kit in about 1914. To the east of the buildings, the Wilsons grew corn, hay, and oats. Wilson family lore also reports the cultivation of cane, perhaps used in crafting wickerwork. In addition, the Wilsons raised horses, cows, chickens, and pigs. They lived here until about 1920. (MC.)

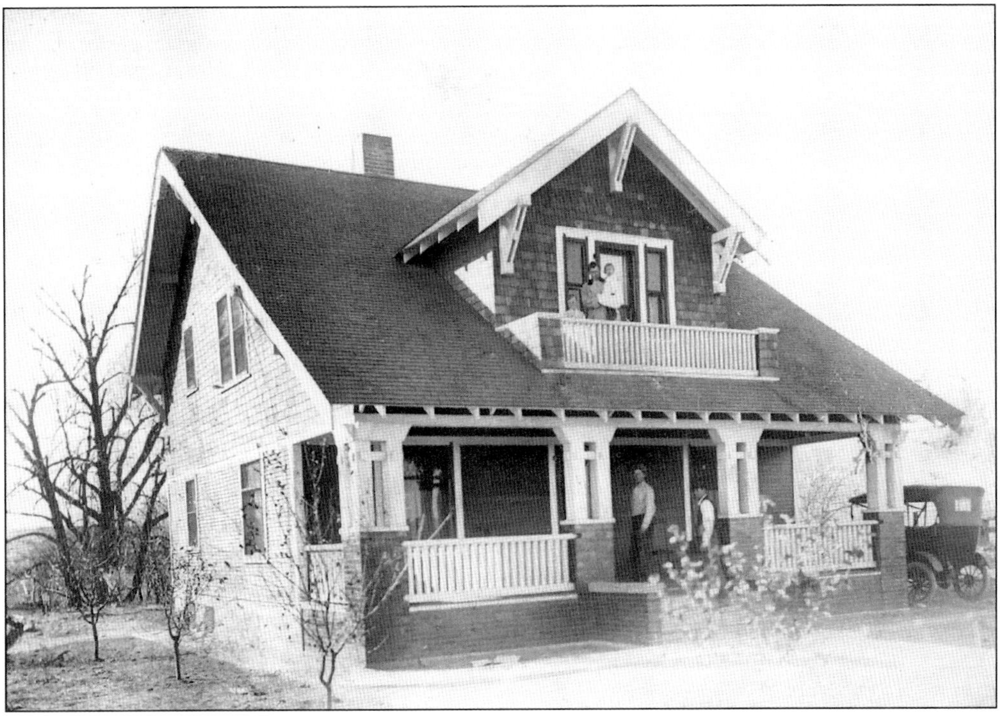

The home pictured here, built by Joseph and Rosa Wilson, is listed in the Colorado State Historical Register. Purchased by mail order from Sears, Roebuck and Co., this ready-to-assemble Westly model kit arrived in railroad boxcars with all the materials needed to construct the house. Commonly, friends, relatives, and neighbors gathered to put such homes together. (MC.)

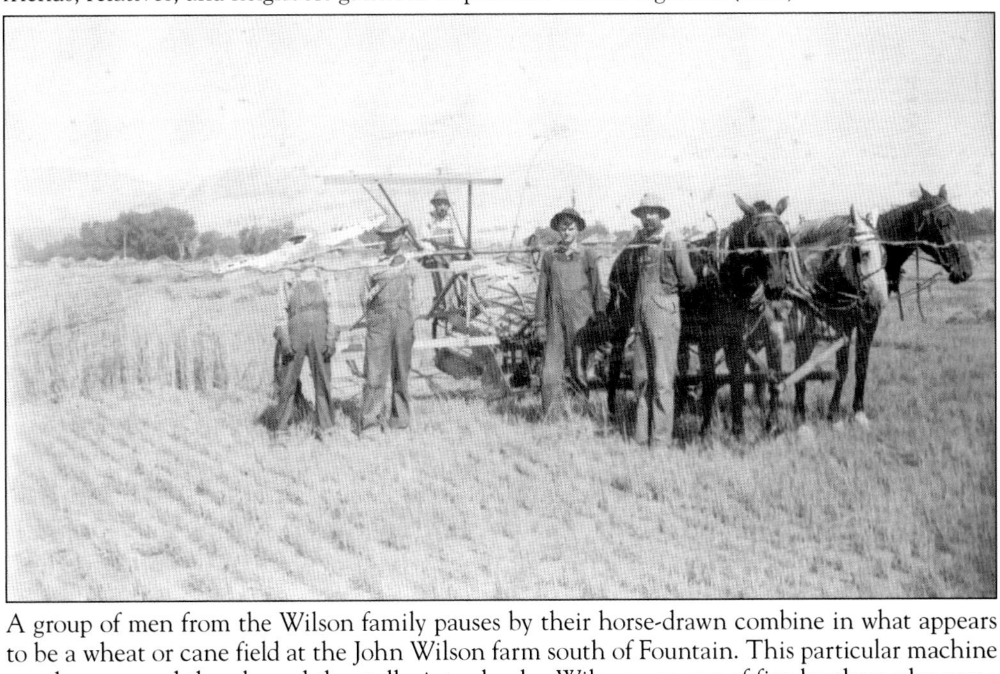

A group of men from the Wilson family pauses by their horse-drawn combine in what appears to be a wheat or cane field at the John Wilson farm south of Fountain. This particular machine cut the crop and then bound the stalks into shocks. Wilson was one of five brothers who came to the valley with their parents sometime before 1900. (MB.)

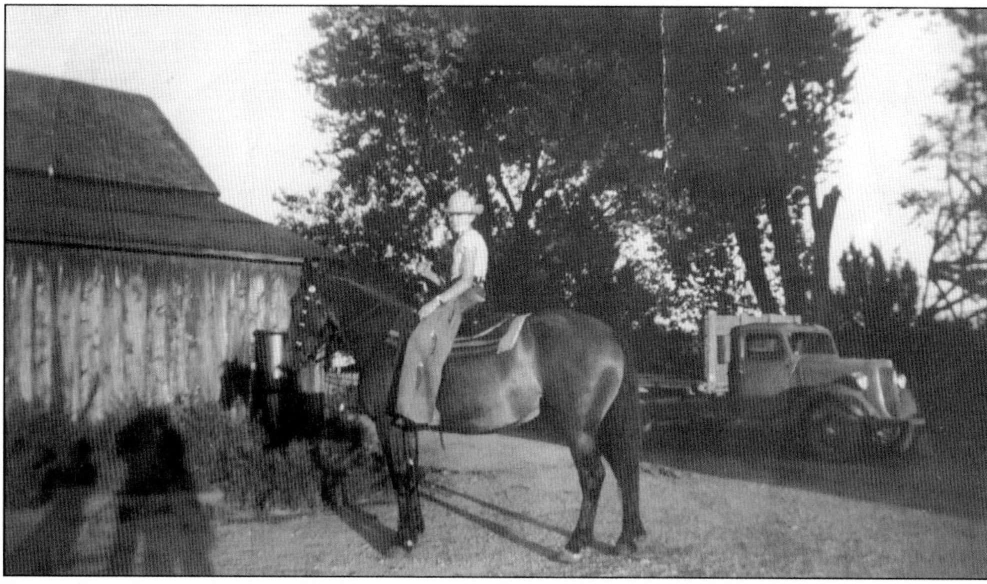

Dressed in chaps, young Bud Seymour sits astride his horse in about 1950 on the farm of his grandfather John Wilson. Seymour lived the dream of many young city boys who could only imagine themselves in the Western movies they saw every week at the theater. (MB.)

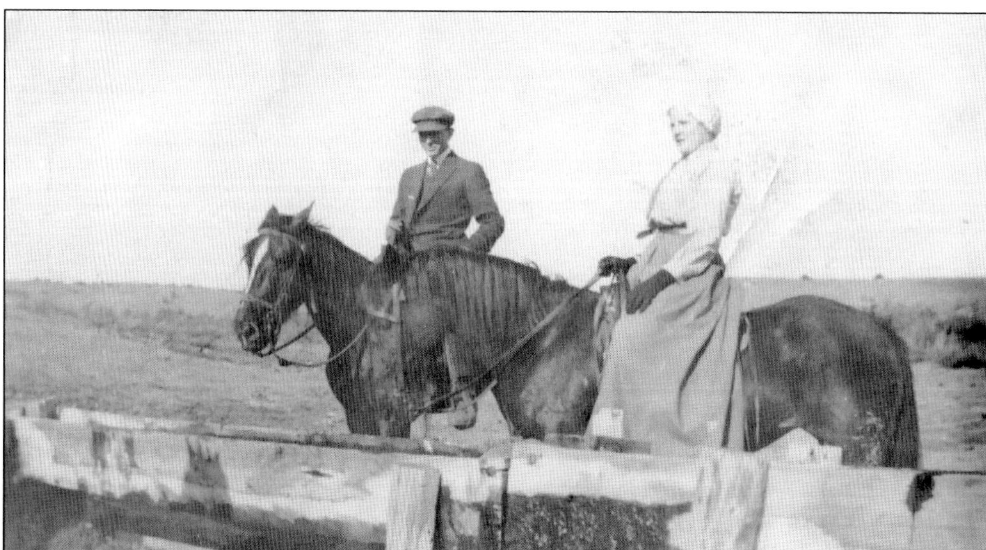

Siblings Elton (left) and Merle Love ride in the west pasture of the family ranch south of town on a crisp day in 1917. The Love family arrived in the valley from Idaho in 1903. Elton Love eventually married and moved away from Fountain, while his sister studied at Colorado College. Graduating in 1923 with a major in biology, she later became a nurse. (NT.)

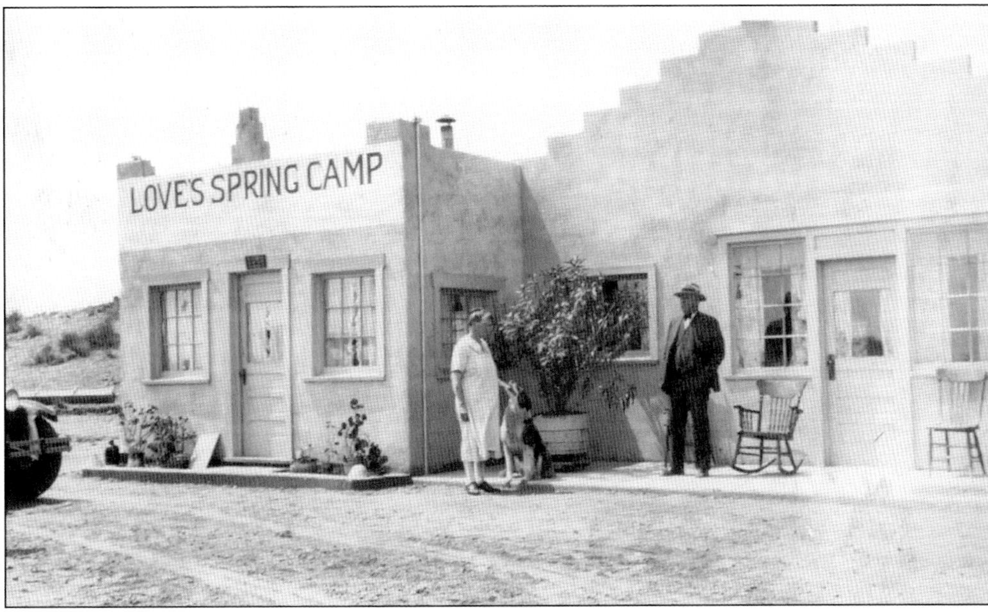

Love's Spring Camp, located south of Fountain against the foothills west of old Highway 85, beckoned to weary and hungry travelers. A series of connected rooms or cabins with doors facing a parking lot was known as a motor court, which first appeared in the 1930s as car travel increased. Love's Spring Camp also included a campground. With its good spring, this rest stop served both motorists and campers. (FVM.)

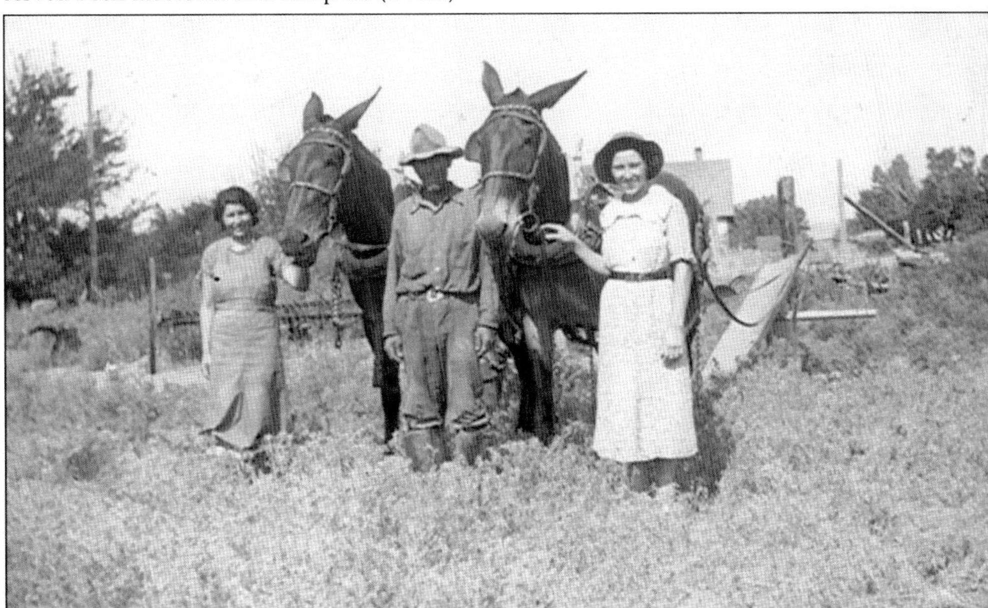

In 1942, Juan Rivera and his daughters Genoveva (left) and Teresa stand with a team of horses on the Love ranch south of Fountain on Old Pueblo Road. The Love family lived in town, and the Riveras farmed the land. The Rivera family arrived in Fountain from New Mexico in about 1924. Customarily, sharecroppers paid for the use of the land with a portion of the crops they produced. (MM.)

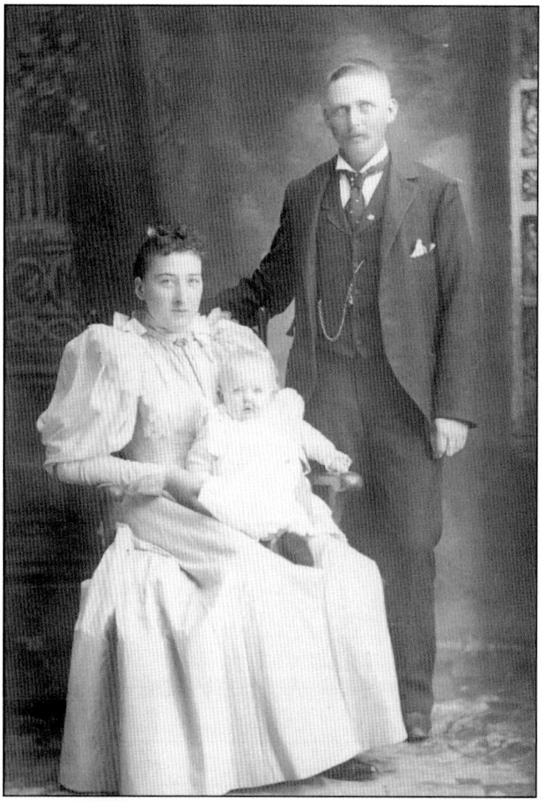

Catherine (Christian) Niles, wearing her lavender wedding dress, poses here with her husband, Louis, and their first daughter, Mildred. They set up house on a farm south of Fountain on the Denver-to-Pueblo Road. Still known by some as the Niles ranch today, the barn continues to advertise hay for sale across its tin roof. (DK.)

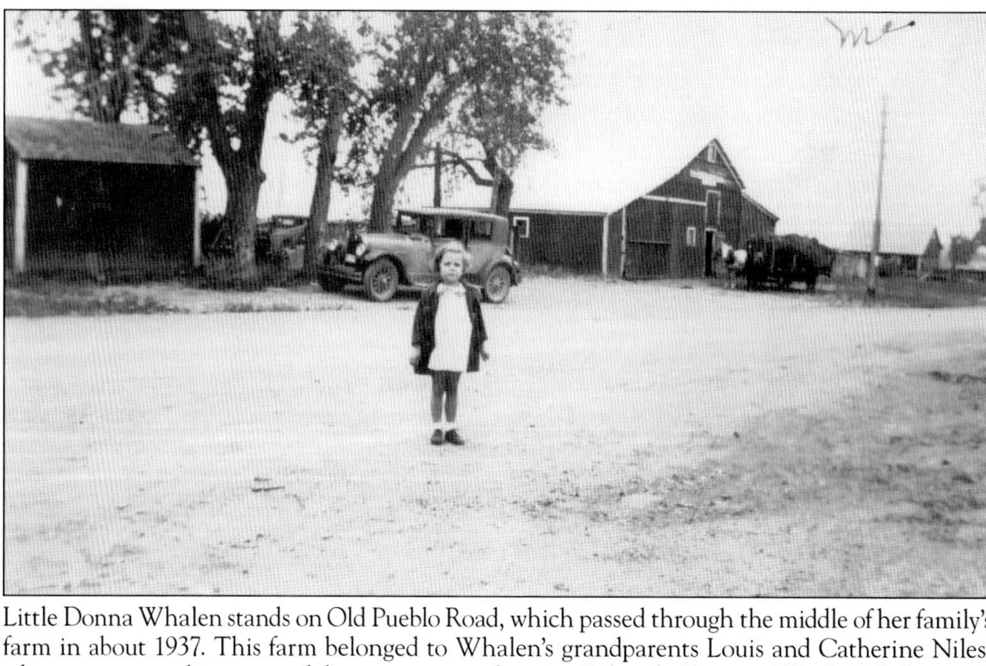

Little Donna Whalen stands on Old Pueblo Road, which passed through the middle of her family's farm in about 1937. This farm belonged to Whalen's grandparents Louis and Catherine Niles, who were away taking care of the county poor farm in Colorado Springs. Whalen's father took the opportunity to work the Niles family's ranch in their absence, knowing his family would have plenty to eat during the tough economic times of the Depression. (DK.)

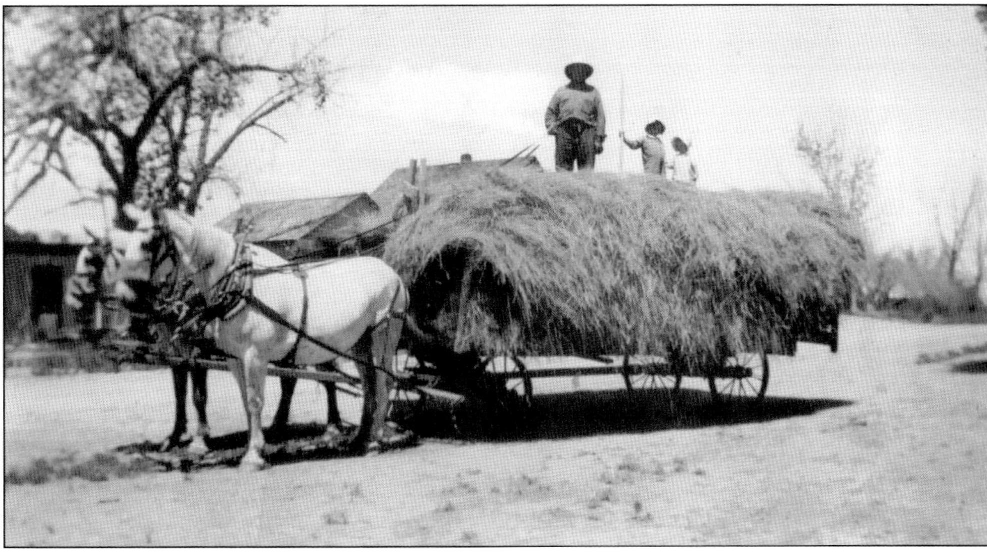

Herb Whalen and his daughters Donna (left) and Romaine stand atop the hay-filled wagon at the Niles ranch on Old Pueblo Road south of Fountain. The valley was known for its natural meadows of bluestem hay, but other farmers grew alfalfa as well. Much of the valley's hay was hauled by rack wagons to dairy farmers farther north. (DK.)

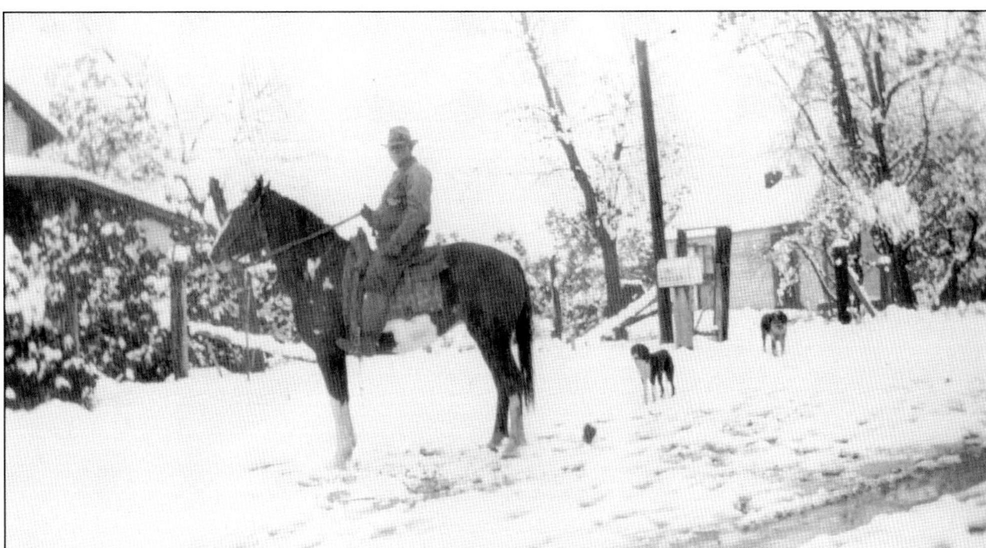

Herb Whalen, dressed in heavy gloves and muck boots, prepares for chores that had to be completed no matter the weather. Accompanied by his farm dogs, Whalen may be preparing to bring the horses and milk cows in for the night. Longtime residents can remember when the region received much more snow than it does today. (DK.)

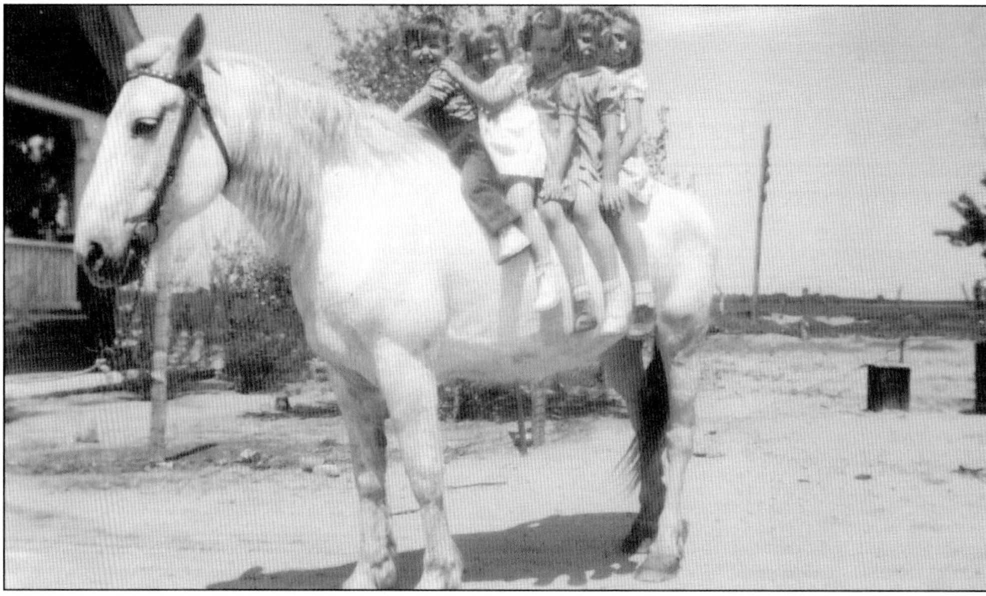

From left to right, cousins Kay Ross Dalby, Darla Mabee, Romaine Whalen, Beverly Mabee, and Donna Whalen sit astride a workhorse named Pet. As opposed to driving, riding, or racing, this dependable and beautiful white horse performed many of the farm labors for the Whalen family. In about 1940, they lived at the Pezolt place, so named for its prior owners, but it was originally built by Joseph and Rosa Wilson. (DK.)

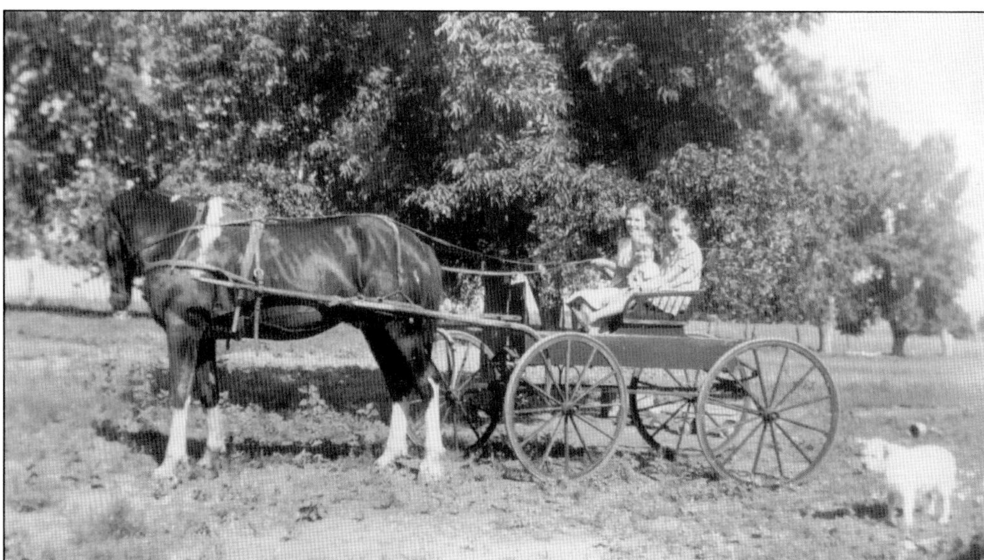

The Whalen children, accompanied by their dog Patsy, are out for a Sunday buggy ride on a beautiful spring day in 1944. From left to right are Donna (with the reins), Niles, and Romaine. (DK.)

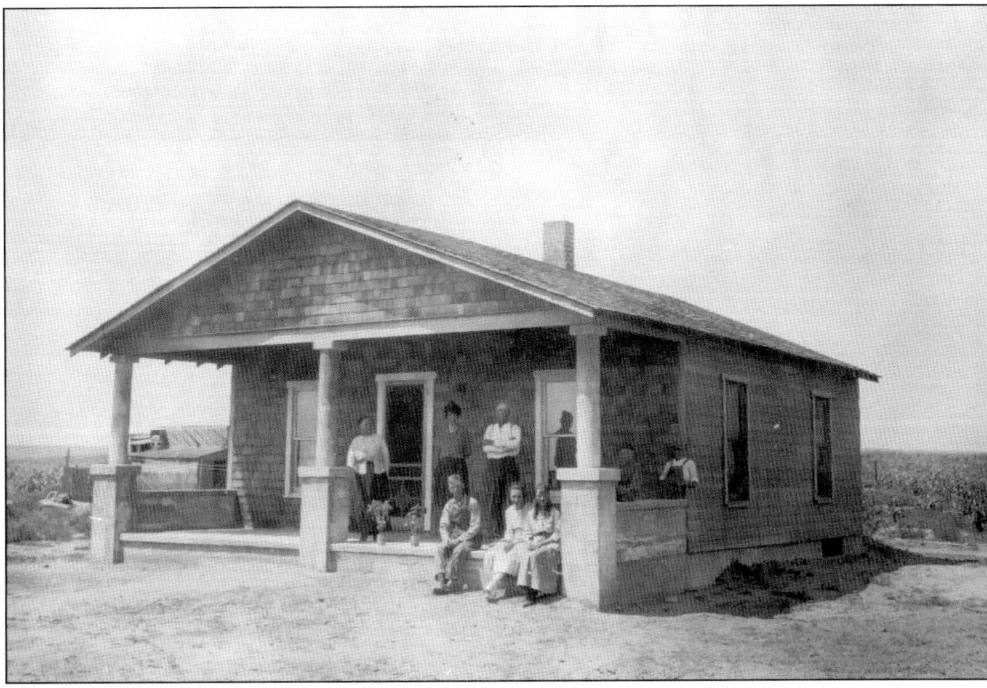

Unidentified people stand on the porch of the Whalens' shingle-sided farmhouse east of Fountain on Link Road at the intersection of Squirrel Creek Road. The Whalens moved to this farm in about 1919 and raised Poland China hogs. Corn grows in the field behind the house. The family also grew hay and barley. (DK.)

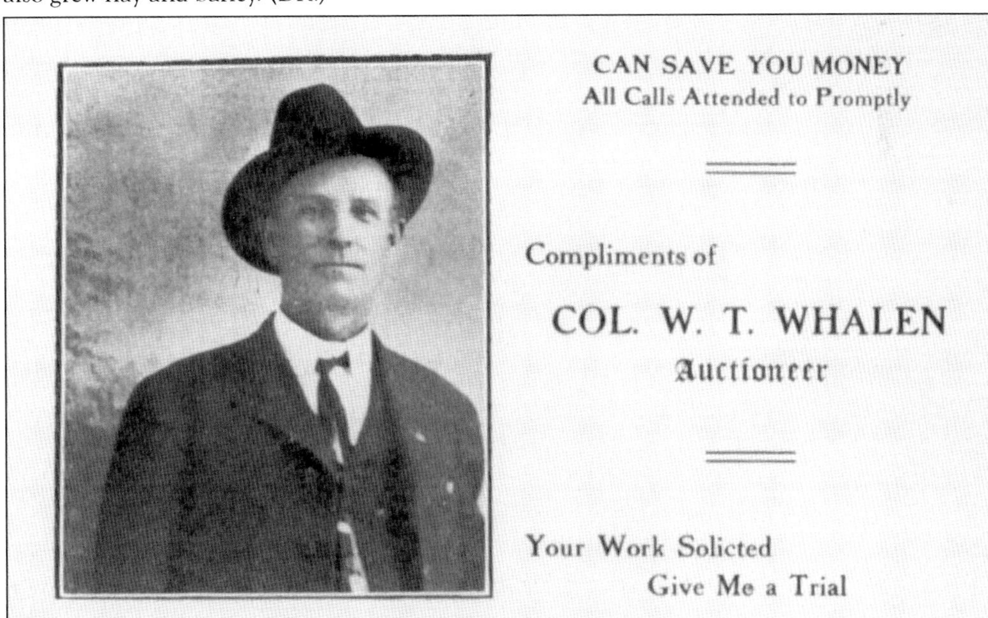

William Whalen, an auctioneer for over 35 years, offered his services with this business card. As an auctioneer, Whalen conducted sales at Fountain and other nearby communities where livestock and farm machinery were sold to the highest bidder. Auctioneers had strong voices and stood on platforms so they could be clearly seen and heard. (DK.)

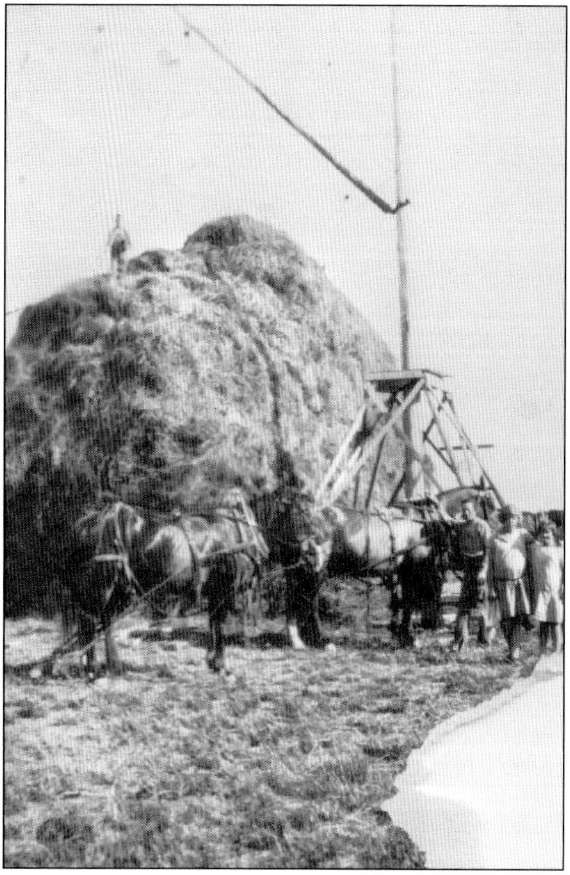

These men on Charles Leroy Charles's farm at Peaceful Valley, east of Fountain, work on the second of what will hopefully be three cuttings of hay in 1929. Hay was pulled by a horse-drawn sled to the haystack. A pulley lifted the bed and dumped the hay on top of the stack, and men at the top spread the hay out flat to make room for more. (LT.)

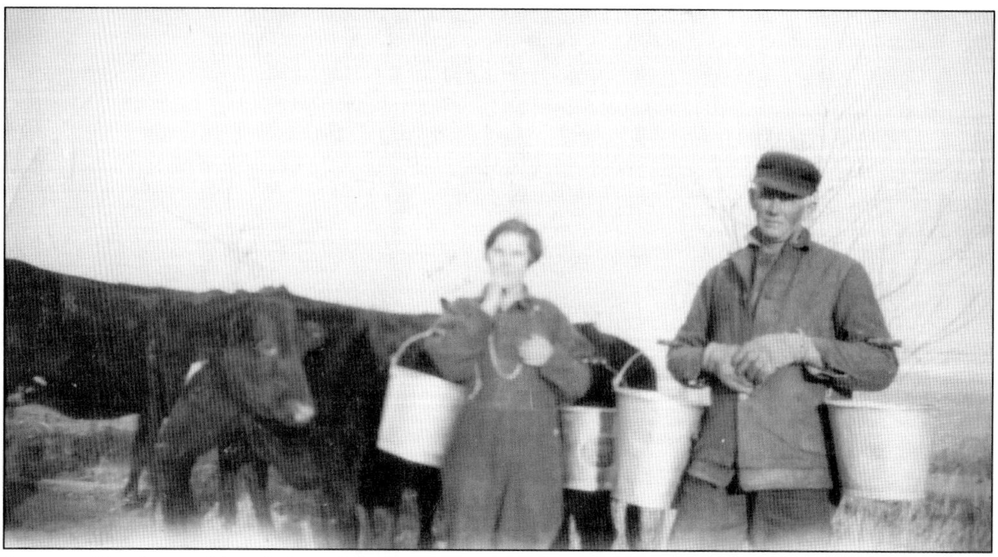

Geneva Charles and her father, Charles Leroy Charles, stand next to their cattle while holding milk buckets. The milking chore was accomplished before breakfast and then again at the end of the day, every day of the year. Milking was often done by farm children like Neve, along with other chores, before going to school. (LT.)

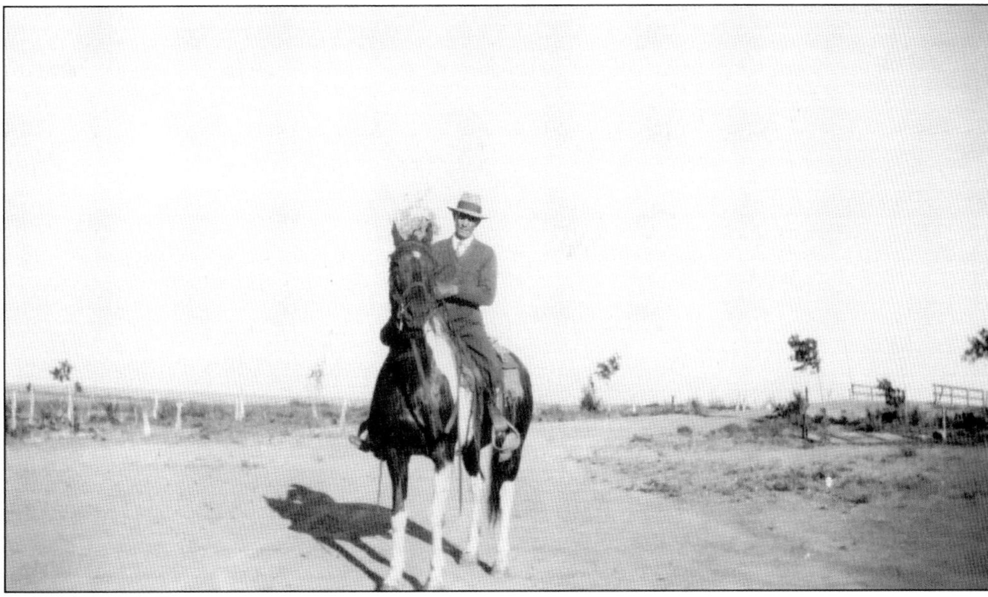

Known simply as "Tag" by the people on his route, this man rides the gas line by horseback in the Peaceful Valley area east of Fountain. Improvements in metals, pipe making, and welding techniques during World War II made pipeline construction more economically attractive. Natural gas was piped in many miles from Texas and Oklahoma to the north as homes began to acquire gas stoves and furnaces. (LT.)

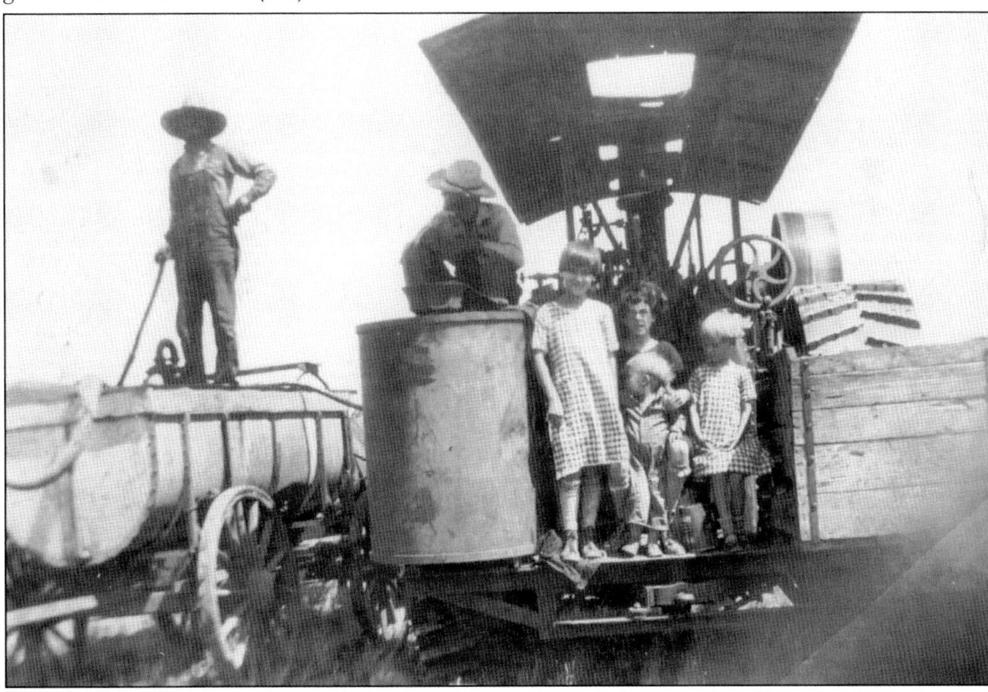

The farmer on top of the water wagon (right) prepares to fill the round tank on the steam-powered tractor as children take advantage of the moment to climb aboard. These powerful tractors were used primarily to pull multiple plow heads when preparing a field for planting. Steam tractors began to be phased out in the 1920s. (FVM.)

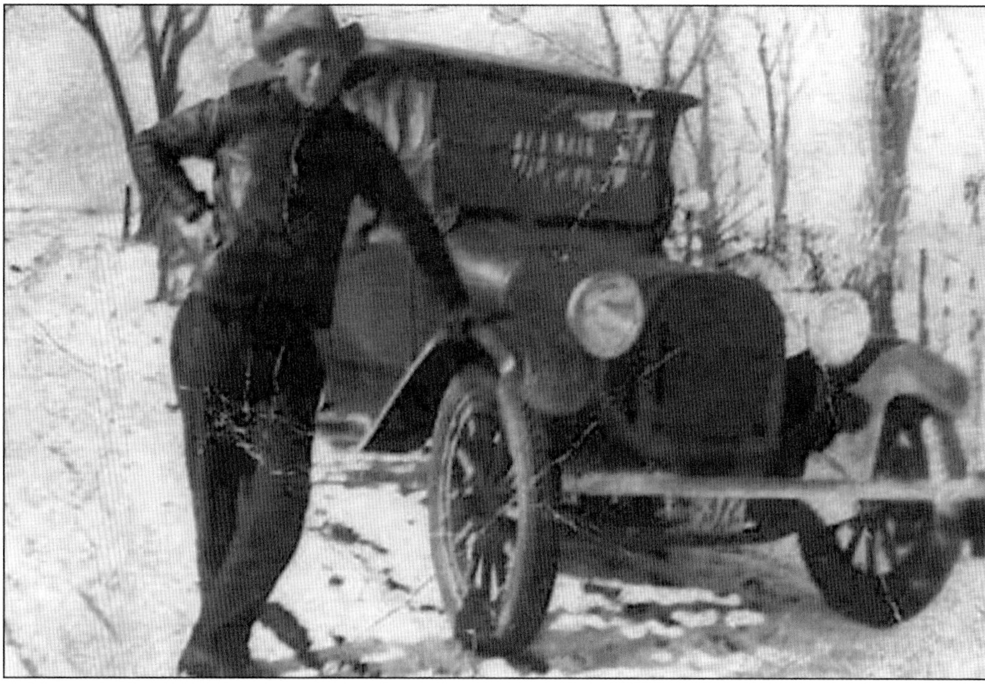

Kenneth Sample stands next to this recently purchased black 1925 Ford Model T Runabout. Built simple, rugged, and cheap, the Model Ts were the first automobiles produced by assembly line. Sample traveled much faster in this Runabout than in his horse-drawn vehicles. This Model T handled mud, snow, and rough country roads and could even ford a small creek if necessary. (FVM.)

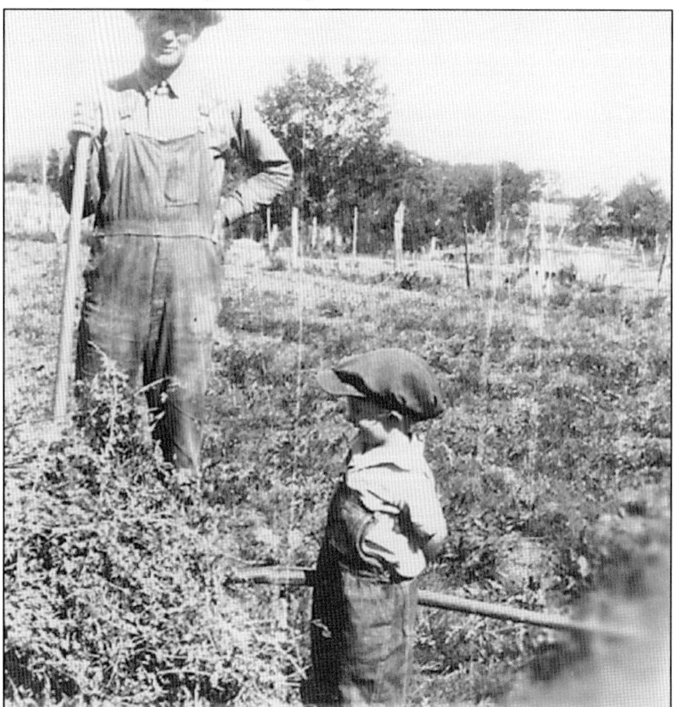

About 1930, little Wendell Sample helps his father, Kenneth, cultivate with hand tools on the farm owned by his grandfather Winford Sample. The Sample family arrived from Kansas in the 1910s and settled on a farm located north of Fountain and west of the river. (WS.)

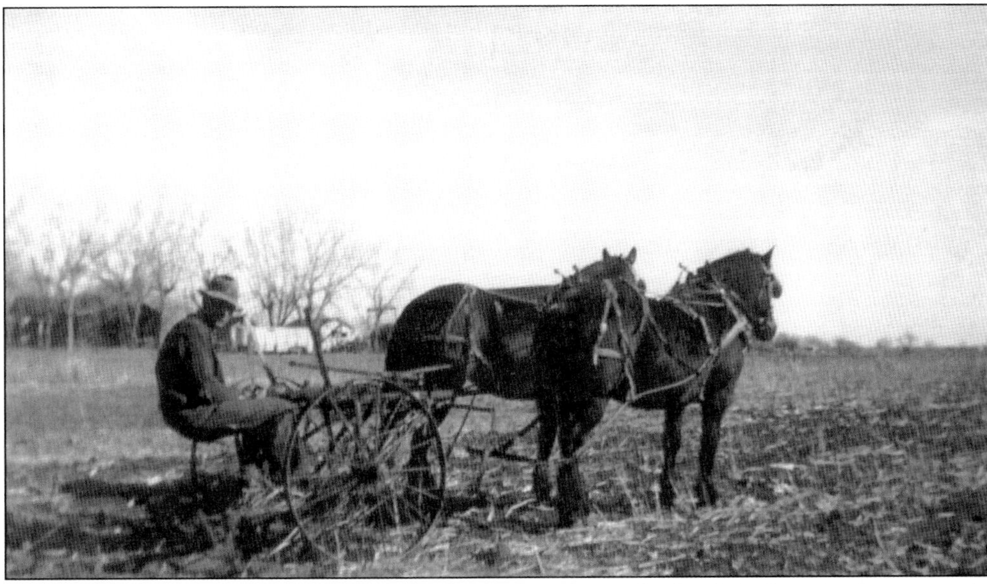

Kenneth Sample rides a horse-drawn cultivator in a cornfield, while laundry hangs in the background. It was probably a mild spring day when this image was captured, as the trees are not quite budded out. After plowing, a one-row cultivator was used to break up the large dirt clods left behind. (WS.)

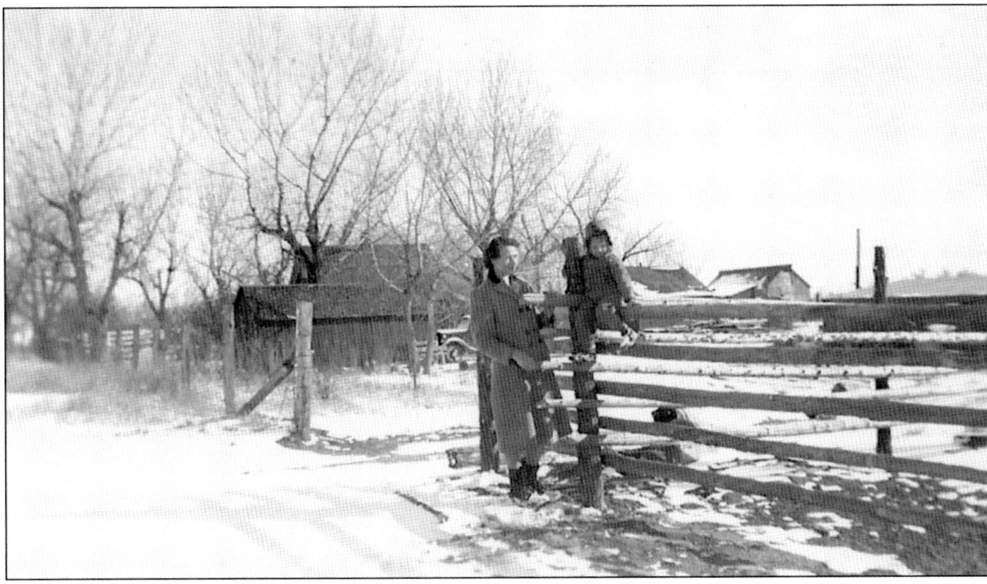

Grace (Ward) Sample stands with her small daughter Joan, who is perched on the fence near their farmhouse, sometime after 1936. Previously known as the Orcutt place, the house still stands on the south end of Fountain on Old Pueblo Road. The Samples operated a dairy with about 18 cows. Sample's son Wendell delivered the raw milk to the townsfolk on his bicycle. (WS.)

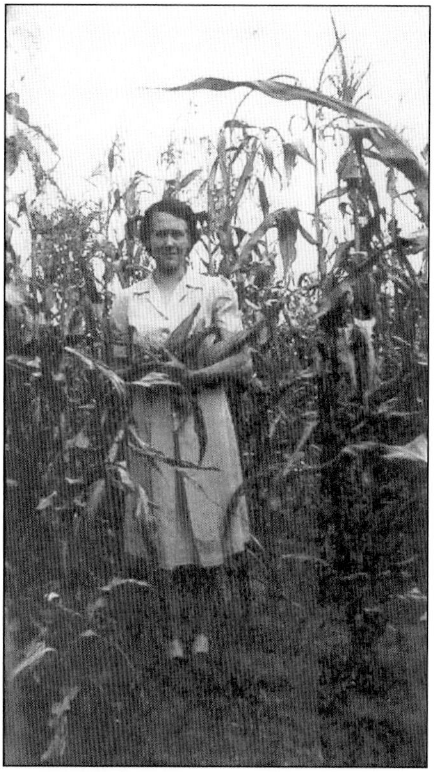

In 1935, Grace (Ward) Sample picks corn in her field from stalks that are taller than she is. Corn grew well on her fertile ground near where Jimmy Camp Creek, known locally as Sand Creek, joins Fountain Creek. Fountain is located on an otherwise arid plain, but Sample's husband needed only to draw water from one of the two creeks to irrigate the field. (FVM.)

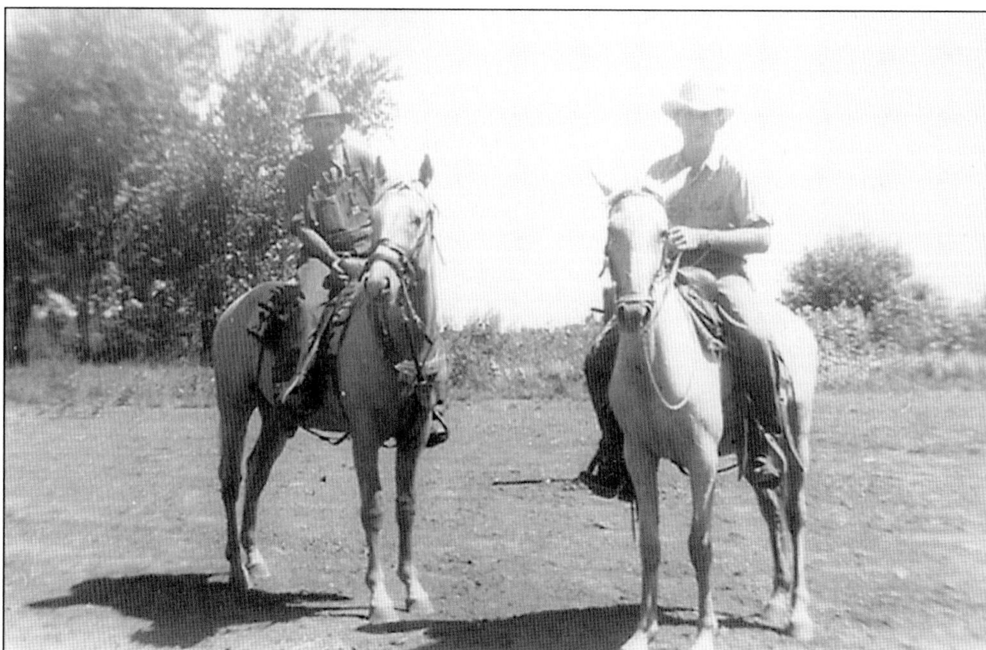

Kenneth Sample (left) and his son Wendell sit astride horses. In the 1940s, rural families still used horses for farmwork, riding into town, and surveying their property. Today, many residents in the valley keep horses for pets and pleasure riding. (WS.)

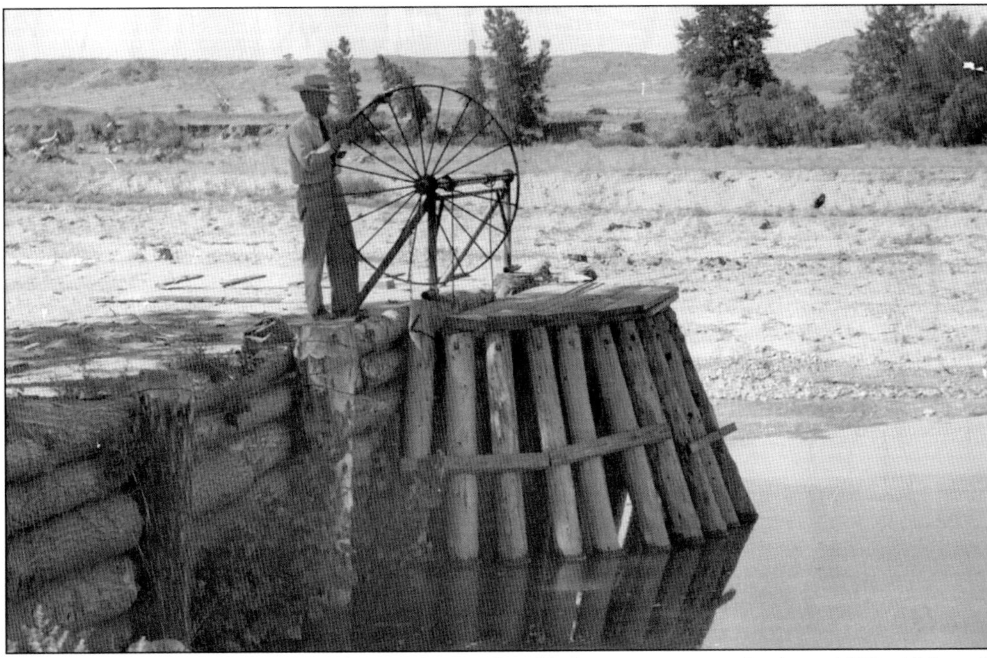

Water from Fountain Creek is diverted into the Chilcott irrigation ditch in 1939. Although the valley was noted for its fertile fields of vegetables, fruits, and hay, it would have been barren without water. Irrigating farmland was essential to food production and required a network of ditches and valves. (FVM.)

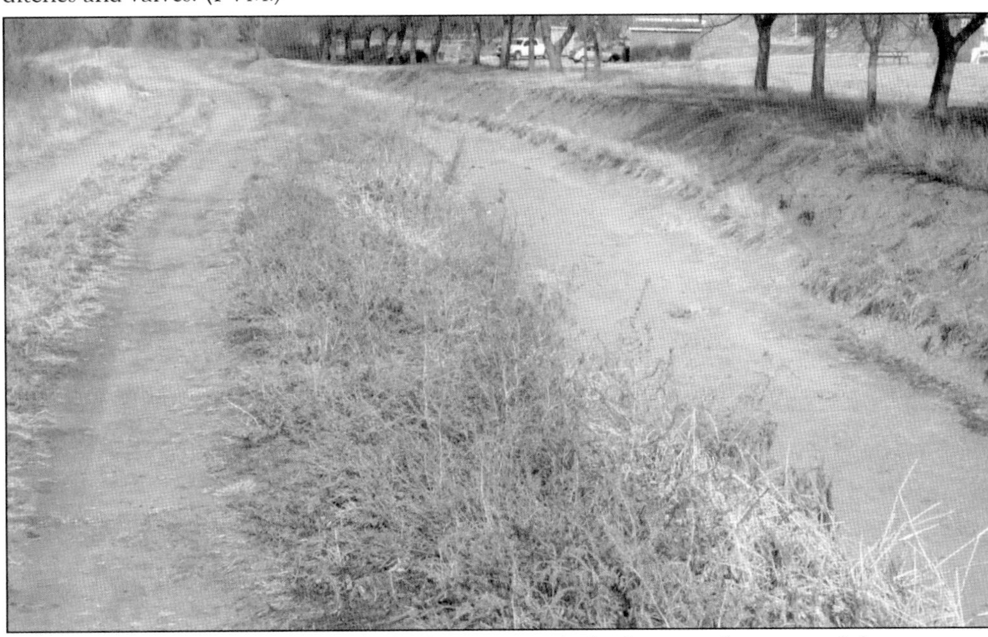

The Fountain region is laced with ditches, many of which are no longer used for irrigation. The Chilcott ditch, dug in the 1870s by hand and horse-drawn plow, brought water from the river to farms below the mesa on the east side of town. A ditch rider traversed sections of the ditch as he looked for obstructions and controlled the flow of water by opening or closing the headgates. (ATH.)

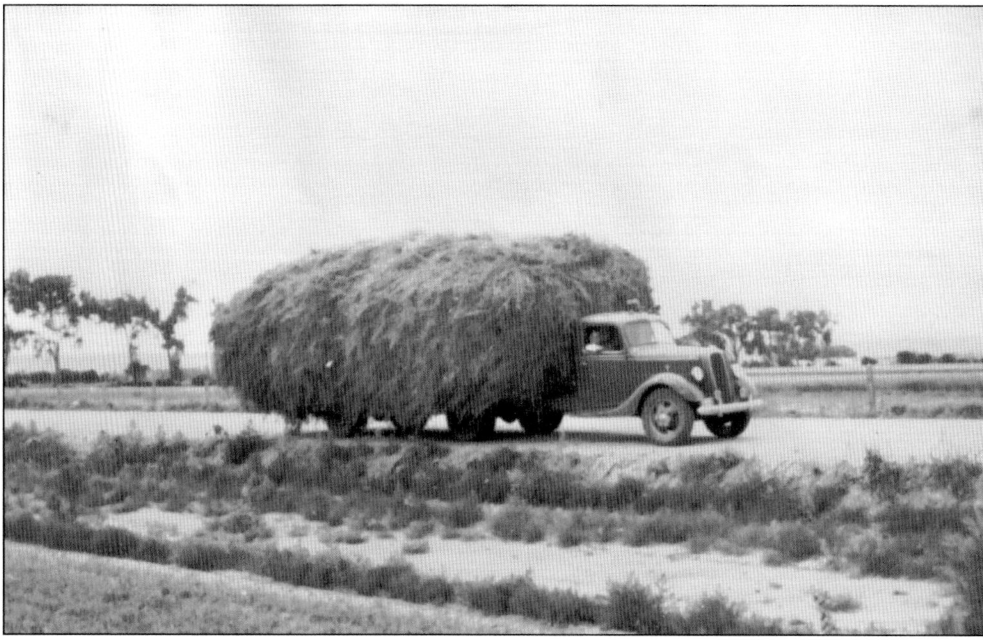

Hay from the natural meadow on the Hinch ranch, once located on the northwest side of town, is trucked away north to dairy farms. In the 1940s, horses did much of the farmwork, as tires and gas were rationed. The 1950s saw a transition to motorized farm vehicles, lending great improvements to farmwork. (FVM.)

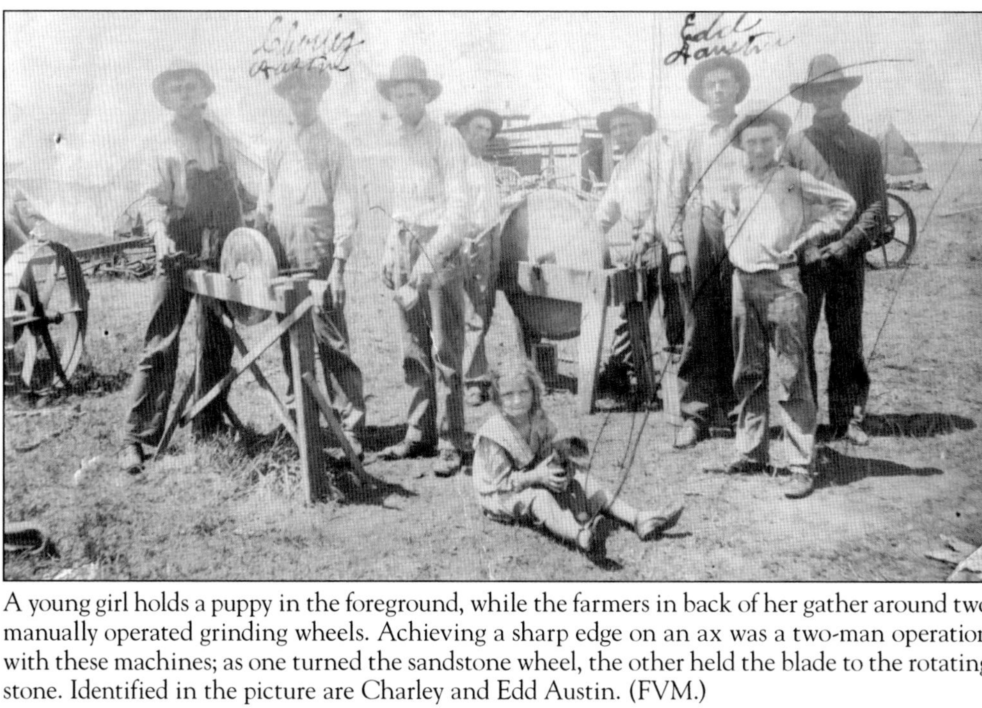

A young girl holds a puppy in the foreground, while the farmers in back of her gather around two manually operated grinding wheels. Achieving a sharp edge on an ax was a two-man operation with these machines; as one turned the sandstone wheel, the other held the blade to the rotating stone. Identified in the picture are Charley and Edd Austin. (FVM.)

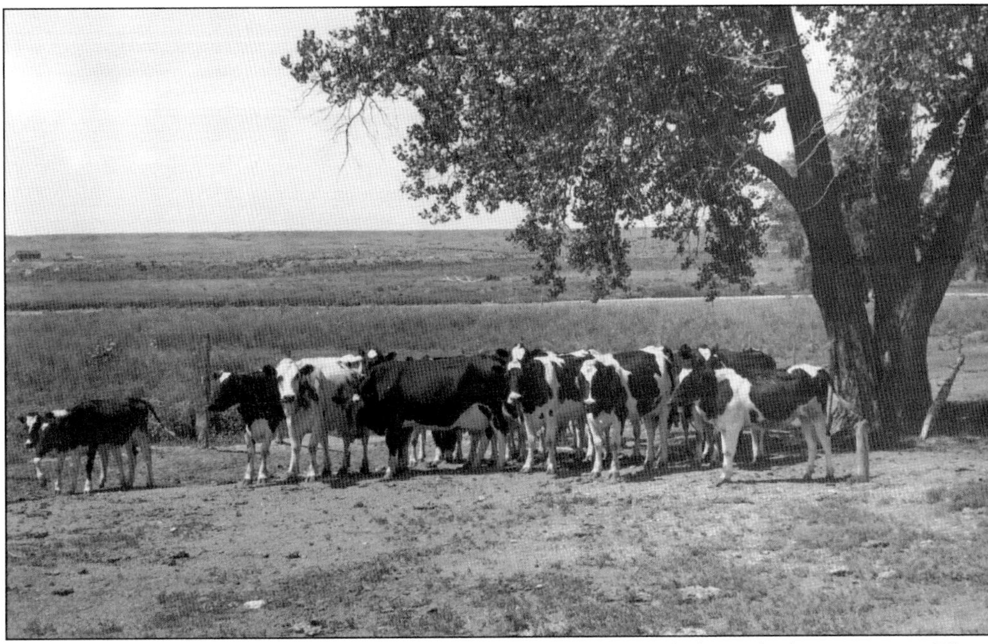

Milk found a ready market near Fountain; therefore, dairy cattle brought large returns. These Holstein milk cows belonged to the R.D. Mundell ranch, located about a mile north of Fountain along the river. It was often a child's chore (with the help of a good shepherd dog) to bring the cows in at night; sometimes they left school early when the days were shorter to get the job done. (FVM.)

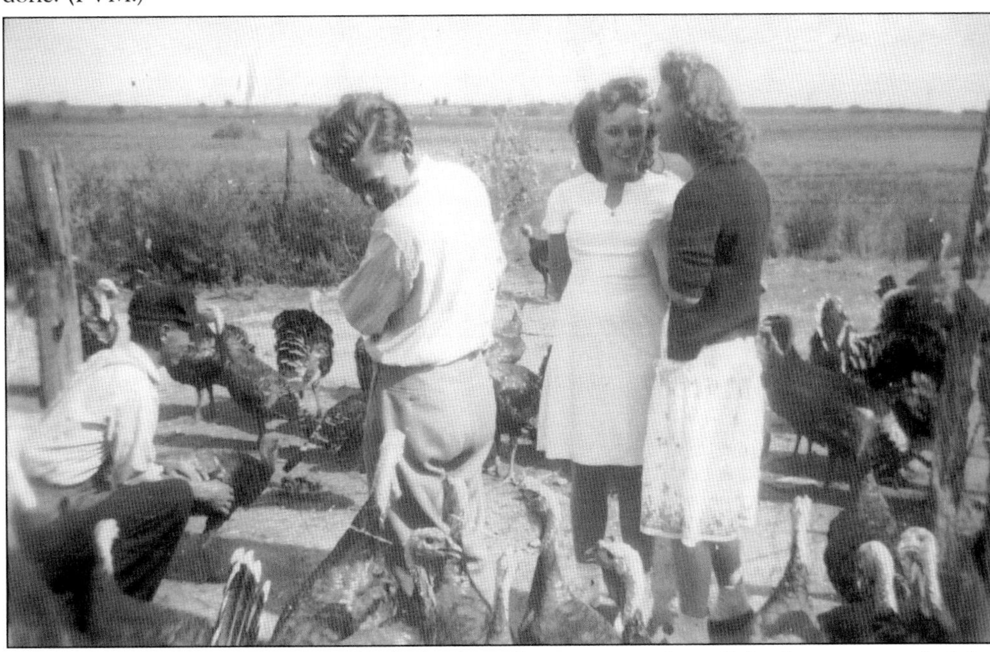

In this September 1946 photograph, the birds are being prepared to sell for the upcoming holiday feasts. Mingling with the turkeys are, from left to right, Herman Chenoweth, Harold Chenoweth, Donna Whalen, and Lorraine Higbee. In addition to many other agricultural endeavors, Fountain was an excellent place to raise poultry. (DK.)

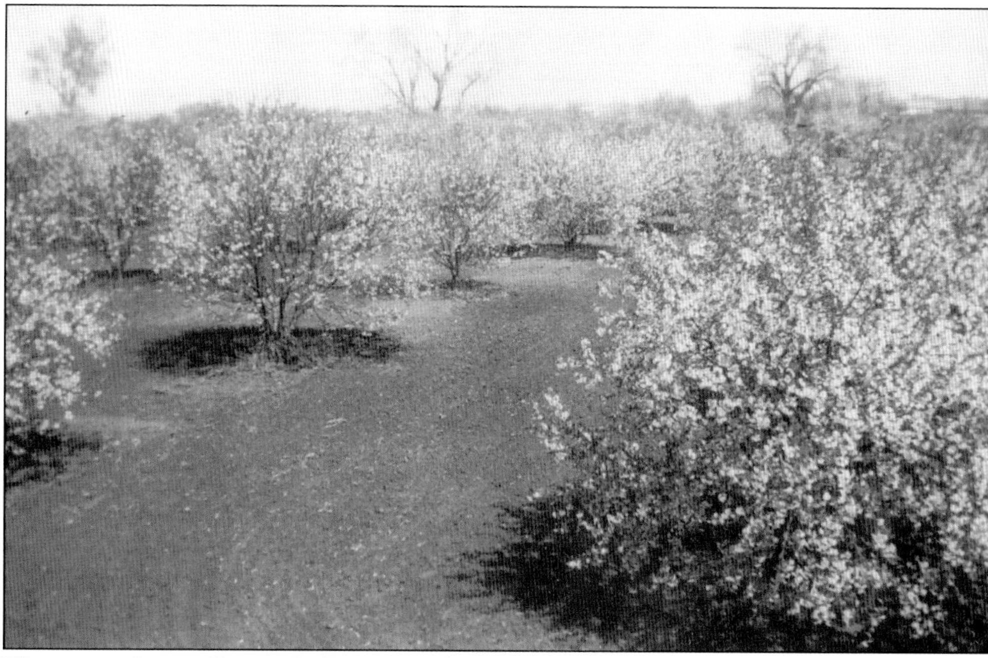

There were plenty of buyers for Fountain's cherries and apples. This cherry orchard on the Wetzel farm was located south of Fountain among several other orchards. Children at the Lock ranch earned their school clothes by picking cherries from the orchard on their ranch. The family set up a roadside stand at the end of their driveway to sell their fruit. (FVM.)

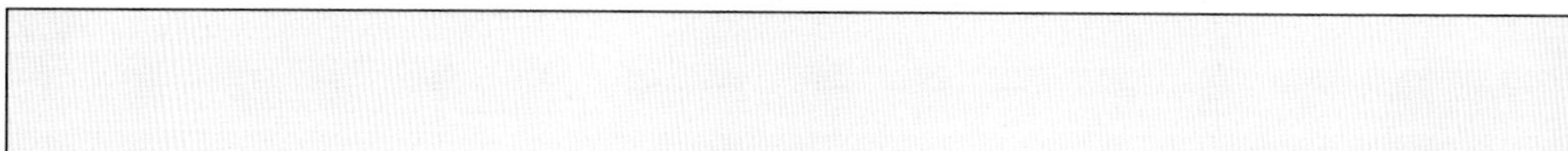

Sugar beets, shown growing on the Colbert Farm on Mesa Road, offered a generous and certain income. The Fountain Valley met the unique requirements for growing sugar beets, which were produced in great quantities. Farms along the mesa were irrigated with water from Johnson Reservoir by the Fountain Mutual Ditch. When harvested, the large white tubers were shipped to the beet sugar factories in the Arkansas Valley farther south. (FVM.)

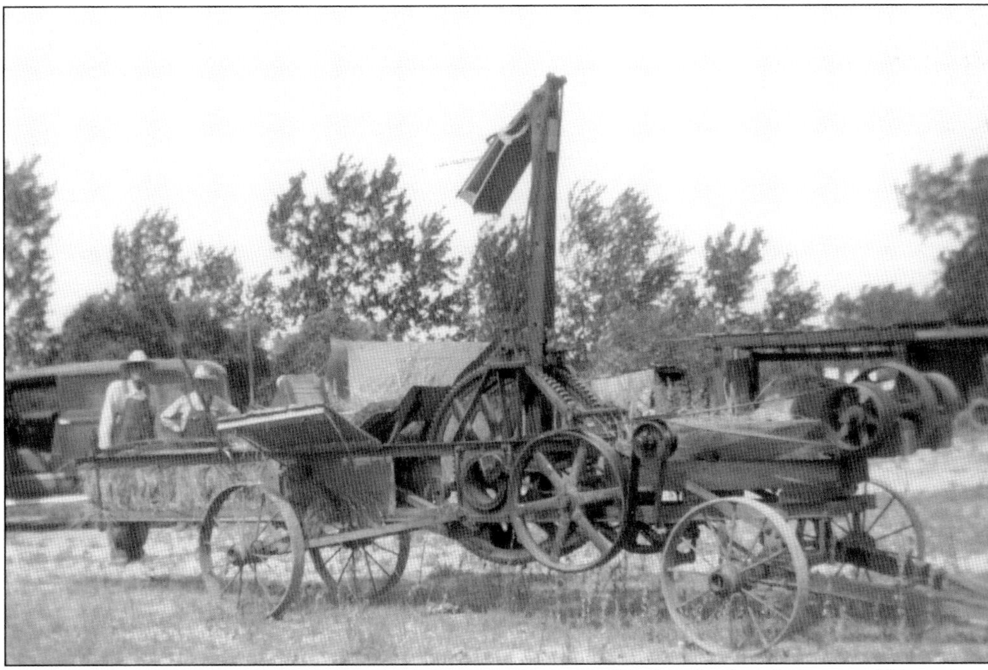

Lee Christian (left) and his son-in-law Clare Peebles stand behind a hay baler in 1930 on land owned by Christian's brother Michael. Located southwest of Fountain, this ranch was later absorbed by Camp Carson. The hay baler was a valuable laborsaving invention that compressed a crop of cut hay into compact bales that were easier to transport and store for winter feed. (DB.)

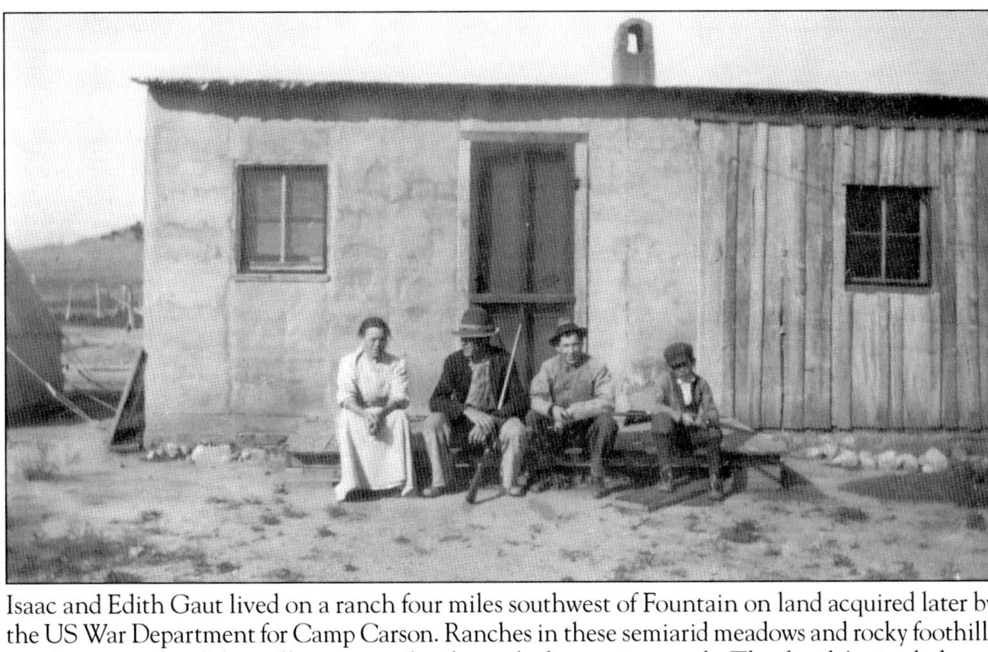

Isaac and Edith Gaut lived on a ranch four miles southwest of Fountain on land acquired later by the US War Department for Camp Carson. Ranches in these semiarid meadows and rocky foothills on the west side of the valley were utilized mostly for grazing stock. The family's simple home appears to be partially constructed of adobe, a common building material in the area. (FVM.)

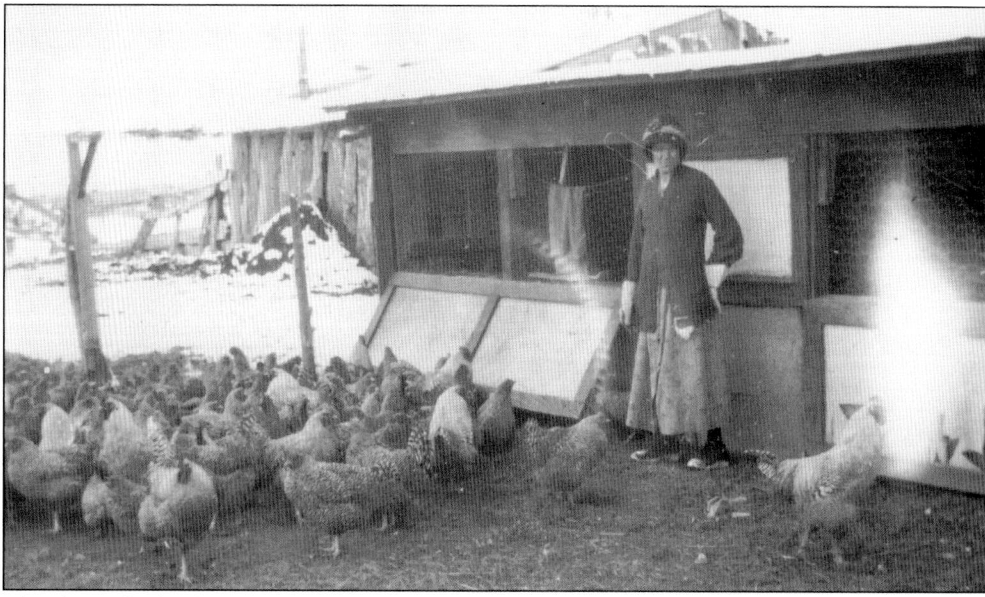

This large flock of chickens at the Gaut ranch is tended by a woman dressed warmly against the winter chill. Tending animals was a daily chore, no matter the weather, which could be very severe in the hills next to the mountains. The spacious coop allows for fresh air ventilation by day and can be closed up against nightly predators. (FVM.)

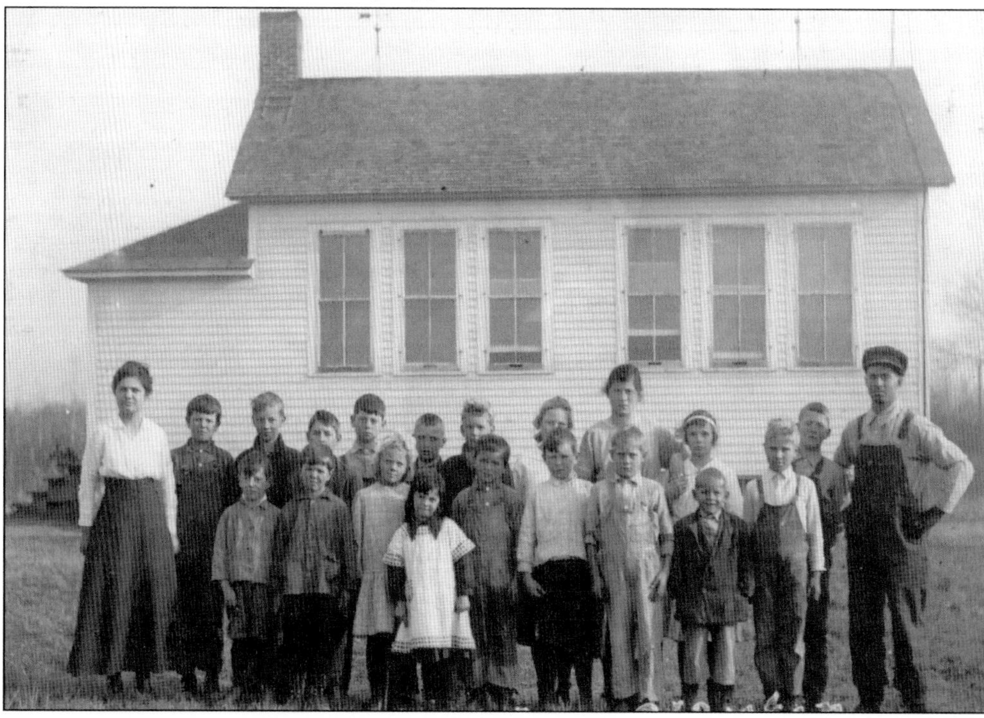

After graduation from high school, Coral Toothman (left) taught at the Lytle School, located in the foothills several miles to the west of Fountain. Farm and ranch children who did not live close to town attended one-room schoolhouses in their vicinity. Toothman most likely boarded with one of the families in the Lytle community. (FVM.)

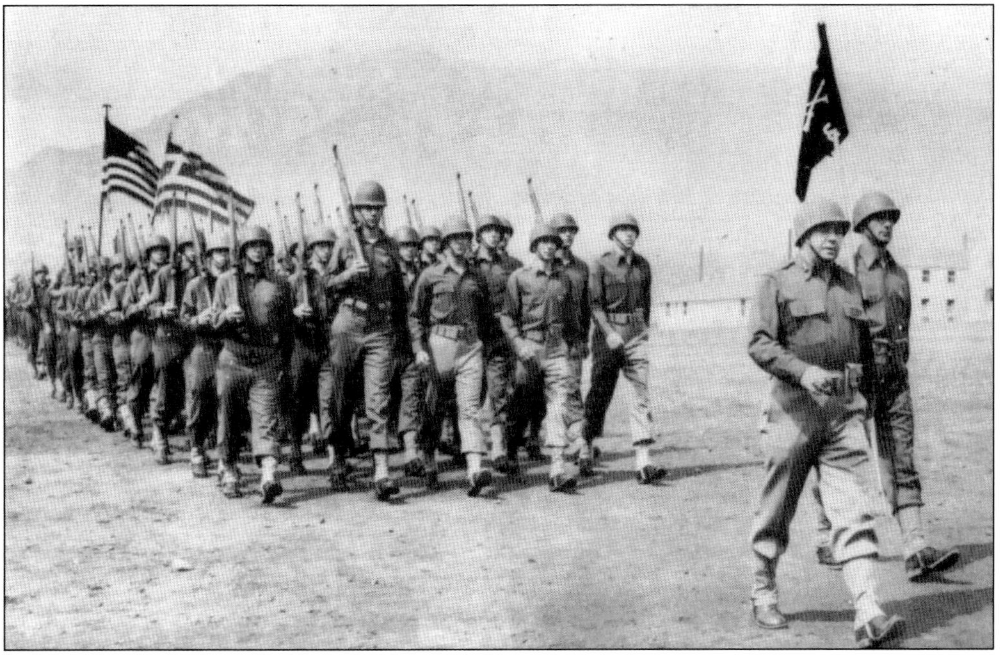

Camp Carson, named for Kit Carson who explored much of the West in the 1880s, was built on land acquired by the US War Department from ranchers west of Fountain. Construction on the new Army training camp began right after the bombing of Pearl Harbor, and the headquarters building was completed in 1942. (FCM.)

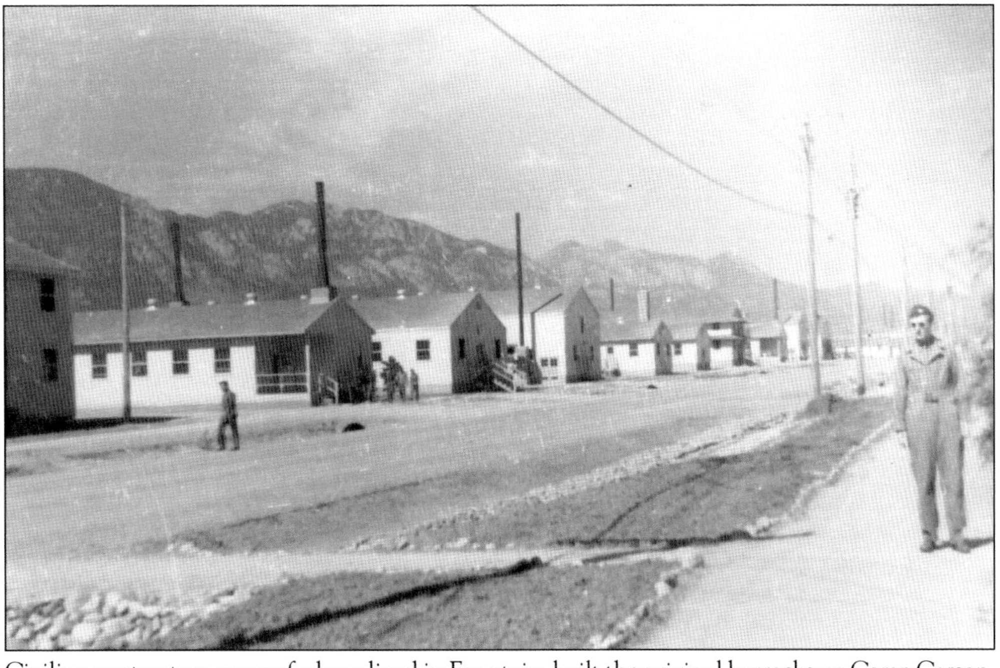

Civilian contractors, some of whom lived in Fountain, built the original barracks on Camp Carson. Construction was completed and ready for the 89th Infantry Division in July 1942. During World War II, while most soldiers were overseas, civilians continued to work on the post in construction jobs, as guards, and as clerks at the Post Exchange. (FCM.)

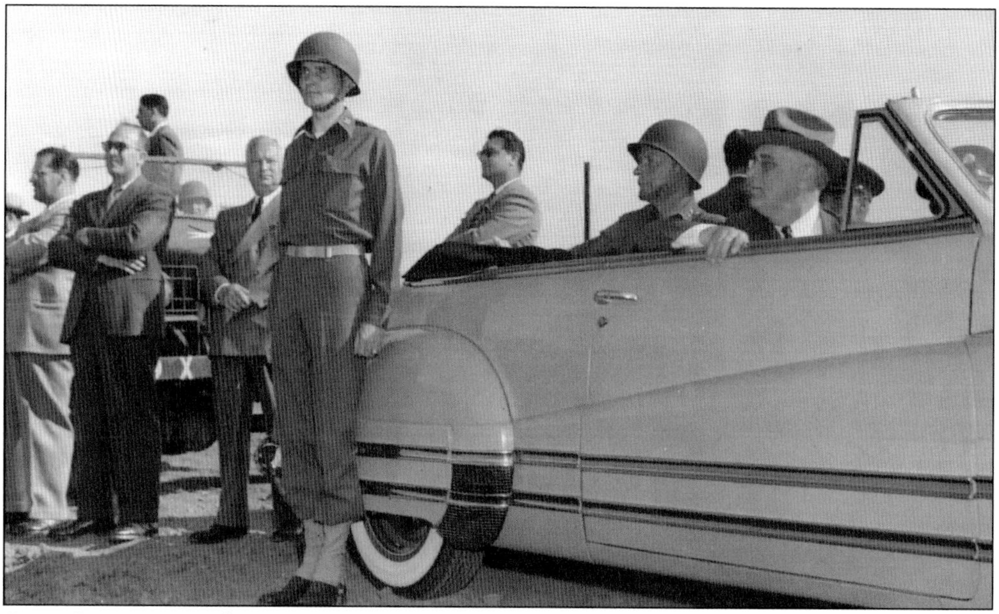

Camp Carson received an important visitor in 1943 when Pres. Franklin Roosevelt came to inspect the 50th General Hospital. Brig. Gen. Thomas Finley, who was in command of the 89th Infantry Division, and post commander Col. Wilfrid Blunt accompanied the president. Perhaps Fountain citizens employed on the post caught a glimpse of this prestigious guest. (FCM.)

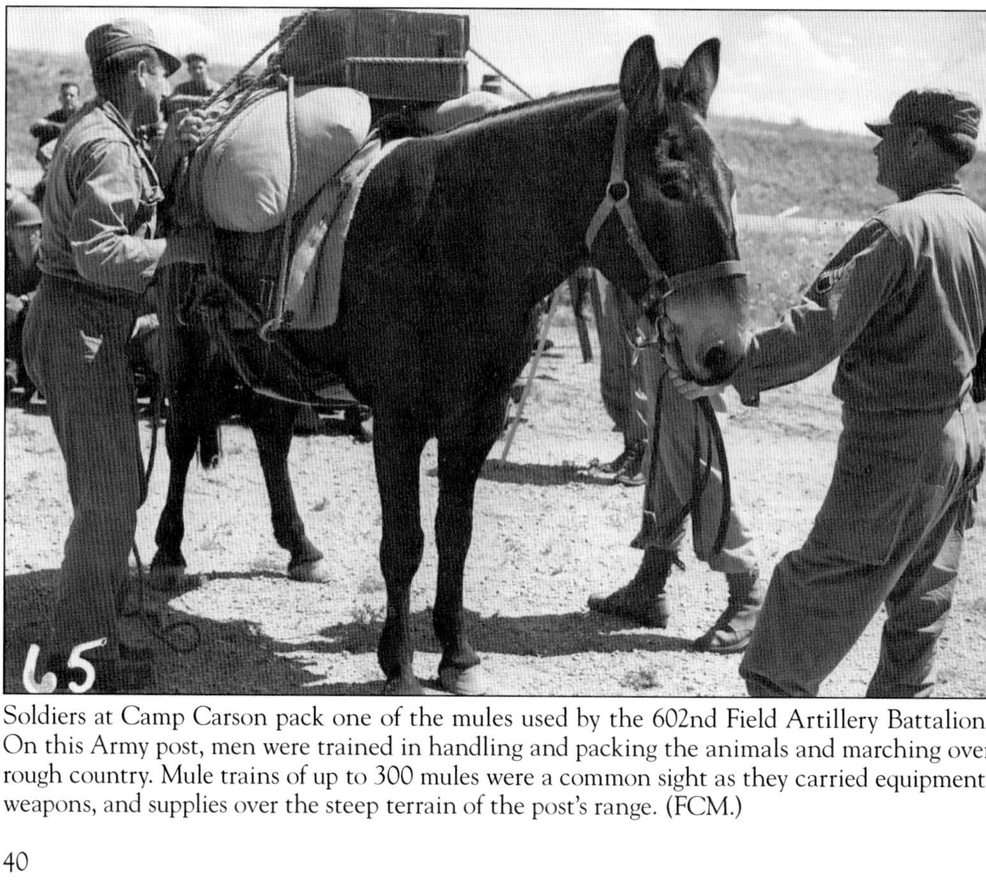

Soldiers at Camp Carson pack one of the mules used by the 602nd Field Artillery Battalion. On this Army post, men were trained in handling and packing the animals and marching over rough country. Mule trains of up to 300 mules were a common sight as they carried equipment, weapons, and supplies over the steep terrain of the post's range. (FCM.)

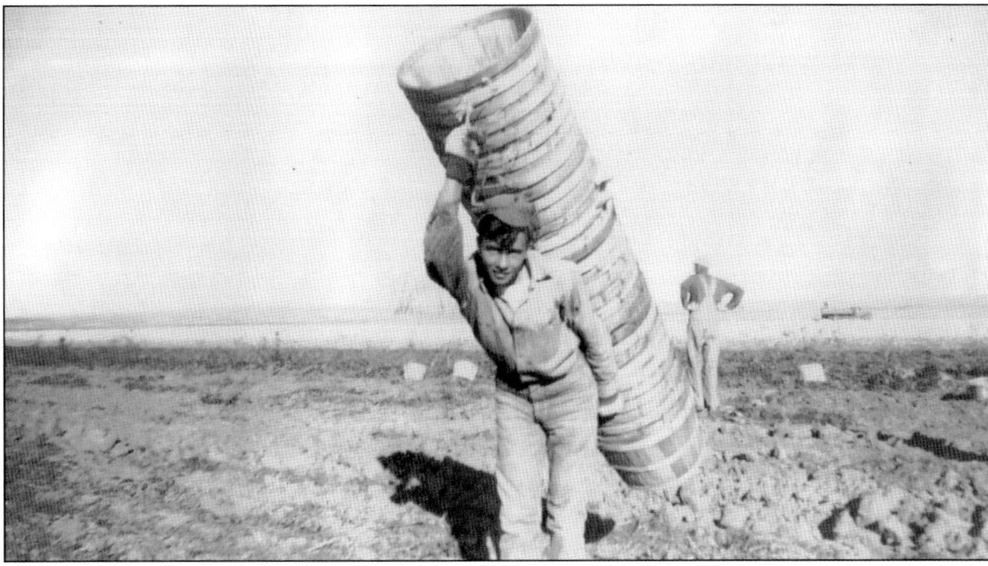

Louis Cimino carries a load of stacked bushel baskets to a field of freshly pulled carrots in this 1934 photograph. In contrast to large grain, dairy, and fruit farms, truck gardens produced a variety of vegetables to be taken to local markets. The Ciminos also produced cabbages. These, along with the carrots and other vegetables, were taken to Pueblo and Colorado Springs markets. (FVM.)

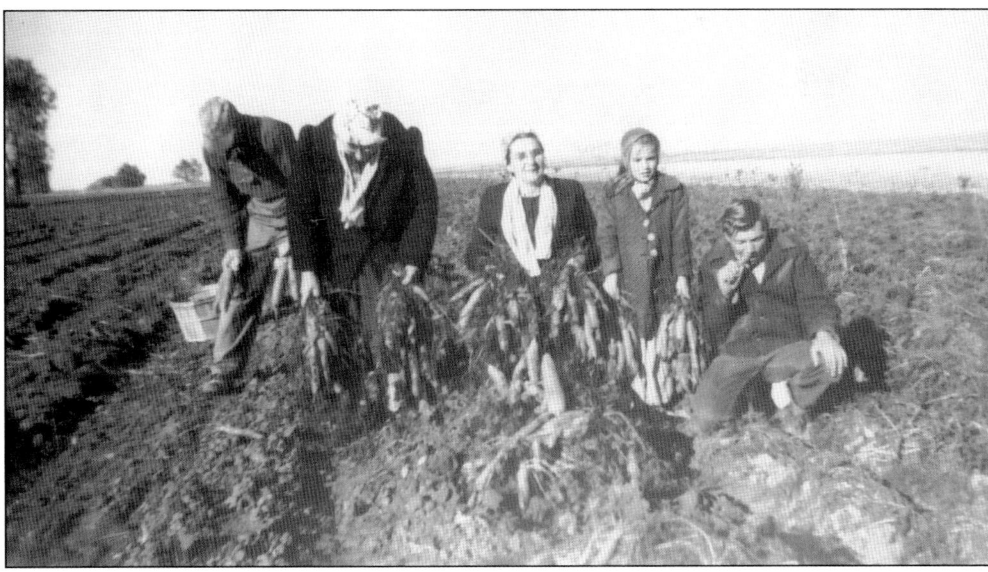

Pictured here in 1934, tourists from Wisconsin enjoy a visit in this carrot field on the Cimino farm. They were surprised to see the variety of crops grown in the Fountain Valley. Purchased in large quantities directly from the farmer, vegetables were taken home and preserved in jars for winter use. (FVM.)

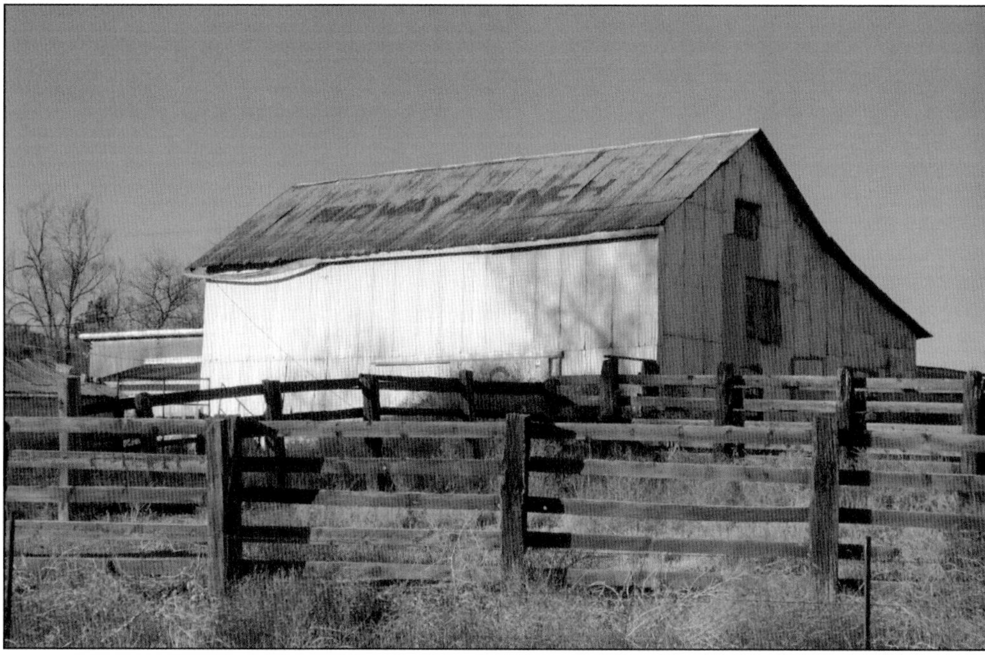

The faded name of the Midway Ranch is displayed across this barn situated south of Fountain. Homesteaded in earlier days by Dr. William Strickler and later by the Link family, this cattle ranch was named for its location midway between Colorado Springs and Pueblo. Purchased by Channing Sweet about 1925, it later fell into the hands of the Ward family. It now is subdivided into five-acre ranchettes. (ATH.)

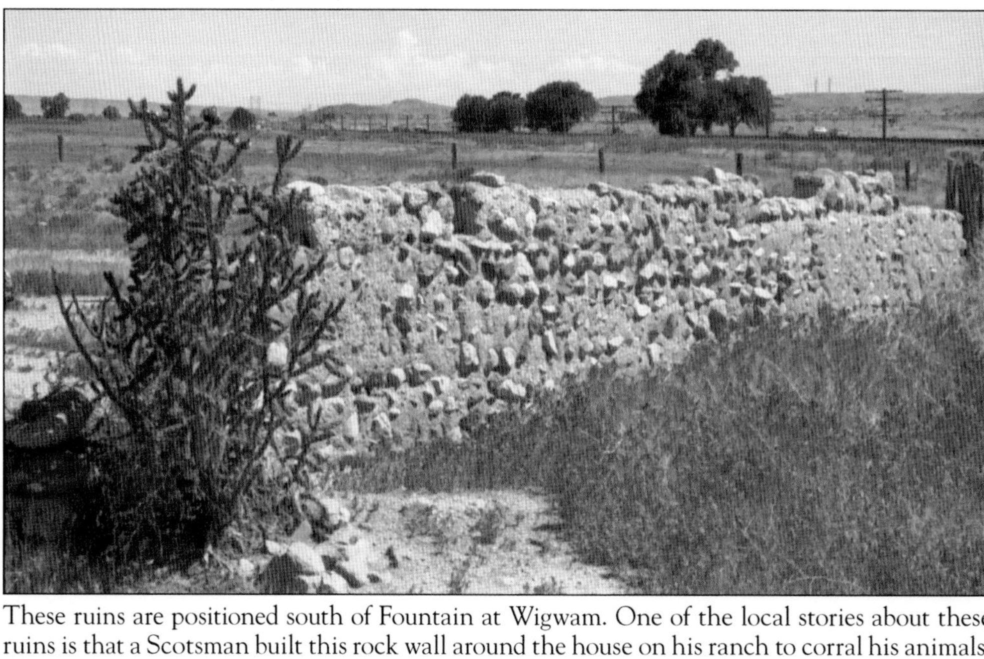

These ruins are positioned south of Fountain at Wigwam. One of the local stories about these ruins is that a Scotsman built this rock wall around the house on his ranch to corral his animals. A trading post and stage stop were later added to the location. Longtime locals say the area derived its name from the many tepees that formed a Ute camping ground at this place along Fountain Creek. (PPLD.)

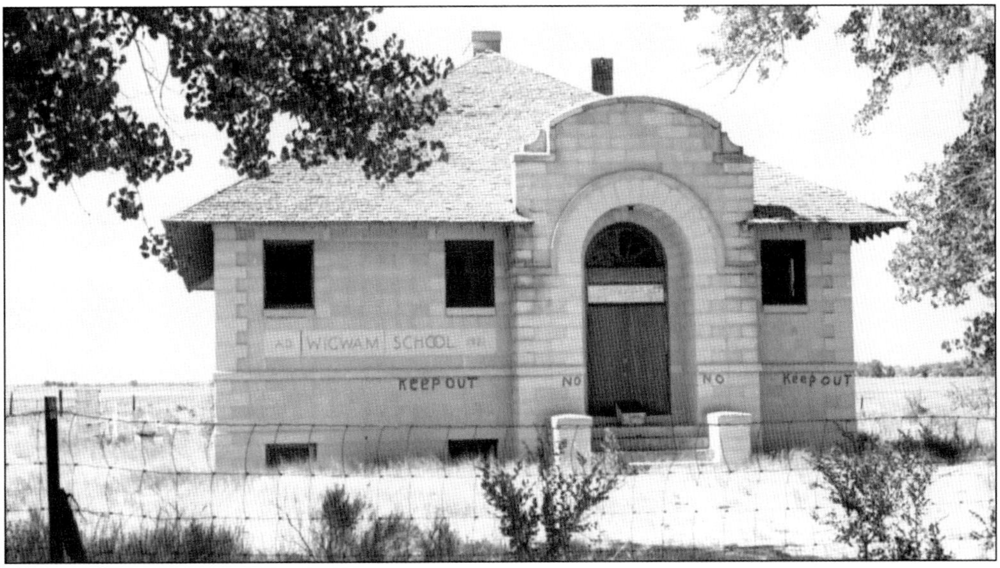

Built in 1921, Wigwam School served the children south of Fountain for only 40 years. The school building was reduced to storage space due to realignment of district boundaries when the Wigwam-area children were sent east to the Hanover School District. Hanover had hoped to open the school again when enrollment in the Wigwam area increased, but the landowner had the building torn down before that could happen. (PPLD).

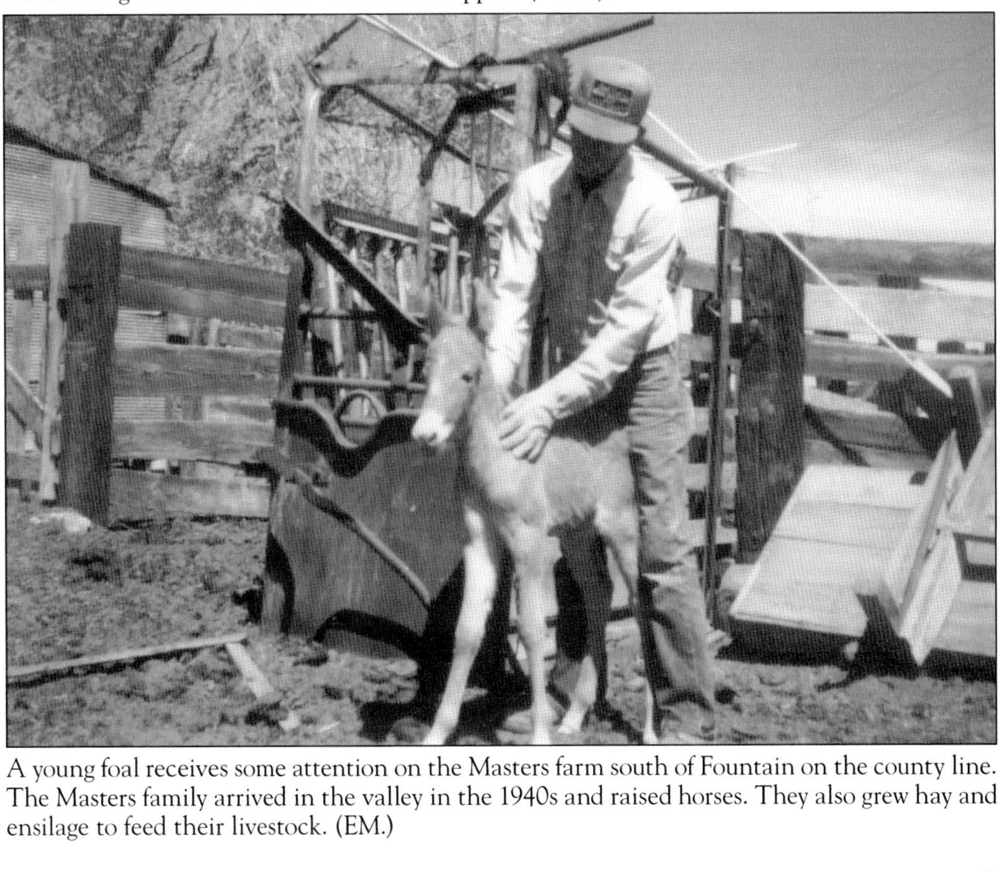

A young foal receives some attention on the Masters farm south of Fountain on the county line. The Masters family arrived in the valley in the 1940s and raised horses. They also grew hay and ensilage to feed their livestock. (EM.)

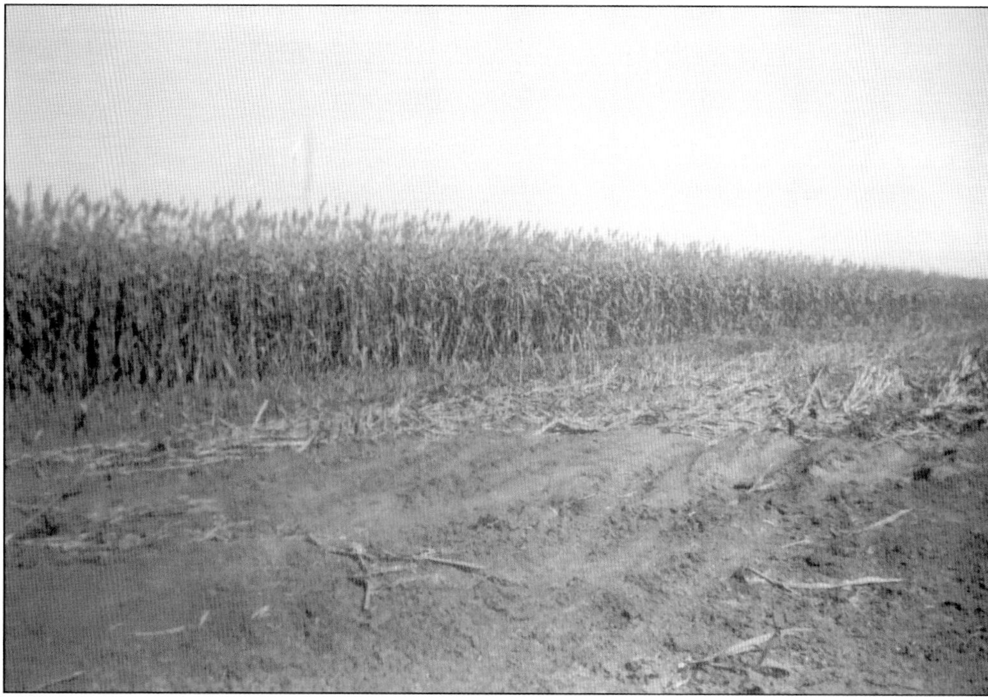

This field of corn grows on the Masters farm near Wigwam. Some of a farmer's corn crop was saved for human consumption, and a portion of the corn was left on the stalk so that the kernels could harden and be fed to horses and pigs. Much of the crop went into ensilage for feeding livestock during the winter months. (EM.)

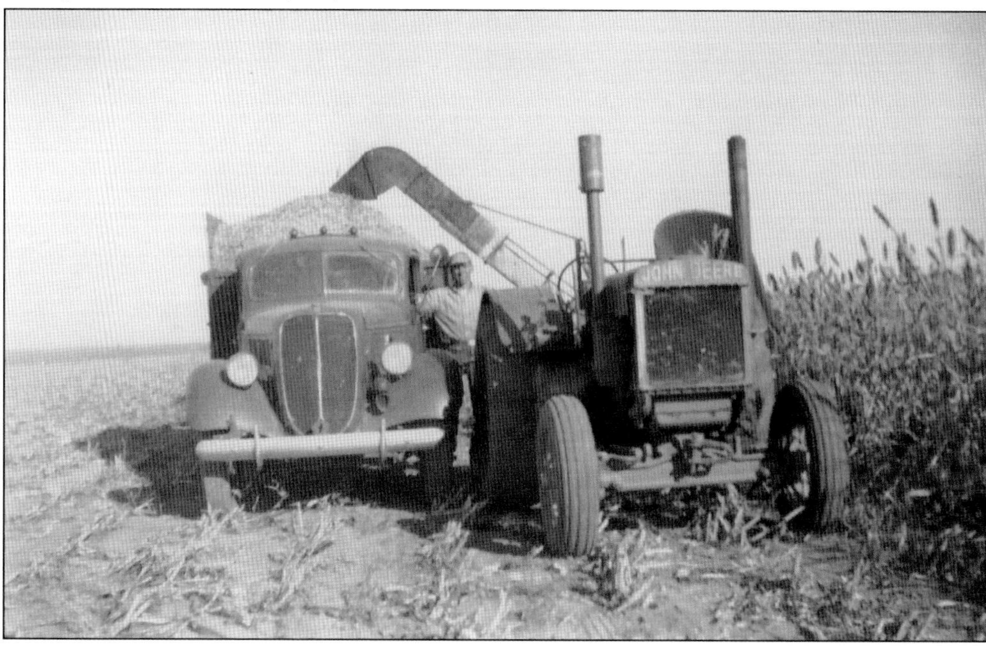

Behind the tractor, an ensilage harvester cuts corn on the Masters farm just before it ripens and then chops it into ensilage before spewing it into the truck bed. The ensilage was taken to a silo, where it was stored for later use. (EM.)

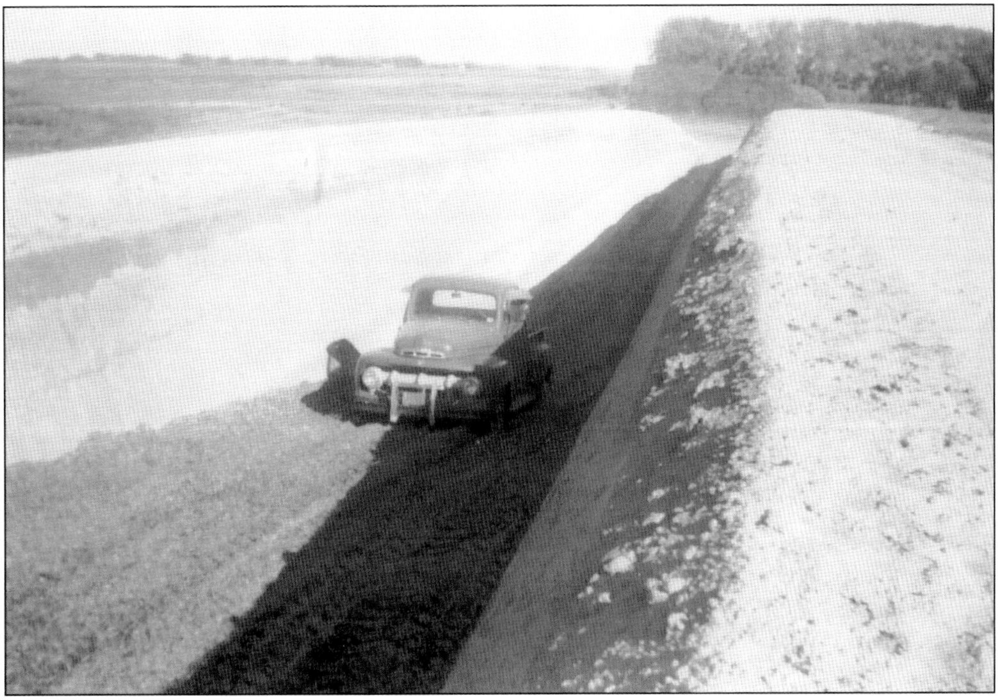

A truck drives over coarsely chopped green corn stalks after they were dumped into a concrete, underground silo on the Masters farm. Pressing the air out of the ensilage preserves the fodder in its green state to be used as food for livestock during the winter months. (EM.)

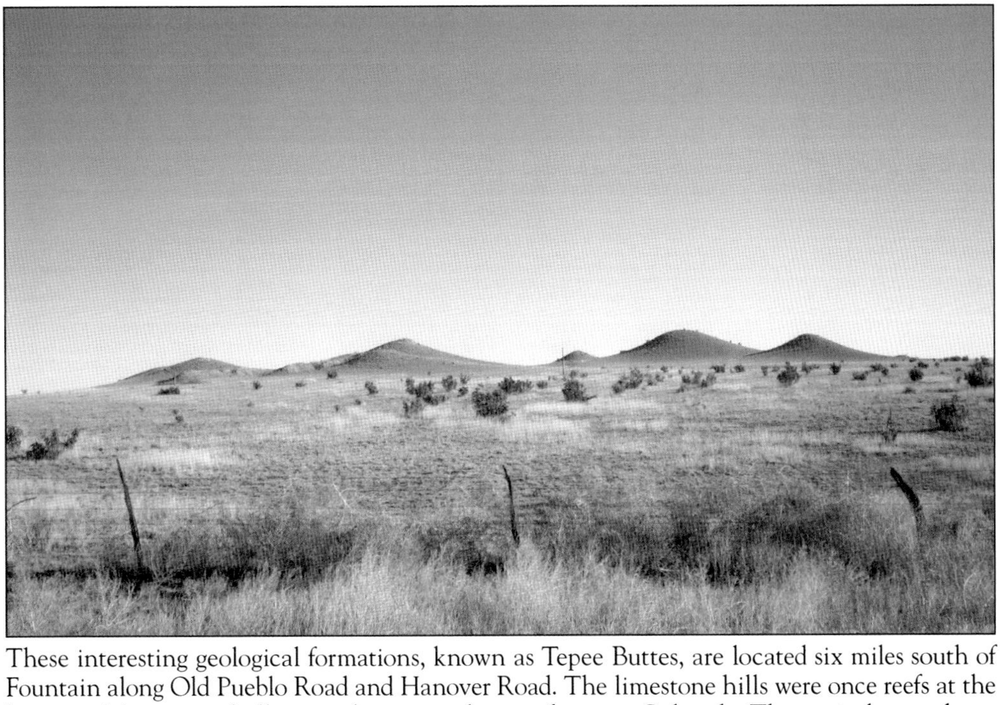

These interesting geological formations, known as Tepee Buttes, are located six miles south of Fountain along Old Pueblo Road and Hanover Road. The limestone hills were once reefs at the bottom of the warm, shallow sea that covered most of eastern Colorado. The conical mounds are packed with cretaceous fossils such as clams, baculites, snails, and worms. (ATH.)

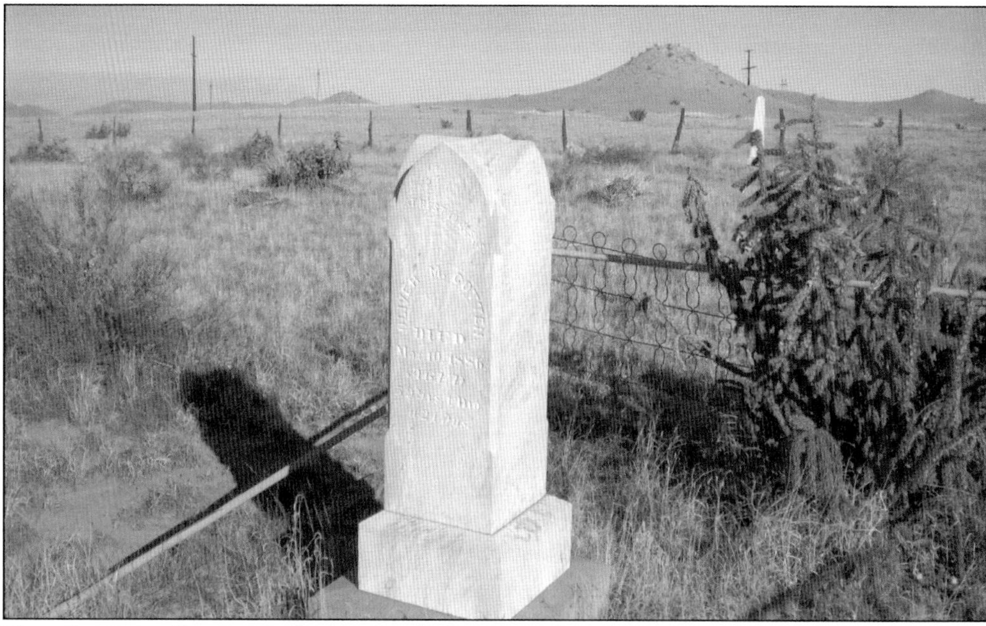

Near the Tepee Buttes, the body of early homesteader Oliver Cotten has been resting in the community cemetery since 1886. Nelson Wilson of Norway, another early settler in the Buttes area, is also buried in this cemetery, believed to be the first in the valley. The Frost ranch now occupies this land, and members of all three families and others of the old Buttes community are buried here. (ATH.)

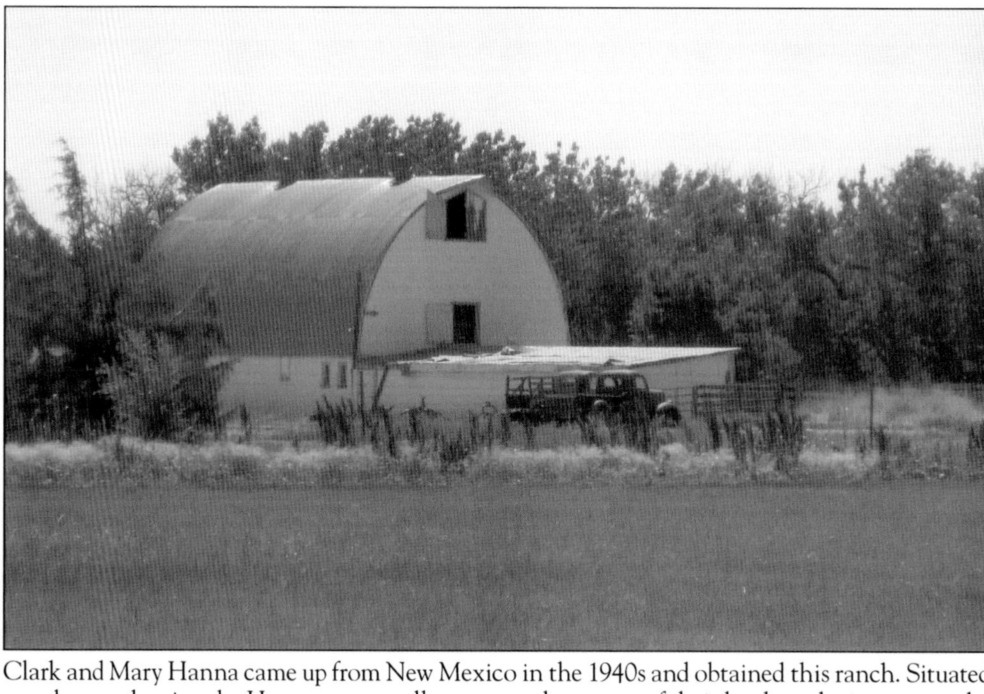

Clark and Mary Hanna came up from New Mexico in the 1940s and obtained this ranch. Situated too close to the city, the Hannas eventually gave up a large part of their lands to the interstate, the racetrack, the power plant and its network of lines, and the City of Colorado Springs. Currently, the old Hanna ranch retains its previous name of Clear Spring. (ATH.)

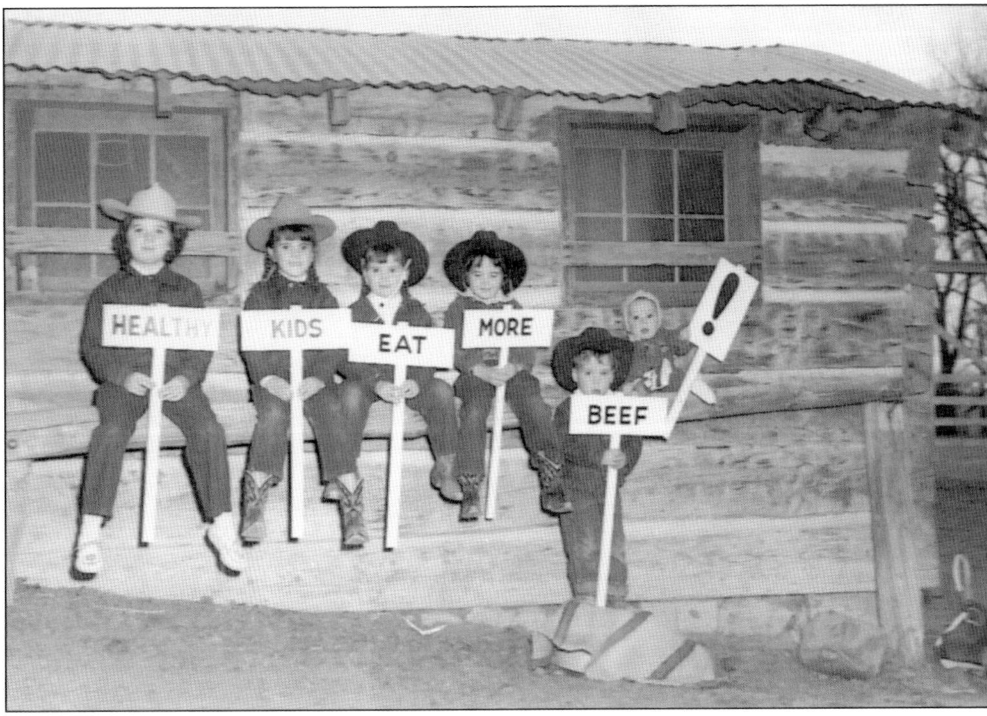

From left to right, Hanna Children Terry, Karen, Randy, Ginger, Steve, and Kirk participate in their own beef campaign. For several decades, Fountain's cattle growers worked with the Cattlemen's Beef Board to promote beef as a source of nutrition. Encouraging consumers to eat beef secured the cattlemen's livelihood, and the "Eat More Beef" campaign intensified with an increase in vegetarianism. (AH.)

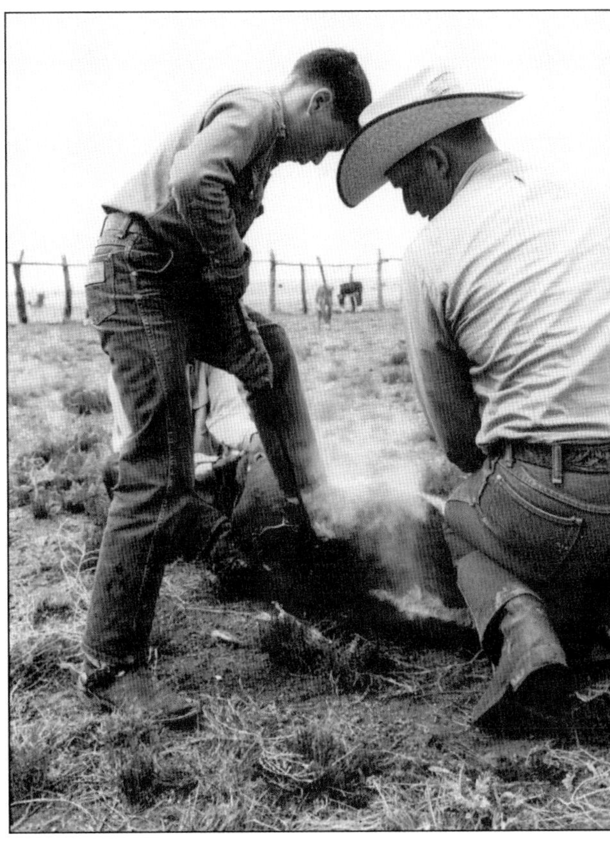

In his spurred boots and Wrangler jeans, young Steve Hanna holds a hot branding iron to a calf in the 1960s with assistance from two ranch hands. This technique of hot branding to identify the owner of the livestock originated in Europe and was improved in the Americas. The unique mark allowed cattle of many ranches to graze together in open range and made separation at roundup time easier. (JF.)

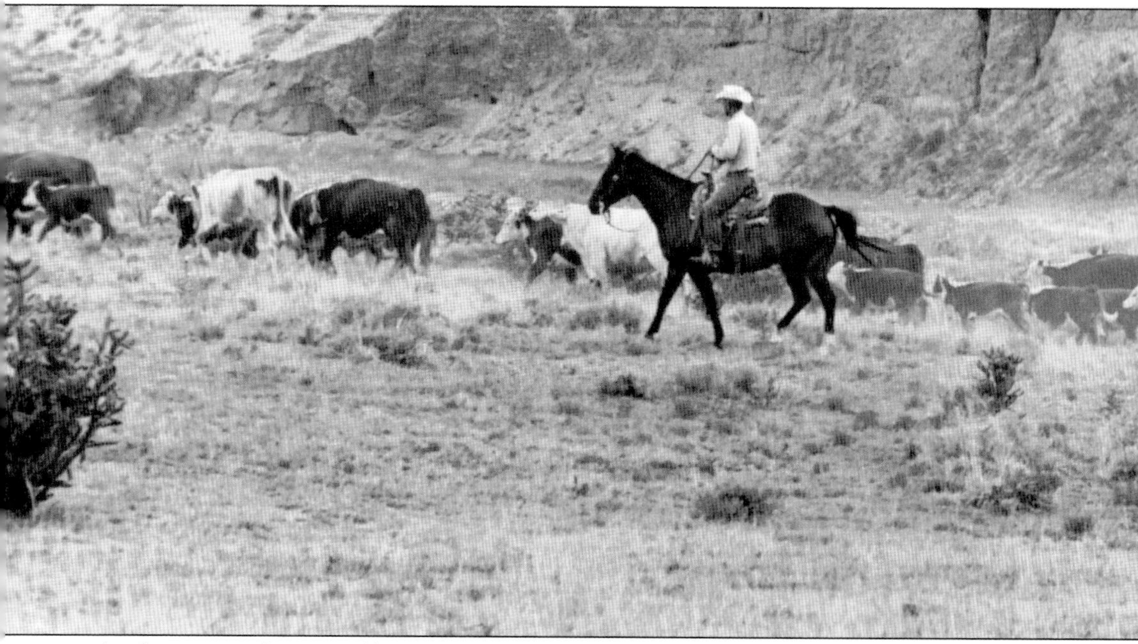

As if in a scene from an old Western movie, conservationist and cowboy Jon Frost (right) rides his range. The Frost ranch is located on Hanover Road southeast of Fountain on lands first homesteaded by the Cottens and Wilsons. Some of the Frost ranch has been chiseled away due to encroaching development, but it has managed to stay in pristine condition. In fact, the owners of this and the neighboring Hanna ranch have succeeded in protecting 1,300 acres of land along

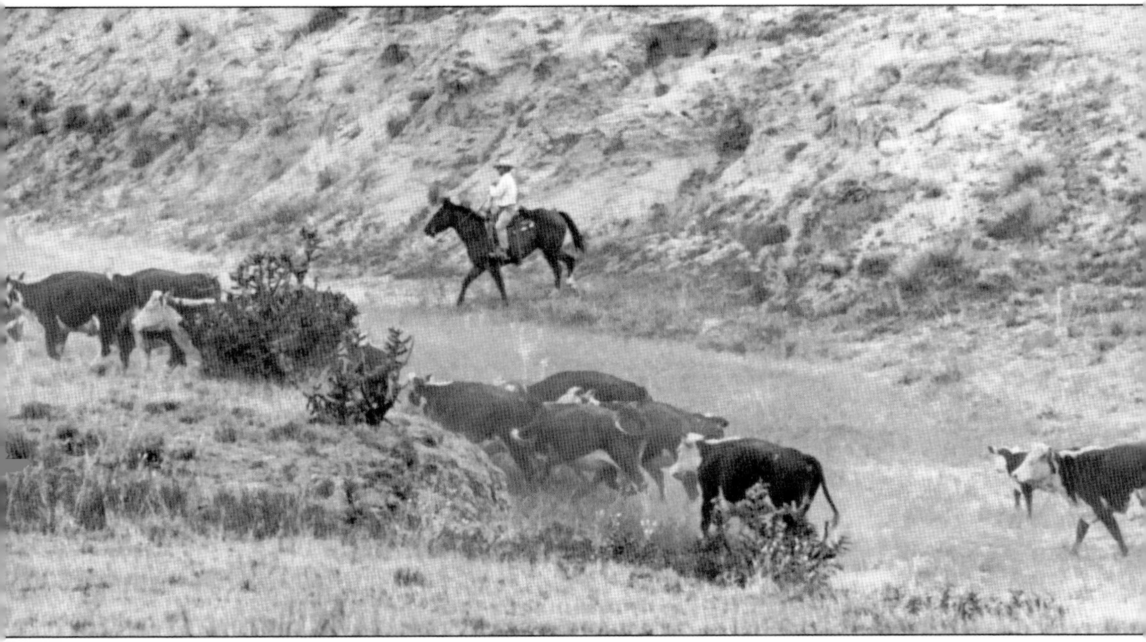

Fountain Creek by placing it under a conservation easement, but it has not been easy. The owners of these ranches must continually keep abreast of the laws governing the land and their right to keep it. Meanwhile, to step onto these ranches is to catch a glimpse of Fountain's historical ranching community. (JF.)

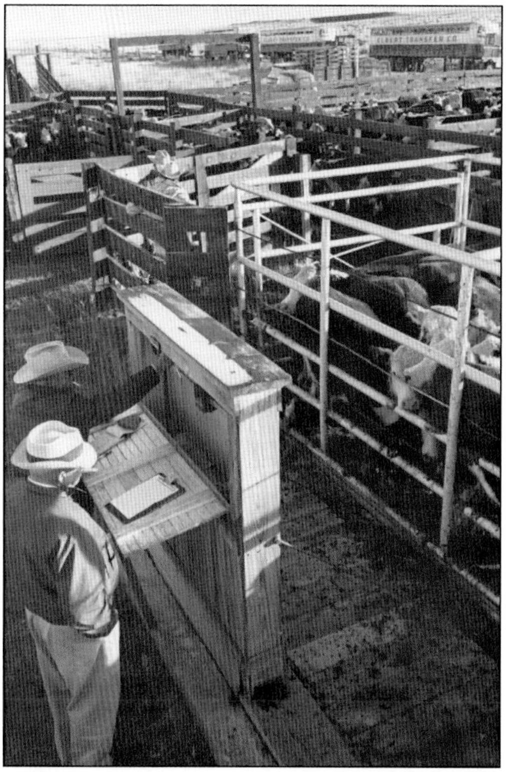

At his ranch in the 1960s, Jon Frost works the scale at the red pens, so named for their red coating of paint, while his father-in-law, Gene Hayward, looks on. The cattle were crowded onto the metal scale directly in front of the men while Frost measured their weight. This information was essential in determining their market worth. (JF.)

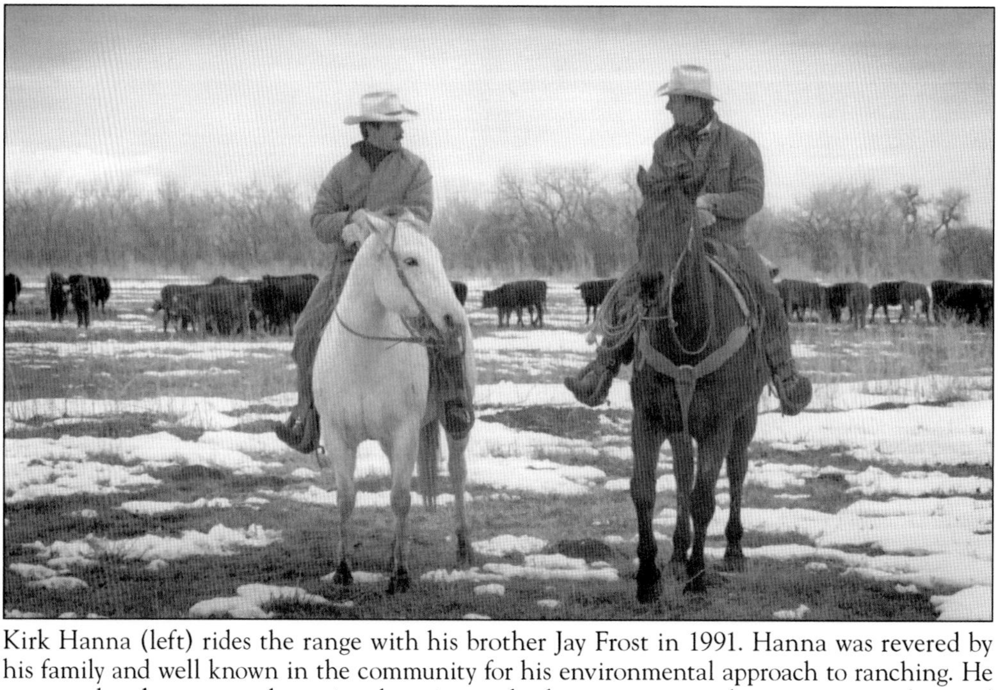

Kirk Hanna (left) rides the range with his brother Jay Frost in 1991. Hanna was revered by his family and well known in the community for his environmental approach to ranching. He promoted and encouraged rotational grazing and other practices, such as using goats for weed control. He remained ever concerned for the river as the city up north continued its assault with steady growth. (AH.)

Three

Working on the Railroad

Fountain became a bustling village with the arrival of the Denver & Rio Grande Railroad and the Atchison, Topeka & Santa Fe Railroad. Depots on both sides of town handled passengers, freight, mail, and the instant messaging of the day: telegrams. Beginning in 1880, the Denver & New Orleans Railroad ran south along Jimmy Camp Creek and passed by on the east side of Fountain on its way to Pueblo. The Colorado & Southern Railway operated on these rails from 1898 to 1913. With all this railroad activity, Fountain naturally became home to quite a few railroad employees and their families.

Uphill trains often stopped to take on water. Railroad sidings every 10 miles or so provided a place for these trains to pull over, allowing the downhill trains to continue on their way. One such siding existed at Buttes about six miles south of Fountain. Sidings also provided a place for work trains to stay off the main rails, while the railroad gangs maintained the tracks during normal usage and cleaned up the aftermath of flooding and accidents.

One such tragic accident occurred in the wee hours of the morning on May 14, 1888, when a few detached train cars in Colorado Springs rolled southward, gradually gaining speed in their descent. At the Santa Fe depot in Fountain, the runaway cars collided with the engine of a passenger train. One of those cars was filled with naphtha gas and exploded in the collision. Burning liquid poured onto the ground and under the depot, setting it ablaze. Men from the town converged on the scene to fight the fire, not realizing another car contained black powder. When the flames reached the powder car, it set off an explosion that was felt for many miles.

One newspaper account reported that every window in town was broken and quite a few homes saw structural damage. Large pieces of twisted iron and splintered wood were hurled several yards in every direction. The accident left 18 people injured and 3 dead, including Henry Hutchin. Undaunted, the town repaired and rebuilt.

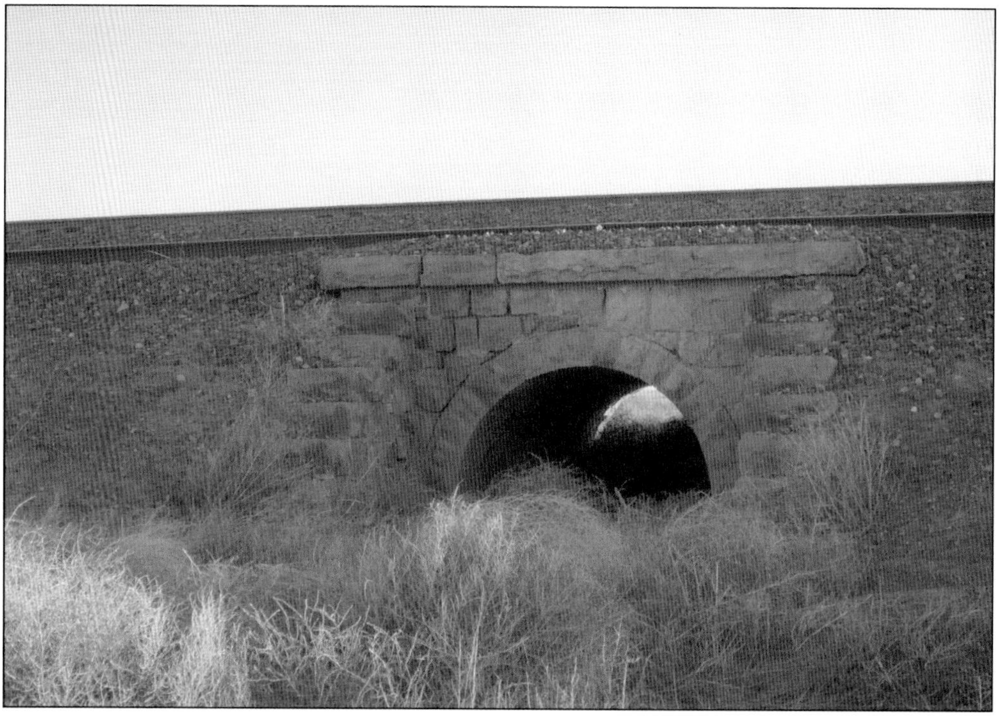

This stone culvert, located south of Fountain near the old Midway ranch, is one of many supporting the railway as it passes over arroyos and gullies. It has been in use since 1887, when it was built for the Santa Fe Railroad by Orman and Crook, a Pueblo road construction company responsible for much of Colorado's early transportation infrastructure. (ATH.)

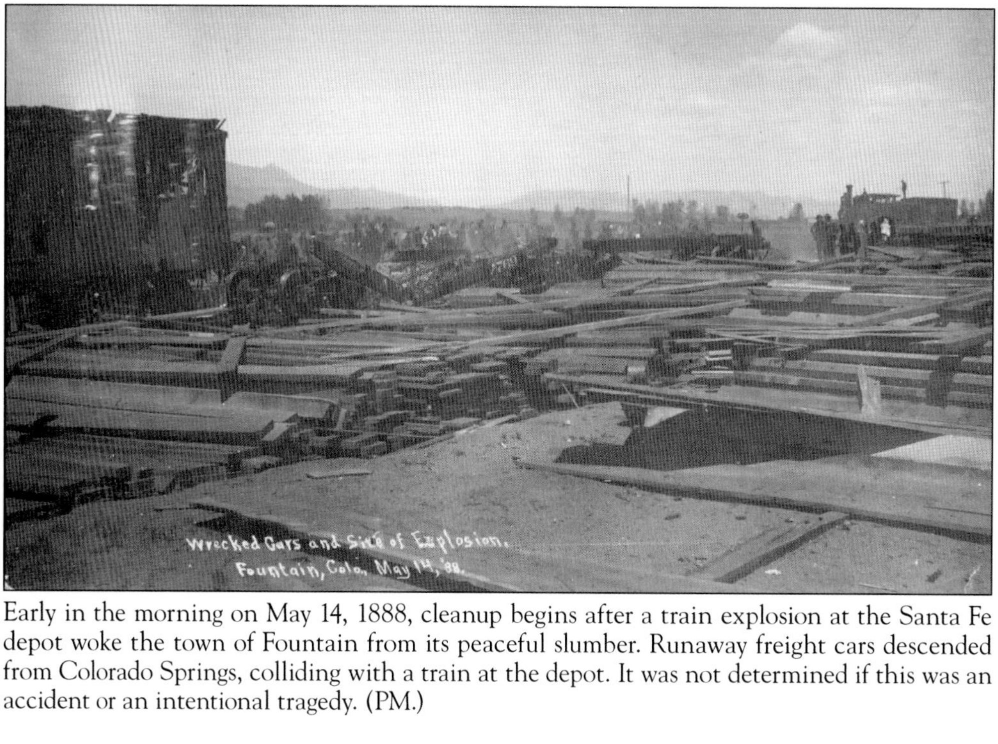

Early in the morning on May 14, 1888, cleanup begins after a train explosion at the Santa Fe depot woke the town of Fountain from its peaceful slumber. Runaway freight cars descended from Colorado Springs, colliding with a train at the depot. It was not determined if this was an accident or an intentional tragedy. (PM.)

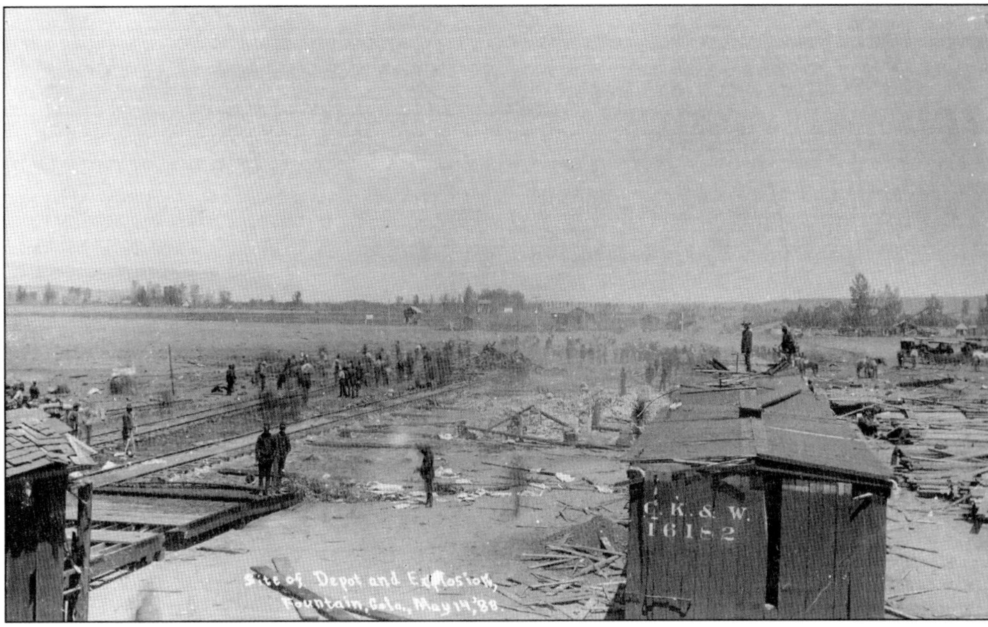

This view of the 1888 wreckage shows the corner of what remained of the depot and its platform (left) and the tracks as they head north past the young town of Fountain. The railroad crew is already cleaning up the debris. (PM.)

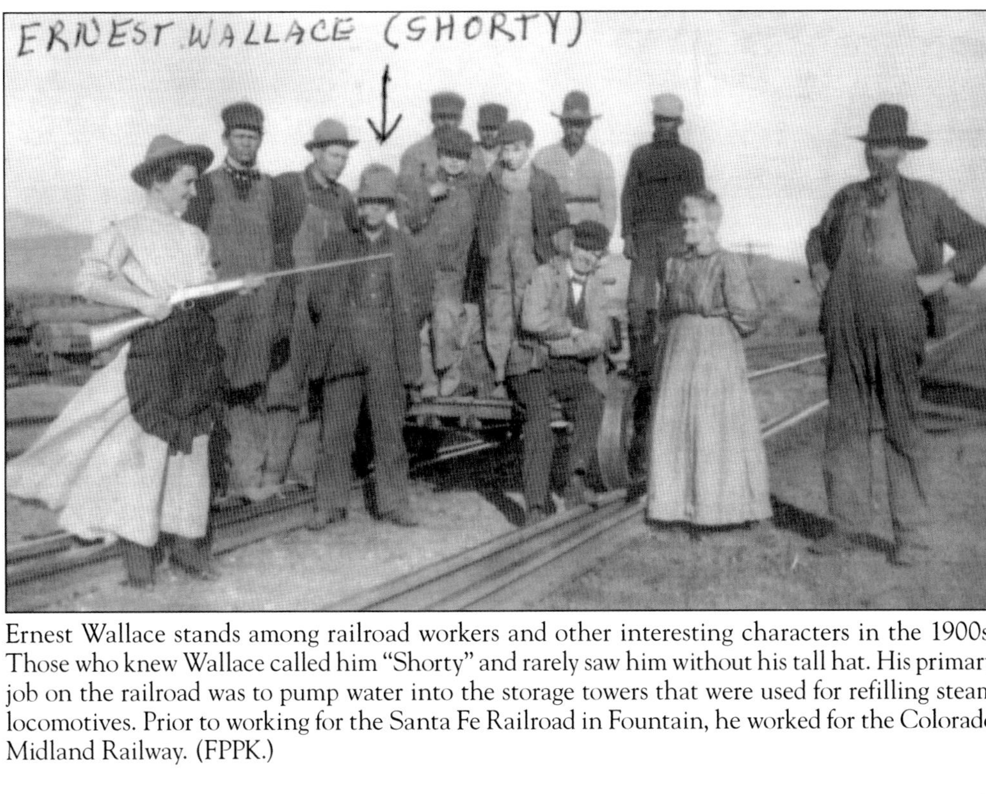

Ernest Wallace stands among railroad workers and other interesting characters in the 1900s. Those who knew Wallace called him "Shorty" and rarely saw him without his tall hat. His primary job on the railroad was to pump water into the storage towers that were used for refilling steam locomotives. Prior to working for the Santa Fe Railroad in Fountain, he worked for the Colorado Midland Railway. (FPPK.)

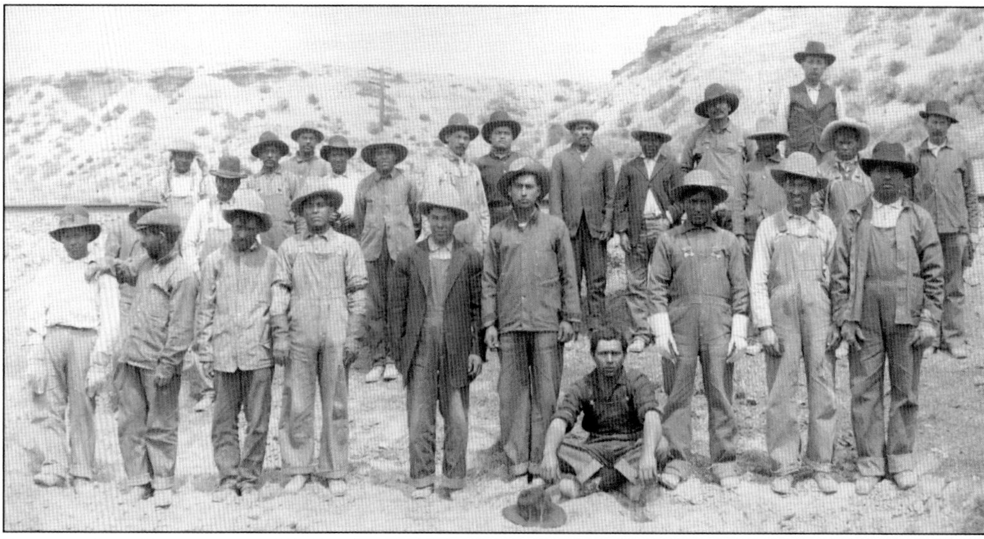

Foreman Lee Christian stands behind and above his Santa Fe Railroad section gang while they stop work long enough to pose for this photograph in the 1910s. A section crew was responsible for the maintenance of a 10-mile section of track. Several families of Mexican ancestry lived on Iowa Avenue in Fountain during 1910, and most of the adult men in these families worked on the railroad. (DB.)

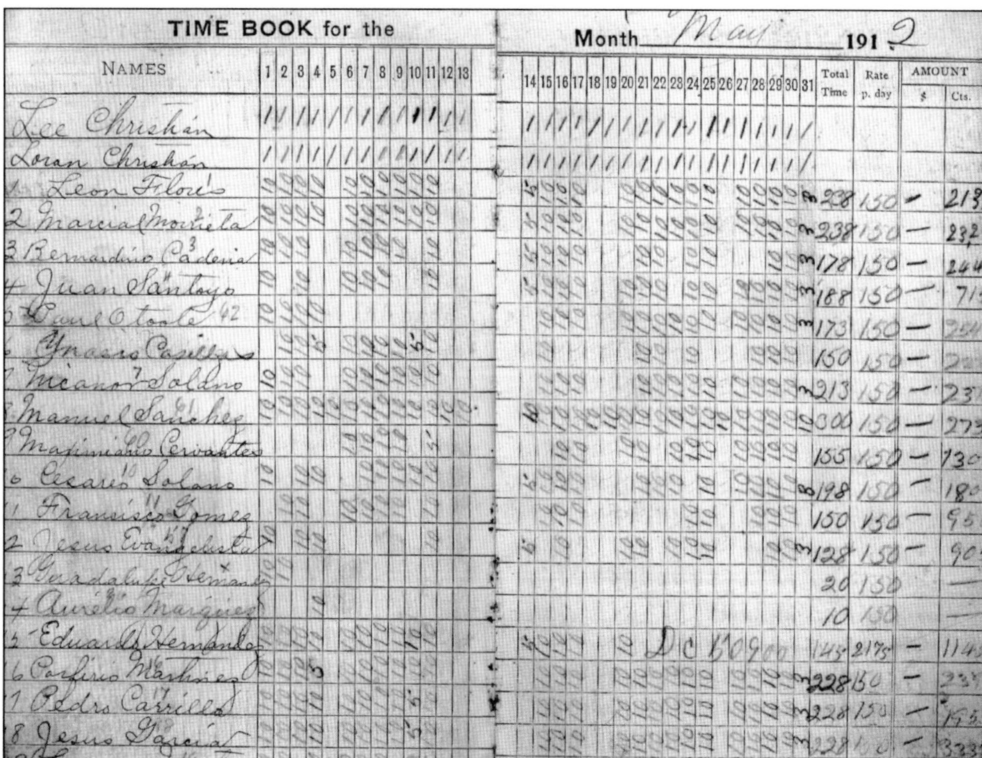

This railroad time book from May 1912 lists Lee Christian and his brother Loran [*sic*] at the top as salaried employees who were credited for every day of the month. Most of the men under them are of Mexican ancestry, and the 10-hour workday seems to be a standard. Working on the railroad was one of a few jobs available to these men. (DB.)

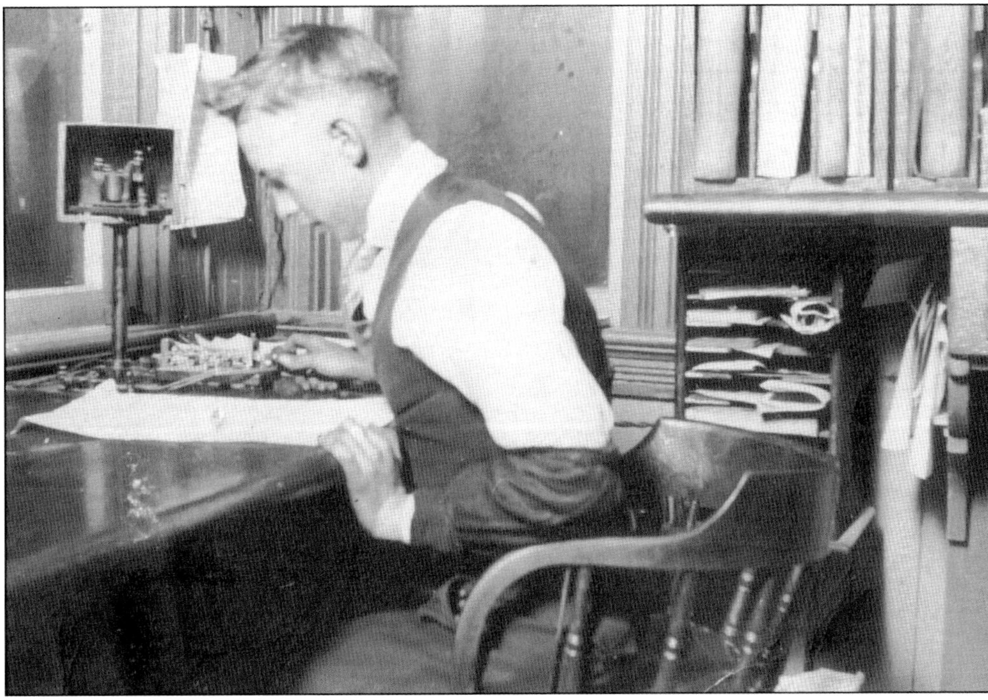

In about 1920, railroad telegrapher John Aldridge sits at his desk, tapping out dot-and-dash signals on the Morse key. His primary duty was to maintain communication between the train dispatcher and the various trains running the track. The skill of telegraphy was usually kept within families but was used less often once the telephone became a common form of communication. (NT.)

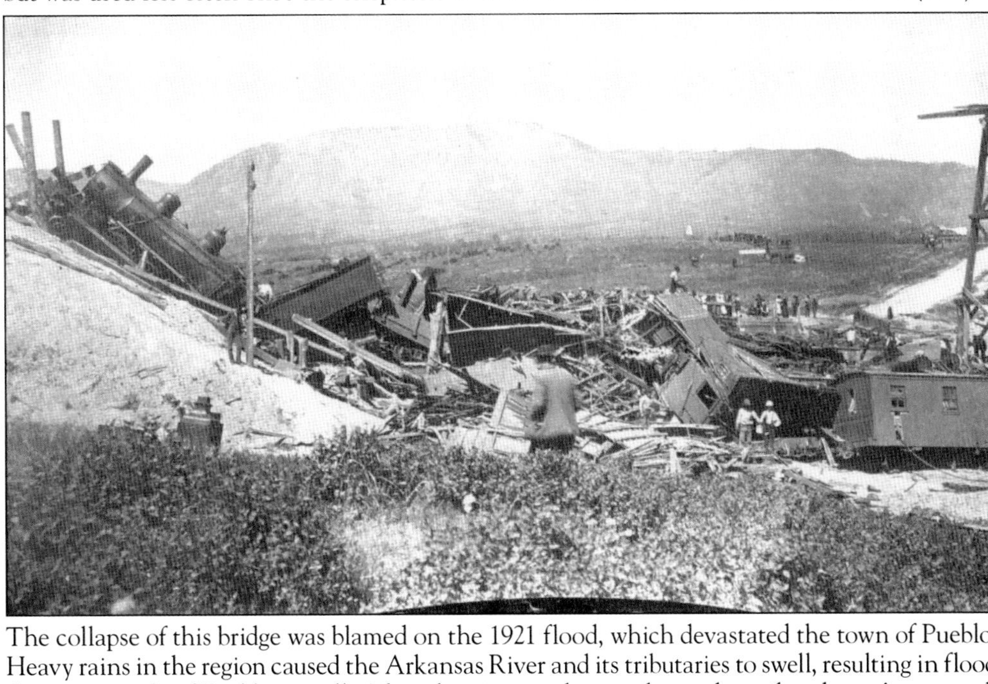

The collapse of this bridge was blamed on the 1921 flood, which devastated the town of Pueblo. Heavy rains in the region caused the Arkansas River and its tributaries to swell, resulting in flood damage outside of Pueblo as well. After cleaning up the wreckage, the railroad crew's next task was to rebuild the bridge. (DB.)

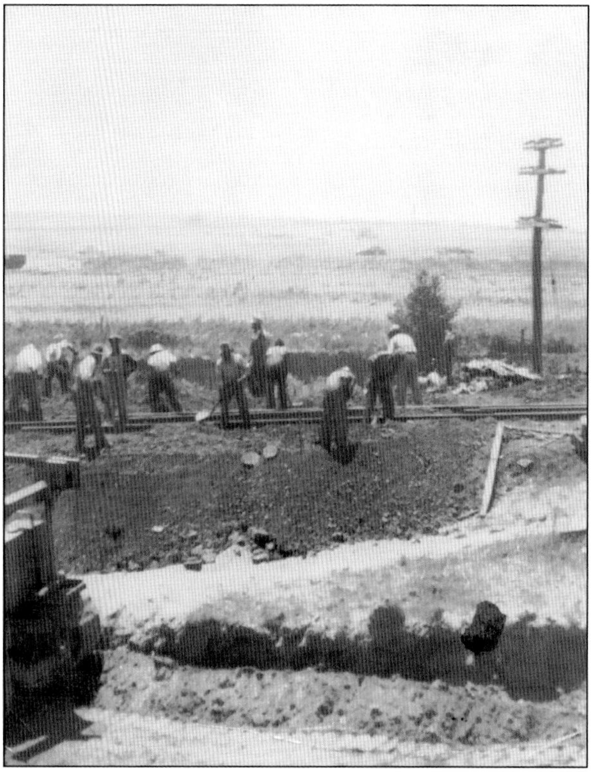

The section gangs that maintained the railroad tracks were known as gandy dancers. Although there are several possibilities for the origin of this term, it is certain that constant maintenance of the tracks was required to prevent derailments, especially along curves. The men struck a rhythm and often sang as they busily lifted the rails with long tools made by the Gandy Company and shoveled ballast back underneath. (FPPK.)

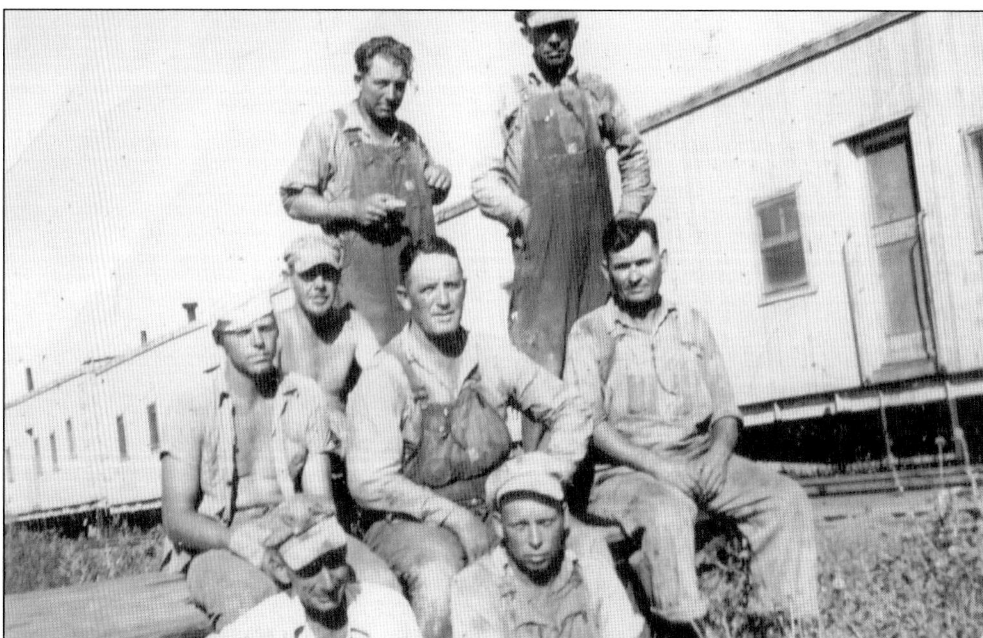

Foreman Fred Wallace (standing left) pauses on a hot day with his section gang for this photograph in the 1940s. Assigned to a certain section of railroad, the crew rode a work train to a siding closest to their section, then hopped on a handcar and pumped it to the work site. Wallace's gang specialized in bridges and trestles, and he eventually became a bridge inspector. (FPPK.)

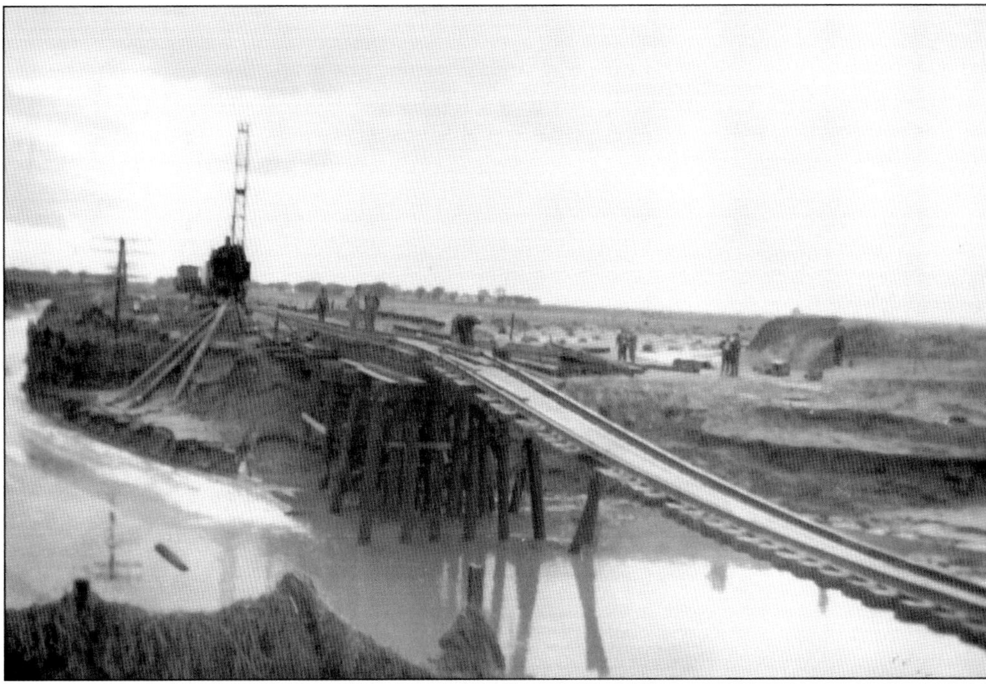

Flooding has caused damage to this railroad bridge. Debris clinging on the fence and water standing off to the side show how high and far the river expanded. A work train has deposited a flatcar and tool car down the track. A pile driver and new timbers will be used by the bridge gang to reconstruct the span. (FPPK.)

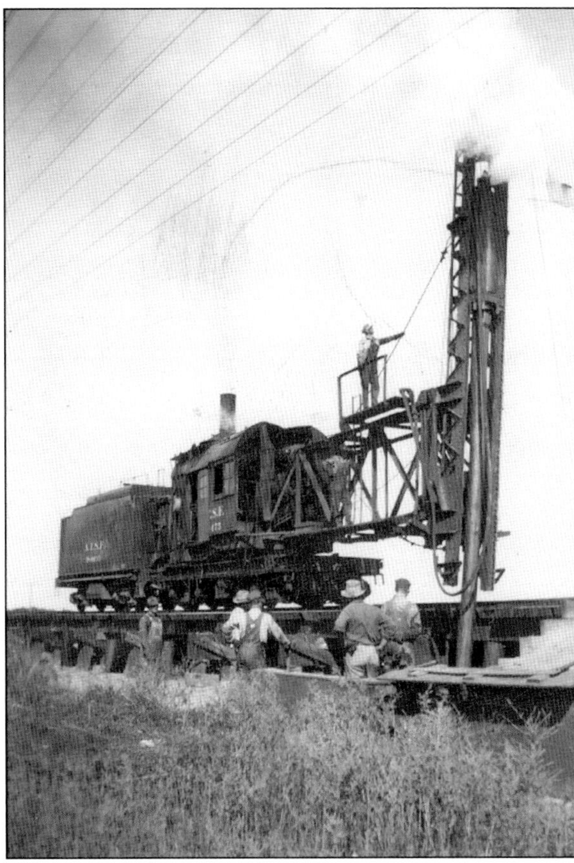

Fueled by coal in the tender car, this Santa Fe pile driver hammers a timber into the ground beside a railroad bridge. Creosote-soaked timbers were protected from the elements and lasted for decades. A cap was set on the top of upright timbers to keep them in place, and the rails were laid across the caps. Since timber bridges tended to weaken with flooding, some were later replaced by steel truss bridges. (FPPK.)

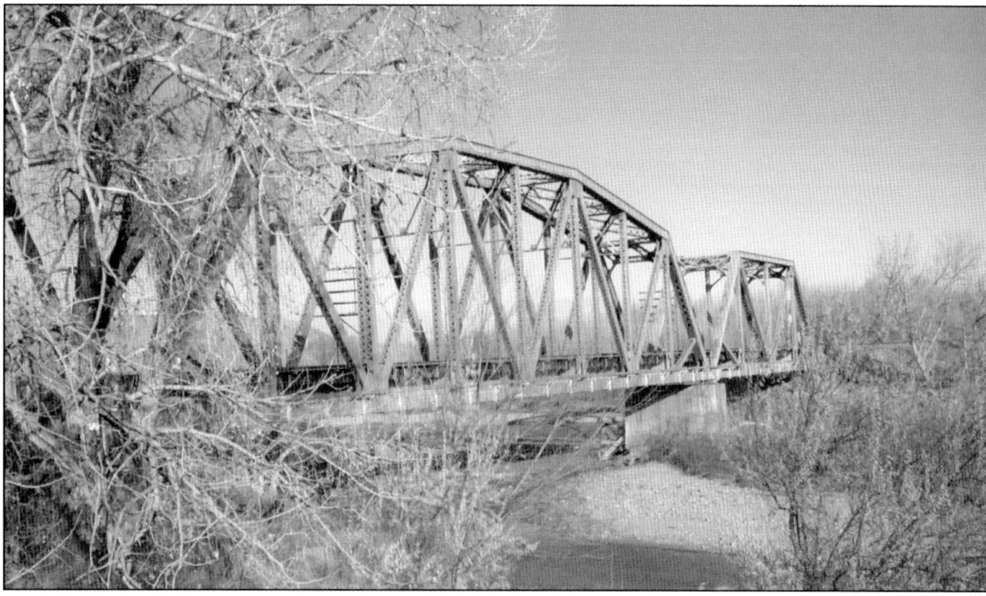

This 1930s railroad bridge crossing Fountain Creek was constructed on the Denver & Rio Grande Railroad near a spot once called Little Buttes. Identified as a through truss bridge, the span is a combination of Pratt and Camelback design. Typically, the steel parts were transported for assembly at the bridge site. This bridge was fastened together by rivets. (ATH.)

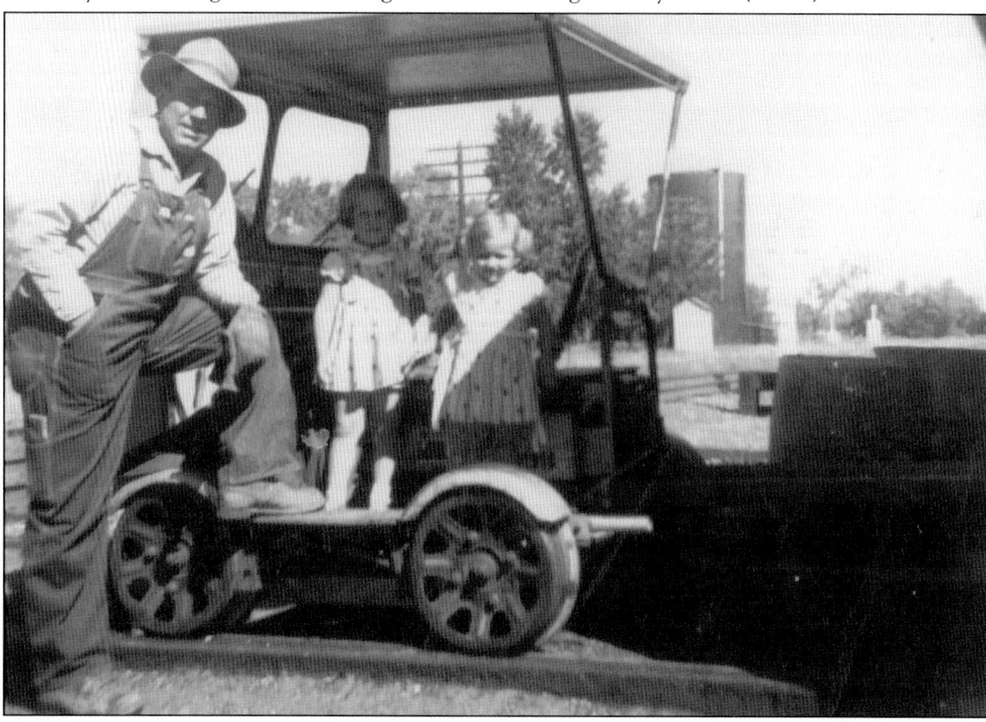

Fred Wallace worked six, sometimes seven, days a week at his job on the railroad. His daughters Florence (left) and Peggy visit him in his "putt-putt car," a motorized version of the hand-pumped car. He used this car to transport himself and when hauling a small trailer of tools and supplies to bridge sites. (FPPK.)

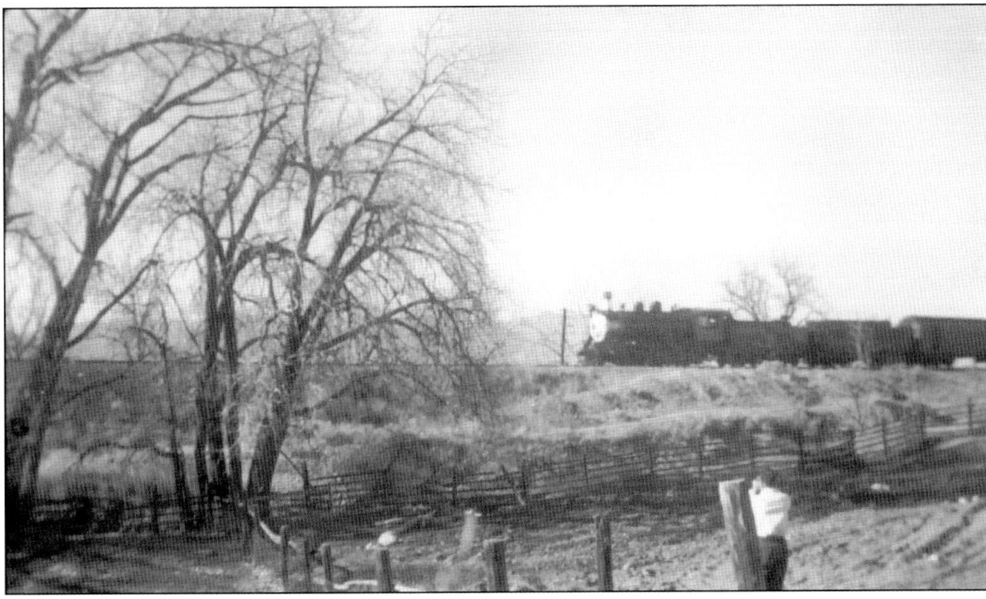

A steam locomotive glides its way south toward Pueblo. Locomotives, such as the one pictured here, were in use by 1910 and phased out in the 1950s. No longer fueled by wood, coal was their source of energy. Many locomotives not only pulled cars full of coal but also hauled a supply of water to avoid stopping so often. (FVM.)

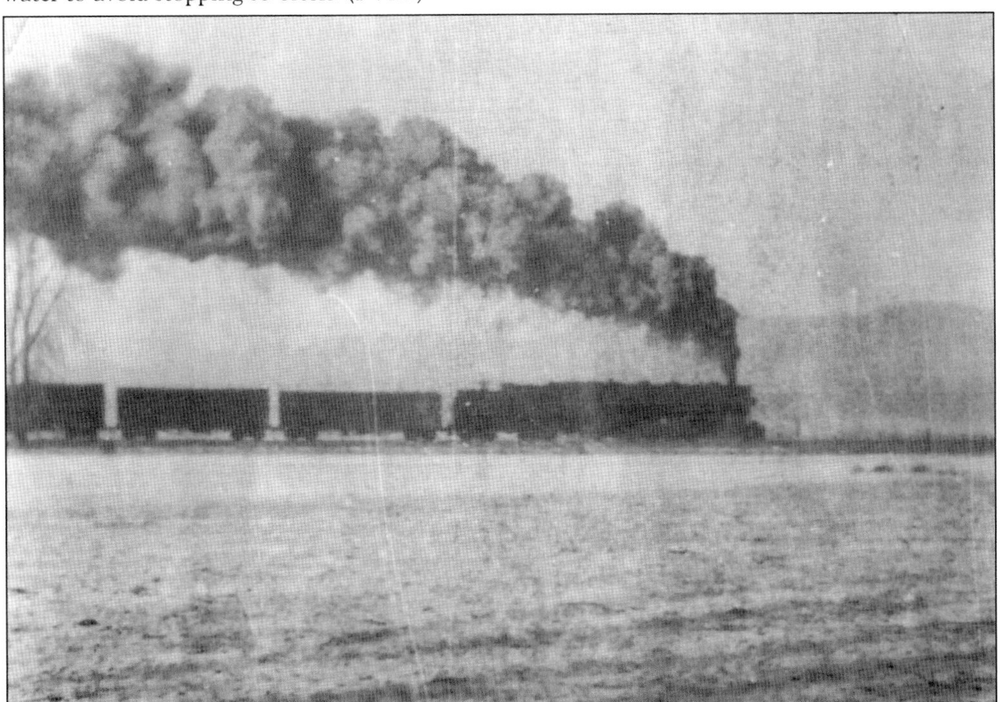

This steam locomotive belches black smoke as it pushes its way north past Fountain farms. Trains traveling north through the valley were presented with a gradual but steady uphill climb to the Palmer Divide. The coal cars are empty, suggesting this train may be on its way to the coal mines in Wyoming. Many valley residents still welcome the lonesome sound of a passing train. (MB.)

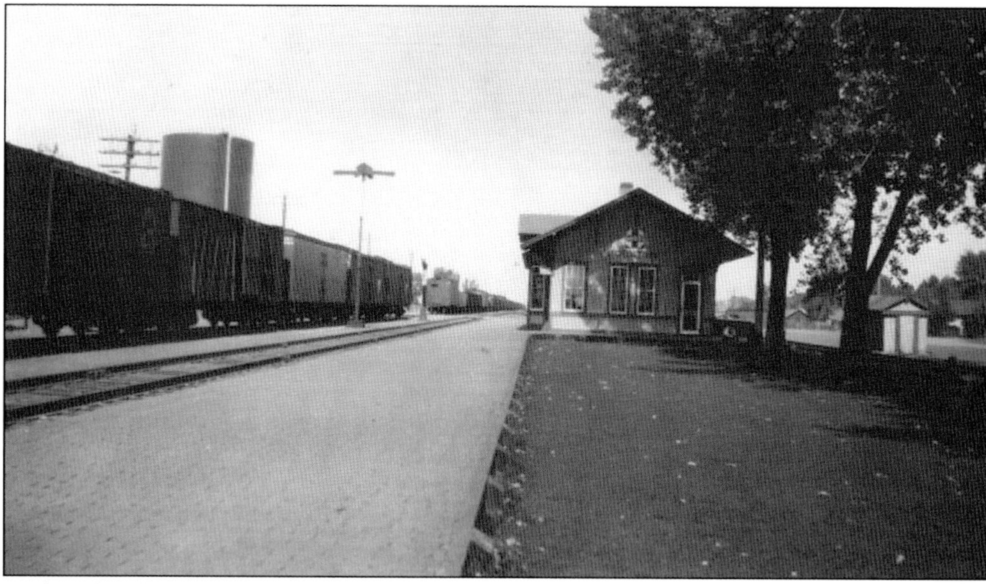

With its handsome brick platform, the second Santa Fe depot sits next to the tracks. The depot was situated on the west side of town until 1953, when the railroad decided it no longer needed it. Fred Wallace purchased the depot for $150 and tasked his children with removing the platform, brick by brick, while he dismantled the building. The materials were reused in subsequent construction projects. (FVM.)

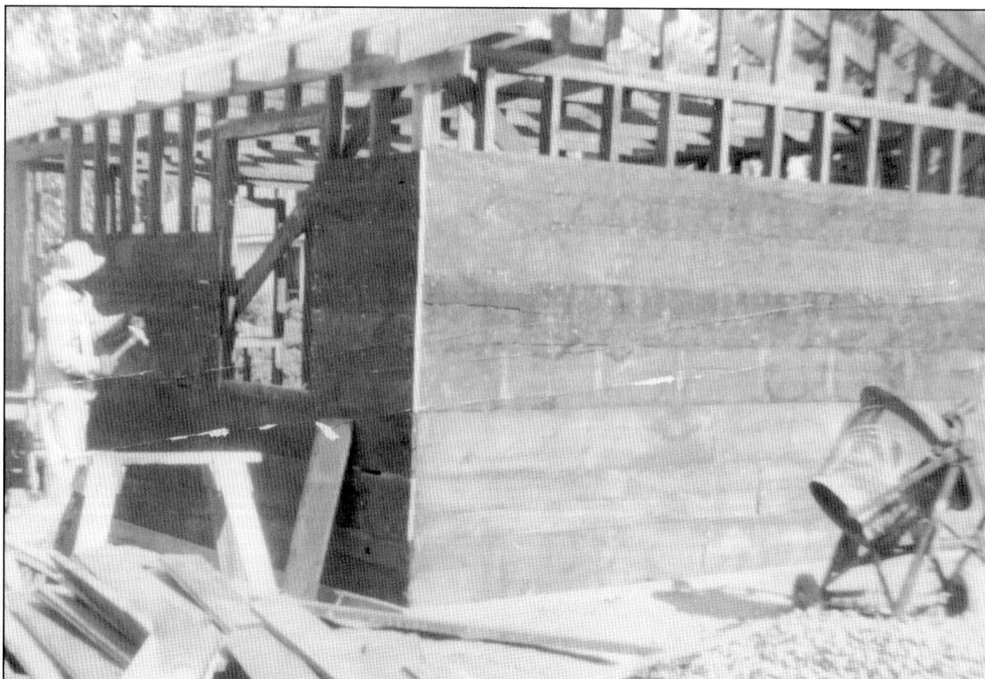

Having learned to waste nothing in his youth, Fred Wallace builds a home out of the remnants of the Santa Fe depot, reusing all the lumber, nails, and bricks. He also refurbished boxcars into apartments, such as the one currently located on the west side of Santa Fe Avenue. These units were then rented to teachers during the school season and tourists in the summer. (FPPK.)

Four

Strolling through the Town

This chapter is designed to take the reader, with the help of a map, through the streets of the old part of town, starting at the main intersection of Main Street and Ohio Avenue. Main Street, formerly the Denver-to-Pueblo Road, heads north past two old churches and many old homes, some built by carpenter L.A. Toothman. Just outside of the historical part of town, Main Street goes north, past old farms, before disappearing into newer Highway 85. The northeast quadrant of the old town features the sites of the old police station, the Denver & Rio Grande depot, and residences once owned by early Hispanic families. Just over the tracks, a road runs north to farmland on the mesa. Iowa Avenue continues on to farms farther east, as well as Link Road and Peaceful Valley.

The southeast quadrant of historical Fountain features Reed Street, which once resembled the old Southwest. The sound of Mexican music and smell of roasting chilies and fresh tortillas permeated the air as the Spanish-speaking *residentes* of adobe homes carried out their daily tasks. Also included in this quarter are the old news office, residential lots owned by early families, and the old hoosegow.

In the southwest quadrant of the old town, South Main Street continued past farms and ranches to Buttes, Wigwam, and Pueblo. Featured in this section are the school block, sites of early family residences, and former businesses such as the Fountain Trading Company and the livery. The explosion of 1888 occurred here on the tracks at the Santa Fe depot. Santa Fe Avenue became the main thoroughfare of the town when it was widened and became Highway 85 in about 1930. The highway heads south across the river and past the cemetery and the old Chancellor place before fading into the newer Interstate 25.

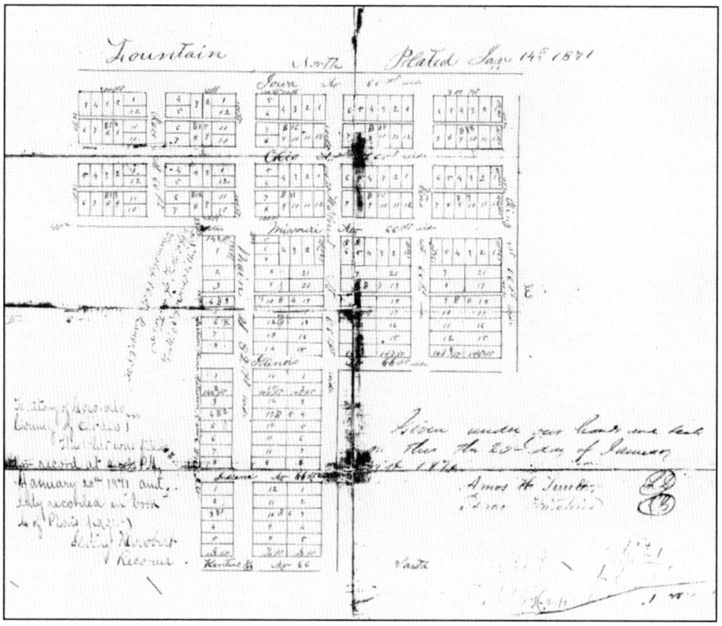

The village of Fountain, consisting of only a few blocks, was platted in 1871 from lands sold by Amos Terrell and Isaac Hutchin, the original homesteaders in this spot. Land surrounding the plat continued to function as farms until later additions to the plat increased the town's size. The town incorporated in 1903 and eventually became a city. Its boundaries now stretch far to the north, with large suburbs sprawling to the east. (EPC.)

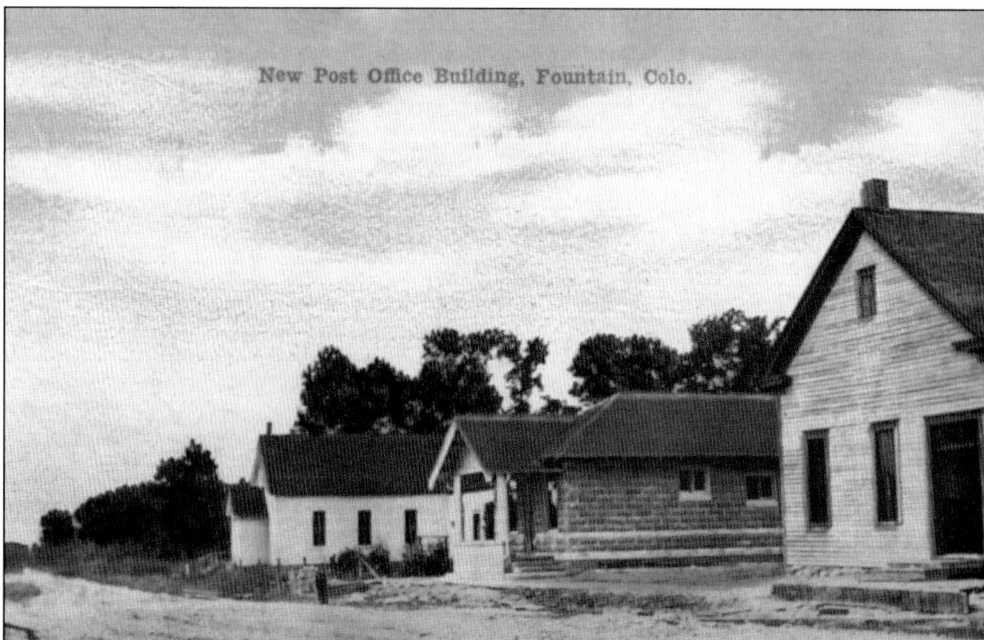

This postcard features the new post office on West Ohio Avenue (center) next to the Free Methodist Church (left). The post office actually occupied a small space in front of the building, which was the home of postmistress Grace Hutchin. Textured cement blocks were used to construct this home in 1904. It was later purchased by the Orcutt family, under whose ownership it has remained for many decades. A section of the old school was moved next door (right) and housed the opera house and later the congregational church. (RW.)

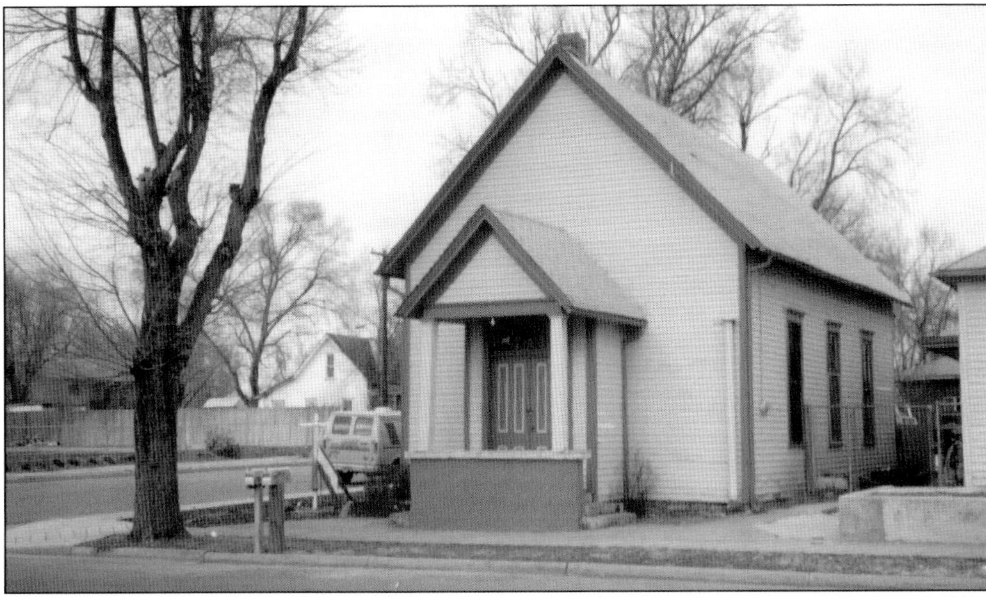

The meetinghouse pictured here in 1996 was originally built in about 1884 as Fountain's Free Methodist Church. The religion was organized in 1860 by former Methodists. Members of this splinter group were free to practice traditional Methodism void of recent adjustments to the doctrine. Barbara Lock's daughter Hovena met John Spicer here while attending church, and they later married in 1885. (ATH.)

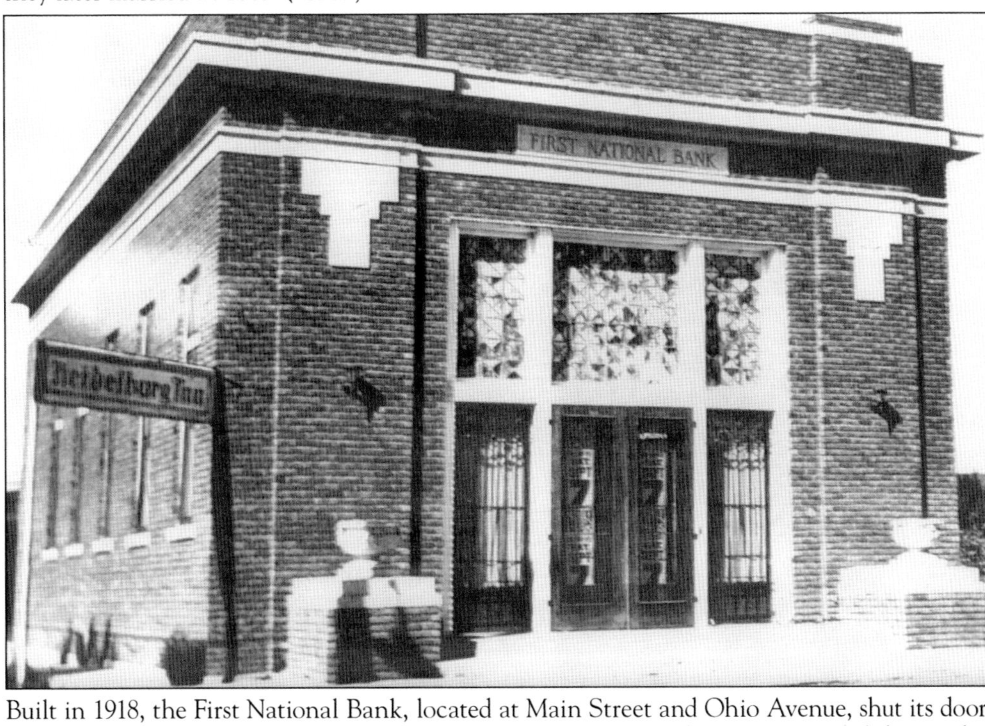

Built in 1918, the First National Bank, located at Main Street and Ohio Avenue, shut its doors in 1929, becoming one of the last of thousands of banks across the country to fail during that decade. A few years later, it was reduced to a saloon called the Heidelberg Inn. The next unlikely owner of the building was the Catholic Church from 1936 until a few years ago. (FVM.)

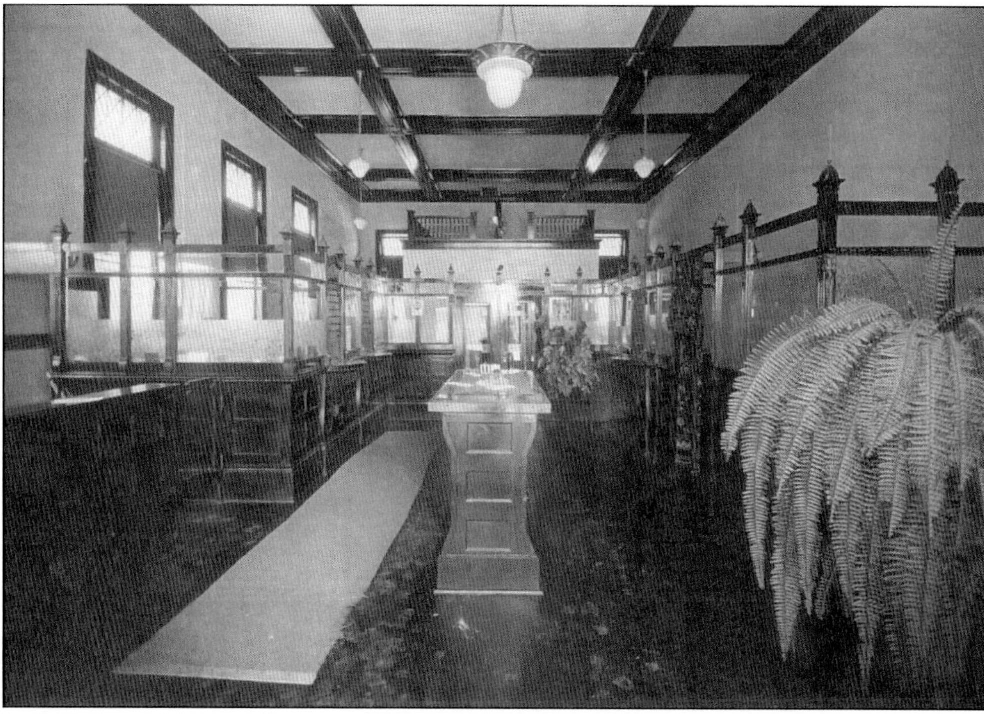

Rich, dark wood framing dominated the interior of Fountain's bank in 1923. The center table was used for filling out deposit and withdrawal requests. Tellers stood in glass booths on the left, lit by the southern sun exposure. Employees and prospective borrowers entered the bank's booths and rear offices through a curtain on the right, leaving dusty shoe prints from the town's sandy streets on the wooden floor. (DK.)

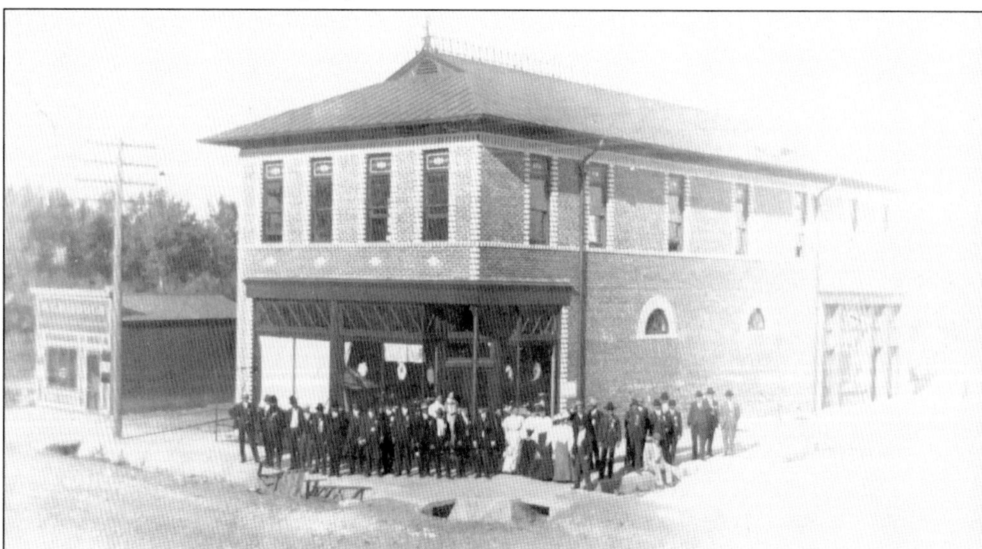

The Woodmen Hall, erected in 1905 by the local lodge of the Woodmen of the World, was located at Main Street and Ohio Avenue. The lower level has been used throughout the years as a store. The hall upstairs was used for civic and club gatherings, and in the 1940s and 1950s, it served as a theater where moviegoers paid 25¢ to watch Westerns and cartoons. (DB.)

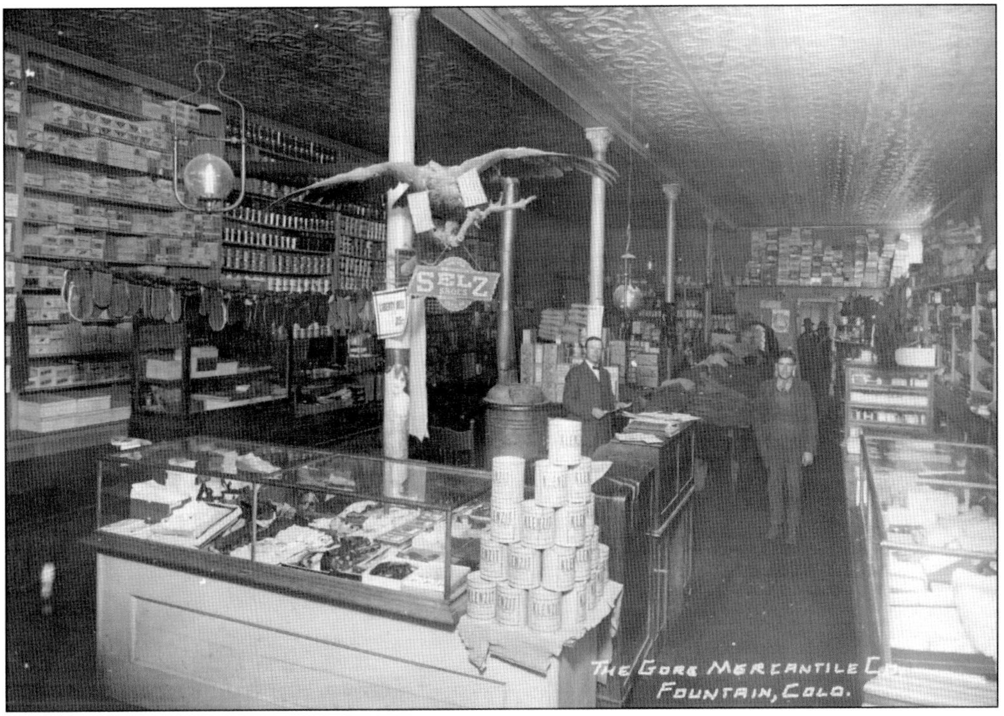

In the 1900s, the Gore Mercantile Company operated out of the first floor of the Woodmen Hall. The general store, warmed by a potbellied stove and owned by Charles Gore, was well stocked with clothing, food, housewares, and fine apparel. The floor-to-ceiling supports and the embossed ceiling panels are still present today. (DB.)

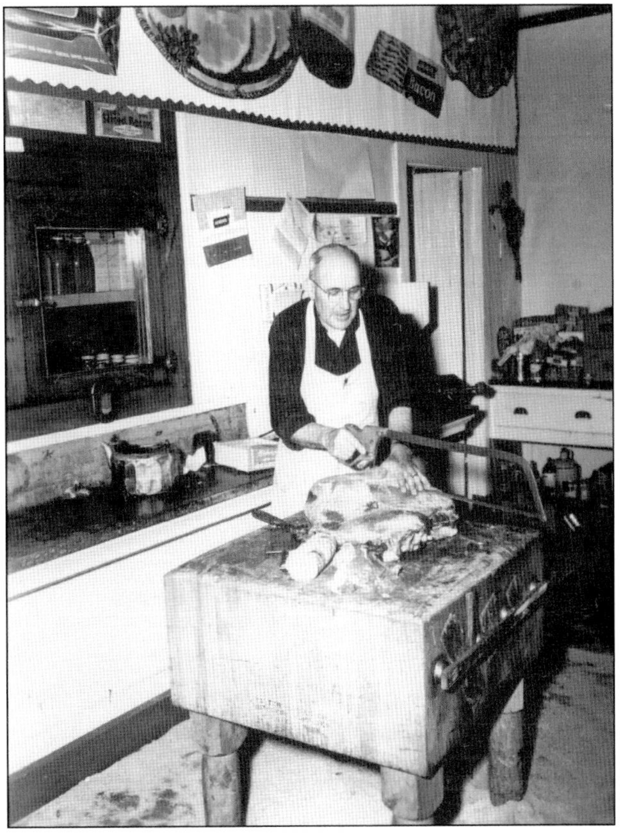

After delivering mail in the morning on his rural route, Charles "Bud" Torbit cut meat on the butcher block at Martin's Store, which operated in the Woodmen Hall in the mid-1900s. Due to lack of refrigeration, customers bought their meat on a daily basis with a visit to the local butcher. Often, the meat was cut to order while the customer waited. (NT.)

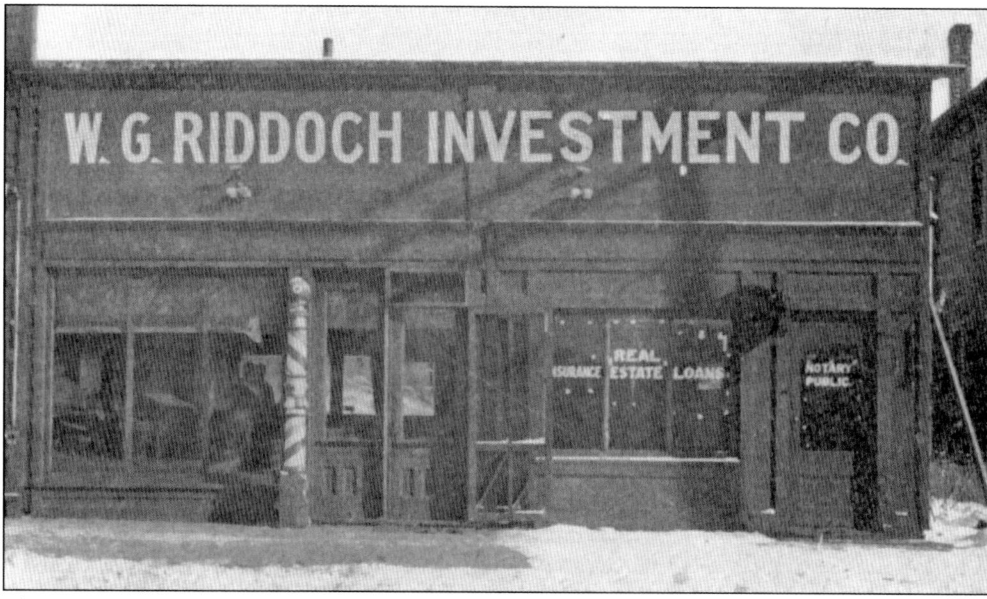

The W.G. Riddoch Investment Company, dealers in insurance, real estate, and loans, was one of the oldest businesses in Fountain and located on the north side of the Woodmen Hall. Riddoch carried a catalog of model homes for prospective buyers to browse. He was also active in the irrigation ditch development of the Fountain area, but his name was prominently connected with the building and development of the town. (CC.)

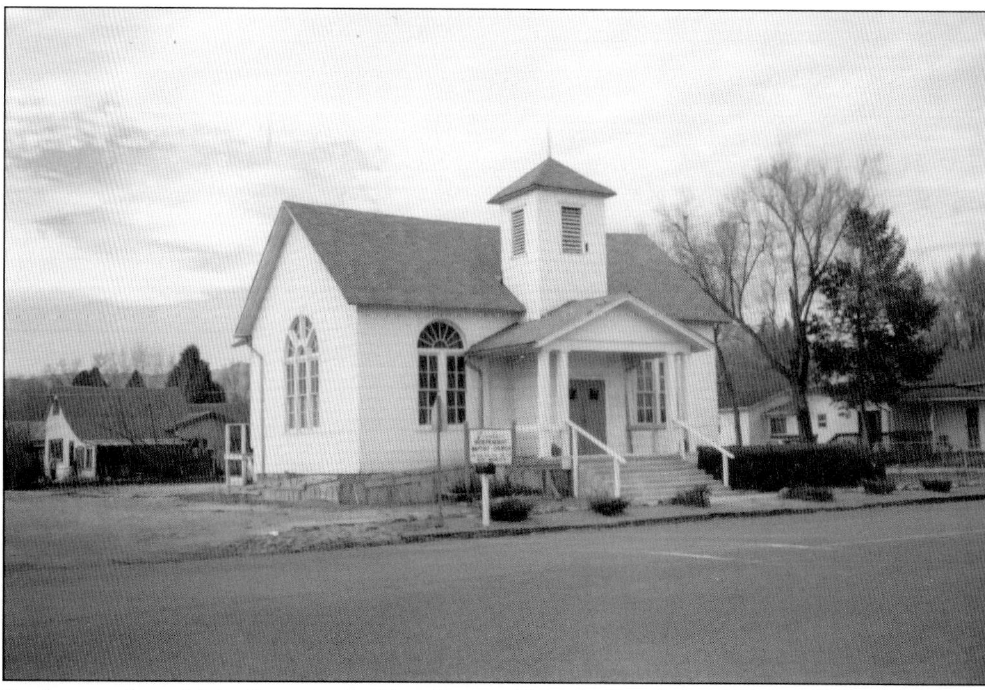

Farther north on Main Street is the First Baptist Church, founded in 1870 and pictured here in 1996. The original building was erected in the 1880s near the Santa Fe depot. After the church was destroyed in the 1888 train explosion, this new edifice was erected in its place. In 1913, the structure was moved to its present location. (ATH.)

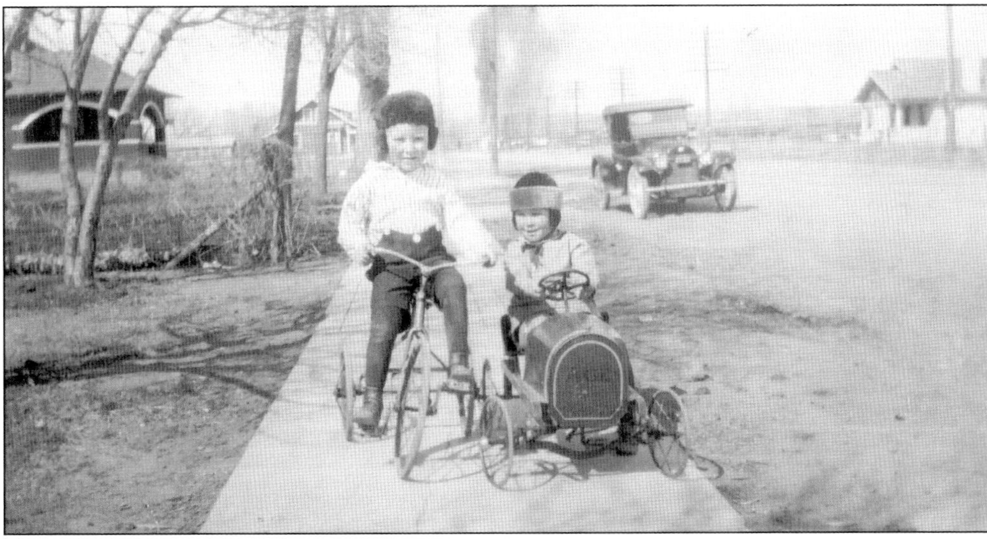

William Whalen rides his tricycle and Brownie Bell drives his pedal car on a crisp, sunny day on North Main Street as they keep their ears covered against the chill. The telephone building (left) now functions as a home. In the background, a train on the Denver & Rio Grande tracks puffs black smoke along the foot of the mesa as it heads north to Colorado Springs. (DK.)

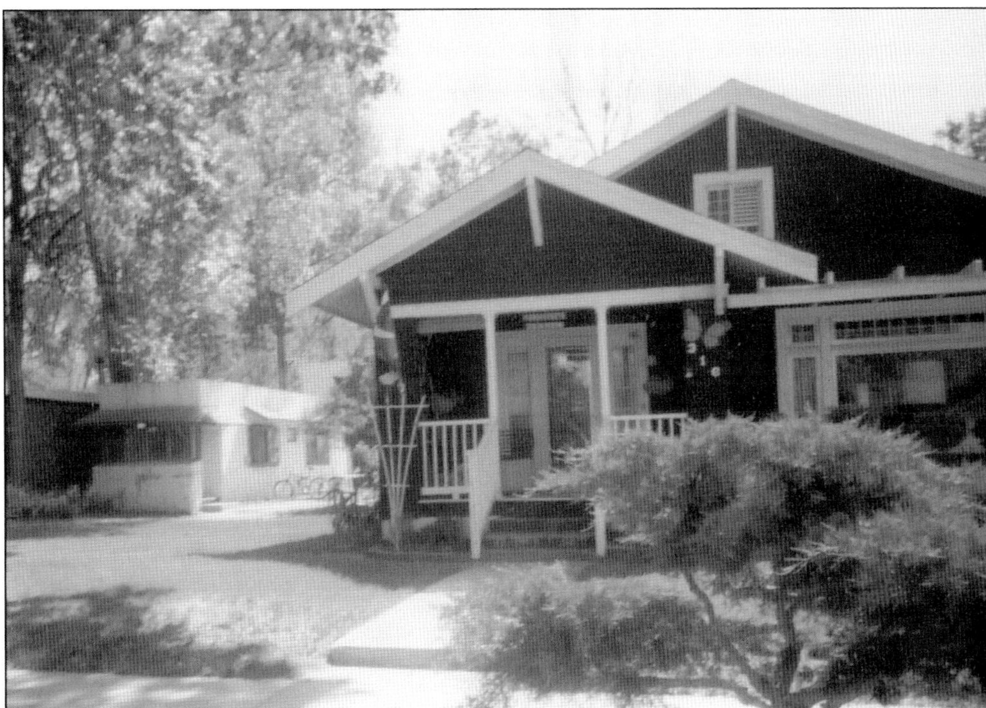

This home, located on North Main Street, was purchased by Fred Wallace in the late 1930s. The one-bedroom apartment to the left was built by Wallace from a Denver streetcar he purchased in 1951. This apartment was most often rented to teachers and is still in use today. Wallace is also responsible for purchasing and remodeling other train cars seen in Fountain into homes. (FPPK.)

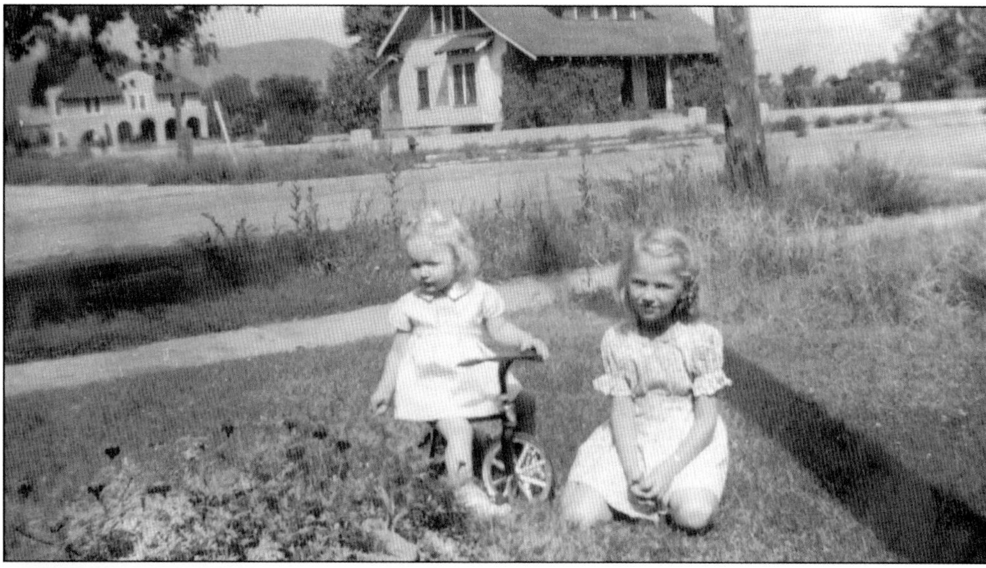

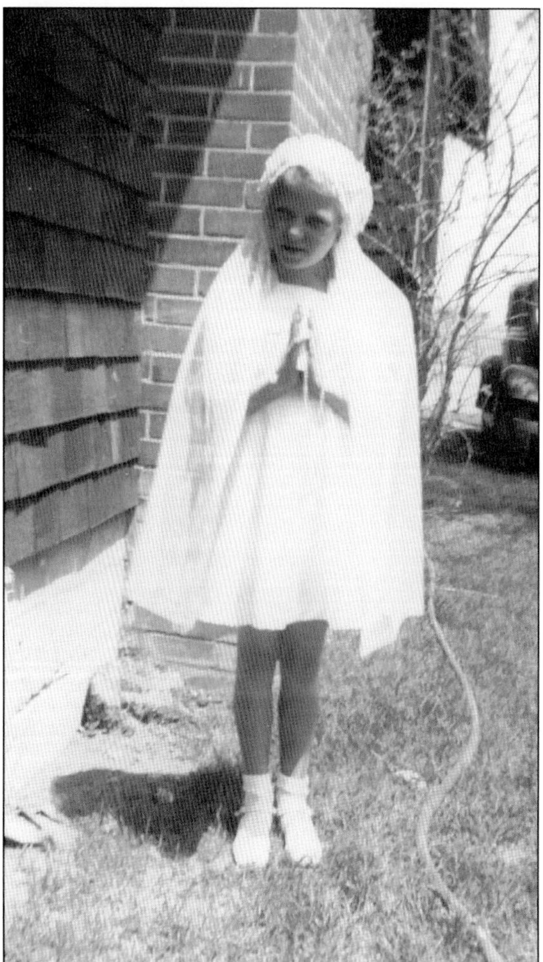

Peggy Wallace (left) and her sister Florence play in the front yard of their home on North Main Street. The two homes behind them still stand today. The ivy-covered house is reportedly built from a kit, and the mansion in back was the home of Wanden Kane, Fountain's first female mayor, at the time this picture was taken in the 1940s. (FPPK.)

Florence Wallace, outside her home on North Main Street, poses for this picture on the day of her first Communion in the early 1940s. Her family consisted of some of the very few Irish Catholics in town, and they attended St. Joseph's Catholic Church with a congregation made up mostly of the town's ethnic Mexican population. (FPPK.)

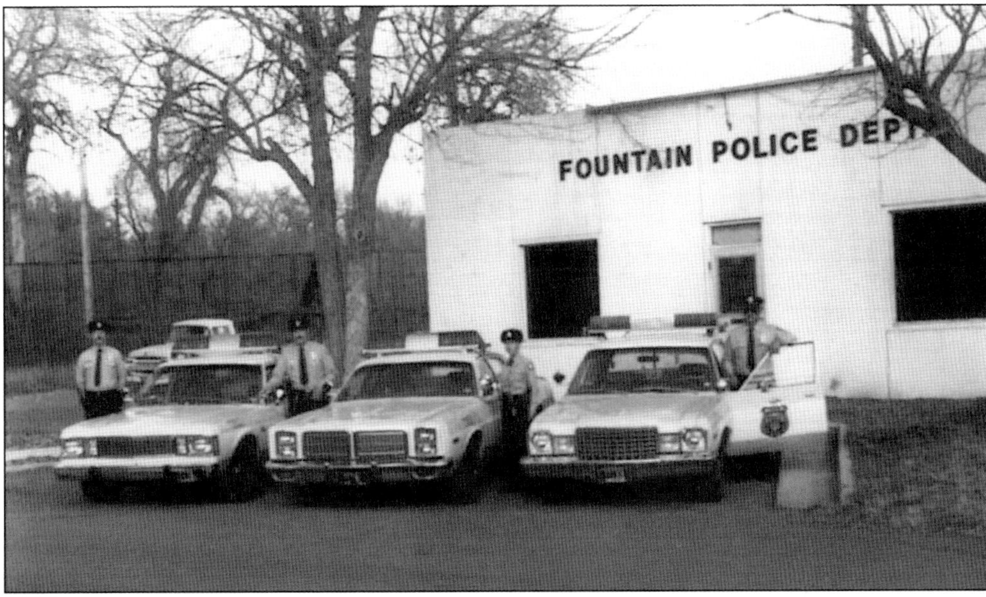

Officers of the Fountain Police Department stand by their patrol cars outside the police station that once stood at the east end of Hanover Street in the 1970s. Fountain has long been fond of their police and fire departments, both of which have grown substantially along with the city's population. (FVM.)

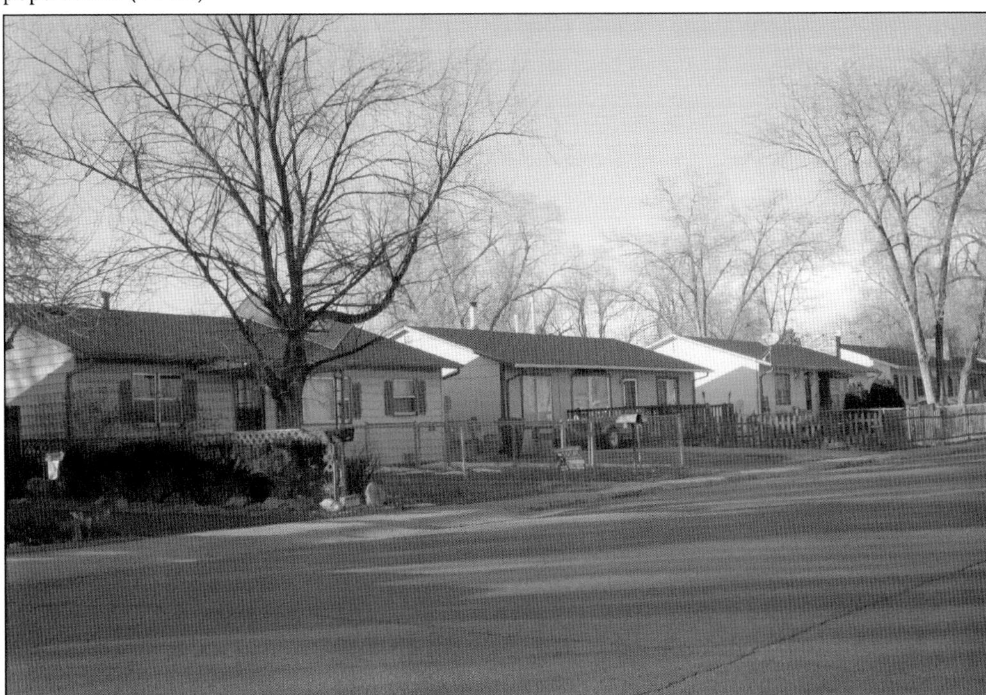

All along North Walnut Street, the houses have the same rectangular shape. In the 1940s, Camp Carson sold these temporary military housing units to home buyers, many of whom became neighbors on this street. Prior to this time, the area was a large cornfield just outside of the town boundary. (ATH.)

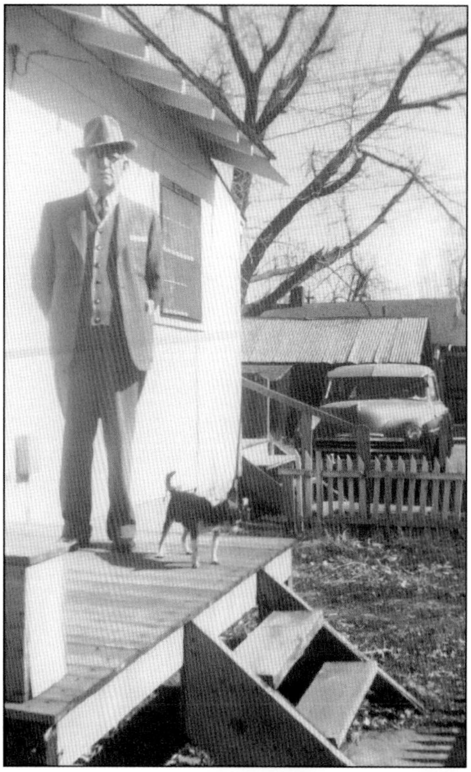

Dr. John Hudson stands on a porch in the 1940s. He came to Fountain from Colorado Springs in the 1920s and served as the town doctor for a number of years. Doctors like Hudson made house calls during morning hours, and after visiting the sick, he would return to his office for afternoon appointments. Many of today's older residents chuckle to think that they were all delivered by Dr. Hudson. (DK.)

The land along East Iowa Avenue and east of the Denver & Rio Grande tracks belonged to the Duran families of Spanish Basque ancestry, who arrived in Fountain from southern Colorado prior to 1920. José Duran's family poses here in about 1907 at their former home. From left to right are (first row) Santana, Maximina, and José; (second row) Francisco, Lucas, and Juan. (FVM.)

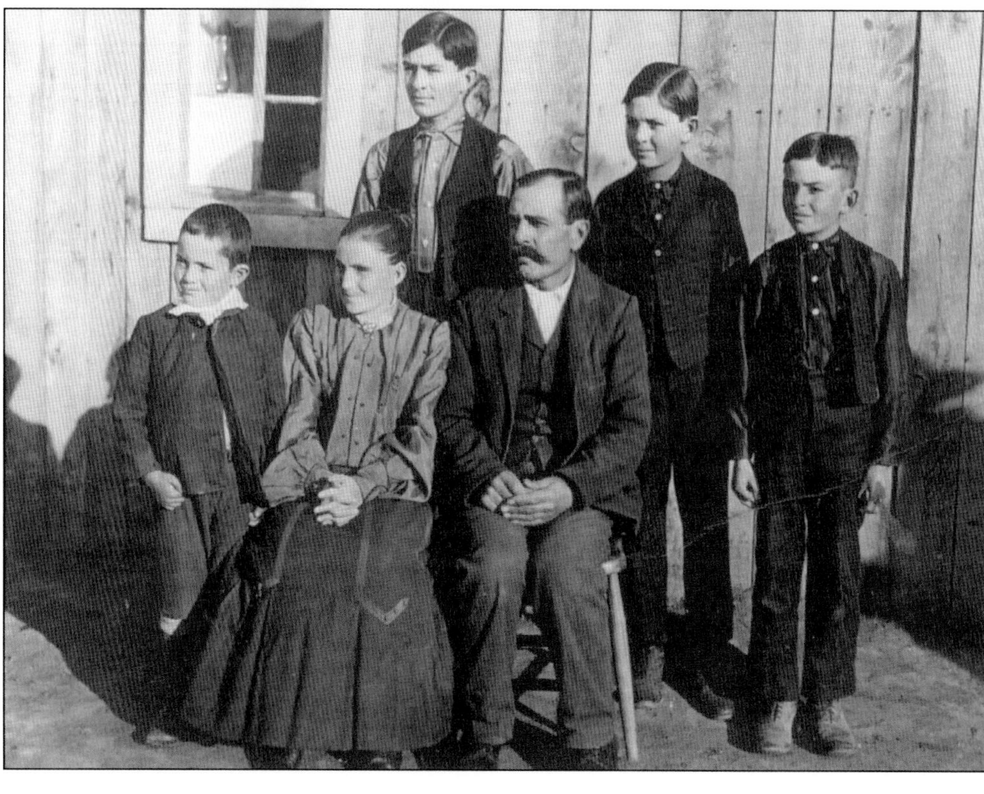

Ernestine Lujan visits with her mother, her sister, and her nephews on a hot summer day. From left to right are Ernestine, Richard Cordova, Perfilia Lujan, Robert Cordova, and Lola Cordova. The Lujan home on East Iowa Avenue was a garden of flowers, bushes, a cherry tree, and other shade trees. (KD.)

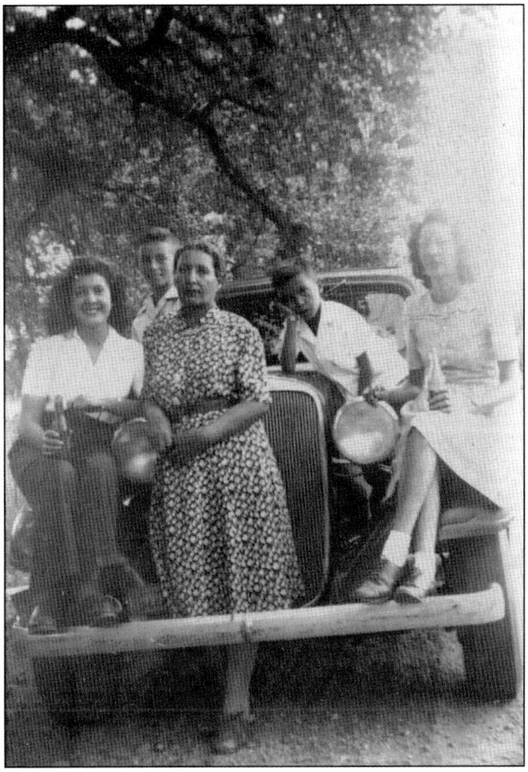

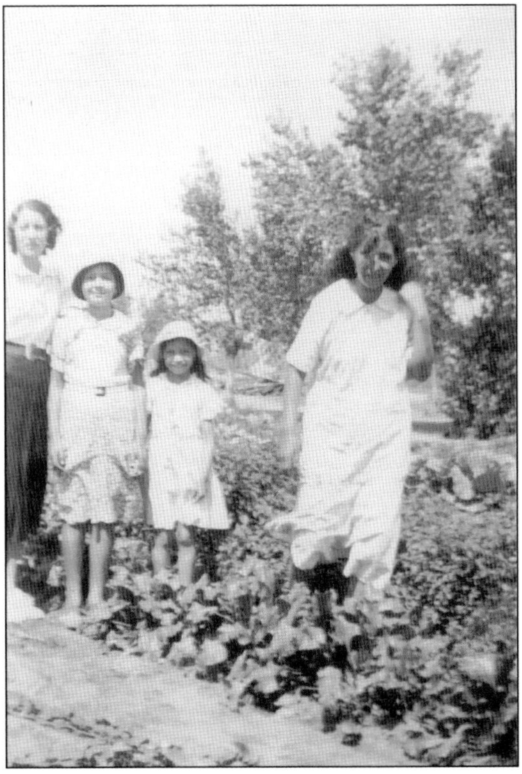

Members of the Lujan family work in their vegetable garden on East Iowa Avenue. From left to right are sisters Lola, Ernestine, and Margaret and their mother, Perfilia. These vegetables supplemented their favorite foods, which included *atole* (porridge made of ground blue cornmeal) and green chilies roasted with onion and garlic. A common cold-weather meal consisted of flour tortillas, pinto beans, and gravy made with red chili powder. (KD.)

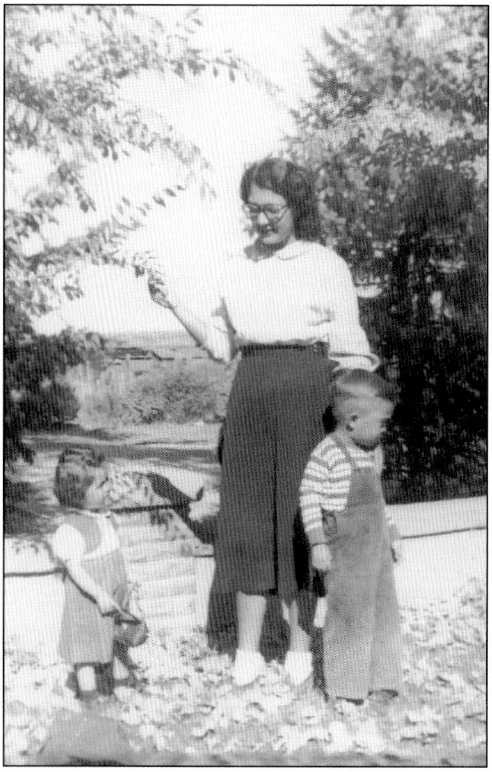

In October 1952, little Katherine Duran stands by the wall in her aunt Lola Cordova's yard with her mother, Ernestine (Lujan), and her brother Joseph. Katherine's family and the Cordova family lived on East Iowa Avenue near the home of Katherine's grandparents Nicanor and Perfilia Lujan. (KD.)

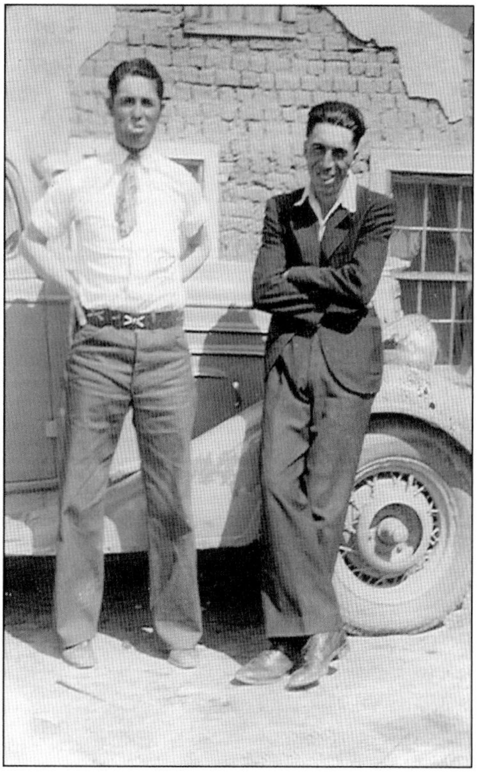

Moises Martinez (right) stands with Juan Mestas outside the home built by Martinez's father-in-law, Juan Rivera, in the 1920s. Rivera and others made the bricks with mud, straw, and water to construct this four-room adobe home once located on the corner of South Reed Street and Missouri Avenue. There was no indoor plumbing or hot water; however, three generations of the Rivera and Martinez families lived here for 40 years. (MM.)

Albino Vasquez and his son enjoy the crisp air on this sunny day near their home on South Reed Street. Behind them are the stockyards along the Denver & Rio Grande tracks at the end of Missouri Avenue. Cattle drives were common in the streets of town, as ranchers brought their animals to the railroads. Another set of stockyards sat near the Santa Fe depot on the west side of town. (MM.)

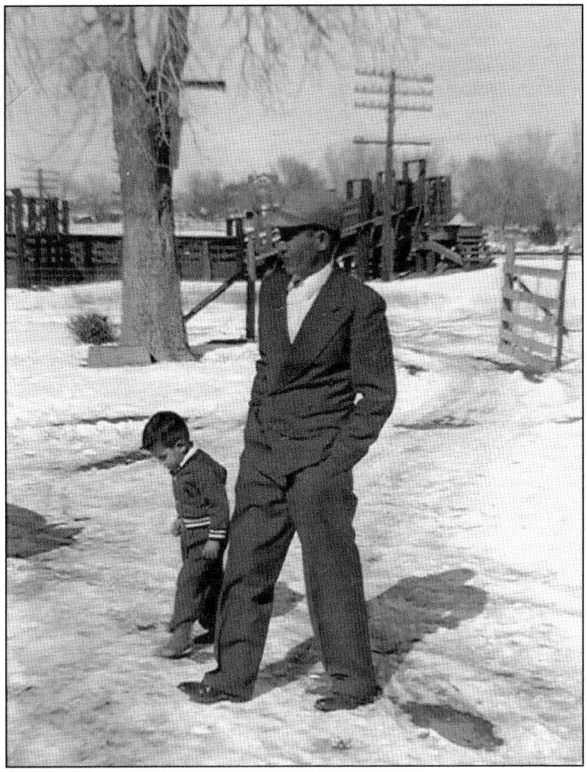

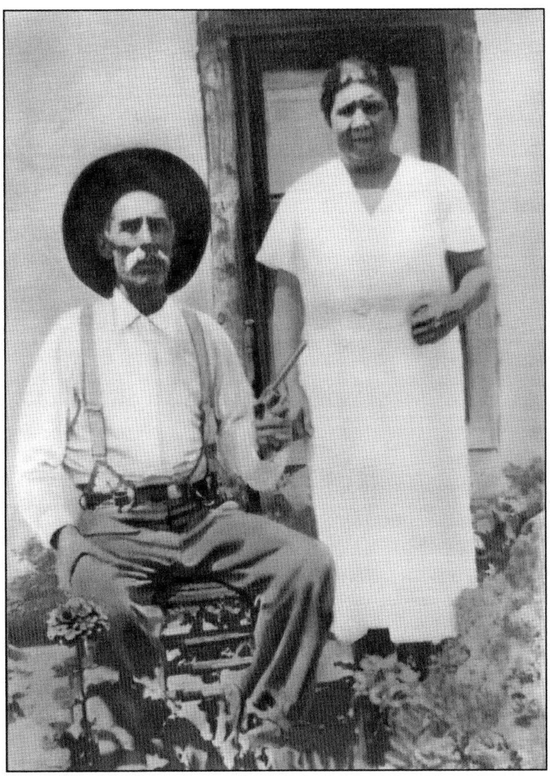

Felix Perea, sitting among the flowers growing outside his adobe home on South Reed Street, proudly displays his pistol that, according to him, was once handled by Billy the Kid. He and his wife, Josefita, and their children came to Fountain in the 1920s from a mining community in New Mexico and lived next door to the Rivera family. Descendants of early Hispanic arrivals still live in Fountain today. (BA.)

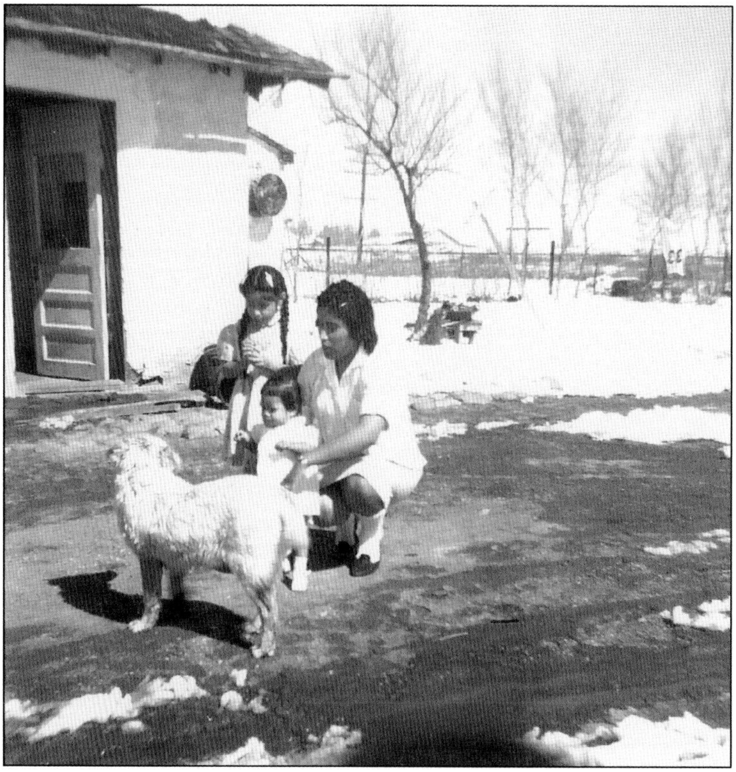

In front of the Arellano's adobe home on South Reed Street in the 1950s, Carmen (Arellano) Roedel introduces her baby Delores to Chico while her younger sister Eva looks on. Most of the residents on this street were of Mexican ancestry and possessed a unique culture. They migrated together from New Mexico and southern Colorado and found homes near each other where they could enjoy their familiar language, food, and customs. (BA.)

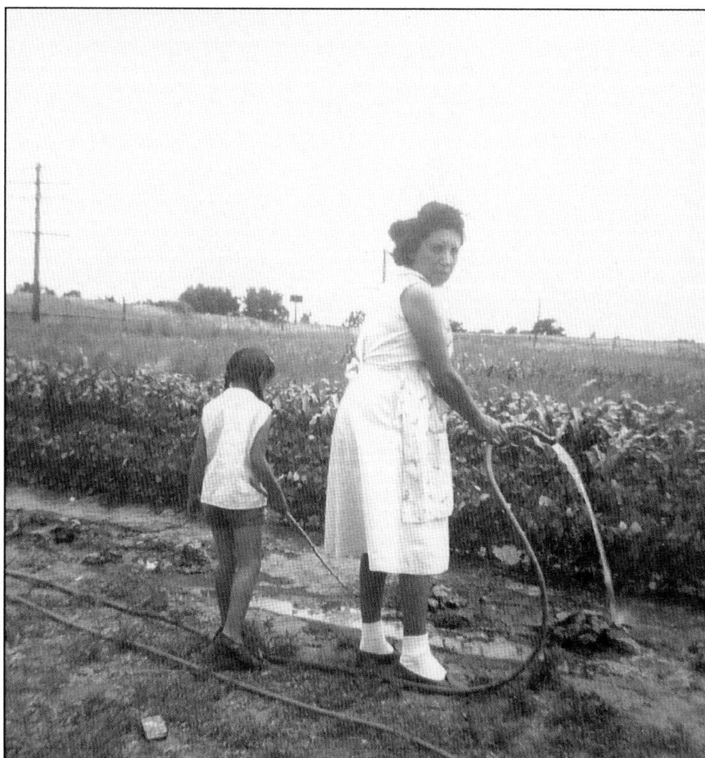

Rita Arellano and her daughter Eva use a hose to water the family garden next to their home on South Reed Street. The Denver & Rio Grande tracks are visible in the background. Arellano was very resourceful, as she grew food for her family to eat fresh and to preserve for later use. (BA.)

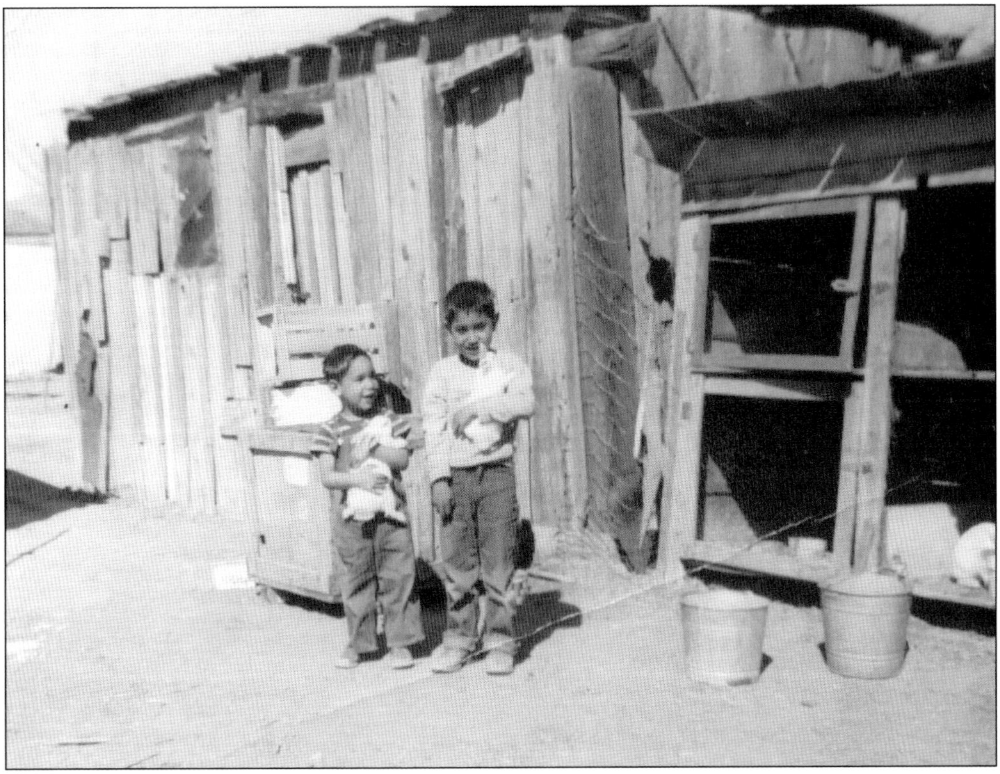

Bennie Arellano (right) and his brother Felix hold their rabbits while standing next to the hutches on the Arellano place. Buckets, probably containing feed and water, wait nearby. The Arellano family raised rabbits and sold the meat and fur; they also raised chickens for eggs and meat. (BA.)

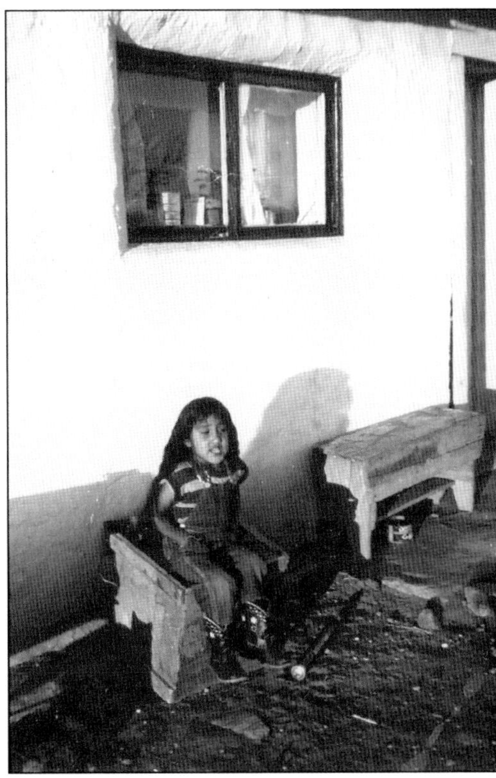

Young Bennie Arellano, wearing overalls and cowboy boots, sits outside his white-washed adobe home on South Reed Street. Bennie's grandmother Josefita Perea was Navajo, and his grandfather Felix was so proud of Bennie's heritage, he insisted that Bennie's hair be kept long in the Indian tradition. (BA.)

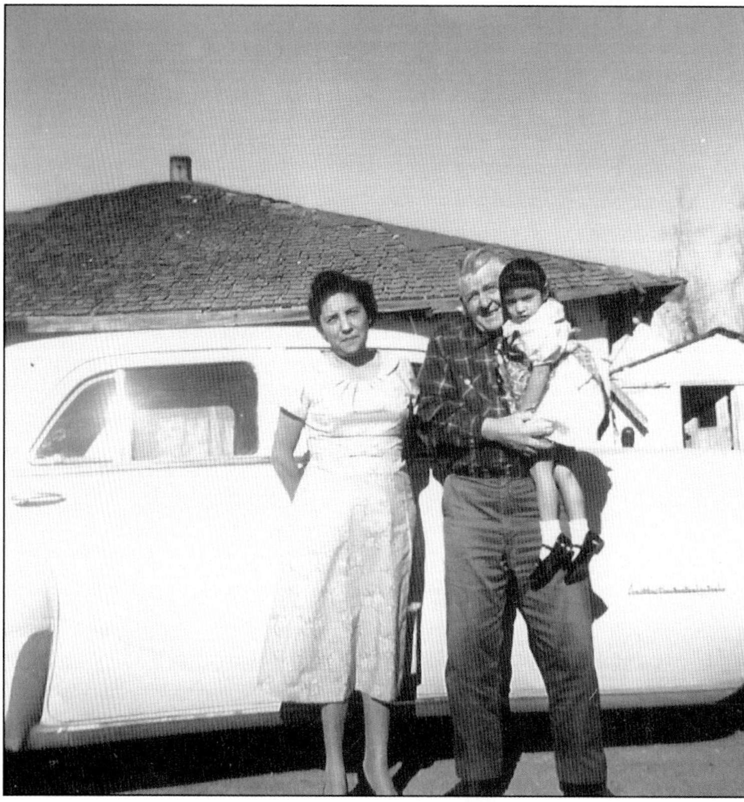

Rita Arellano stands next to Lee Love while he holds her daughter Eva in this 1950s photograph. Love was a friend to the Hispanic population of Fountain. He employed sharecroppers on his ranch south of Fountain and hired Arellano to clean at Love's Spring Camp motor court and campground. (BA.)

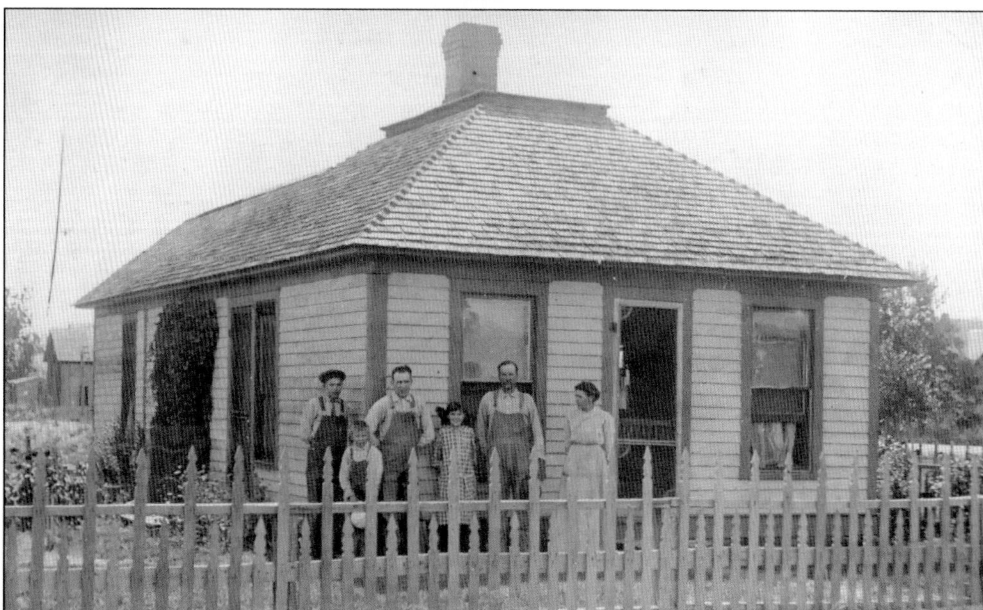

The Torbit family stands outside their trim home fenced in by ornamental pickets on Missouri Avenue, which is typical of Fountain homes in 1915. From left to right are Harry, John, Charlie, Ruth, William, and Nora. William Torbit labored in the railroad yards, and Charlie clerked in the Fountain Trading Company, managed by his uncle F.E. Torbit. (NT.)

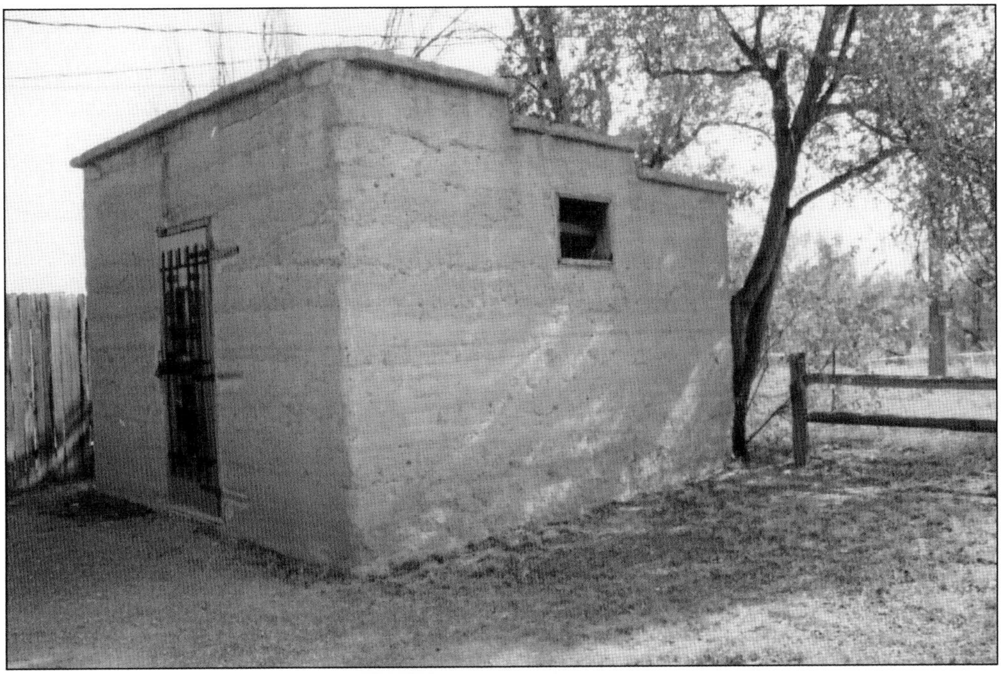

Built in 1903 and restored in 2005, this structure on South Walnut Street, affectionately known as the "Pokey," served as one of Fountain's jails where drunken folks spent the night to sober up. A few occupants recorded their thoughts on the walls. One etching reads, "1-7-1935 It is sure as hell to have been here let alone leave." (NBT.)

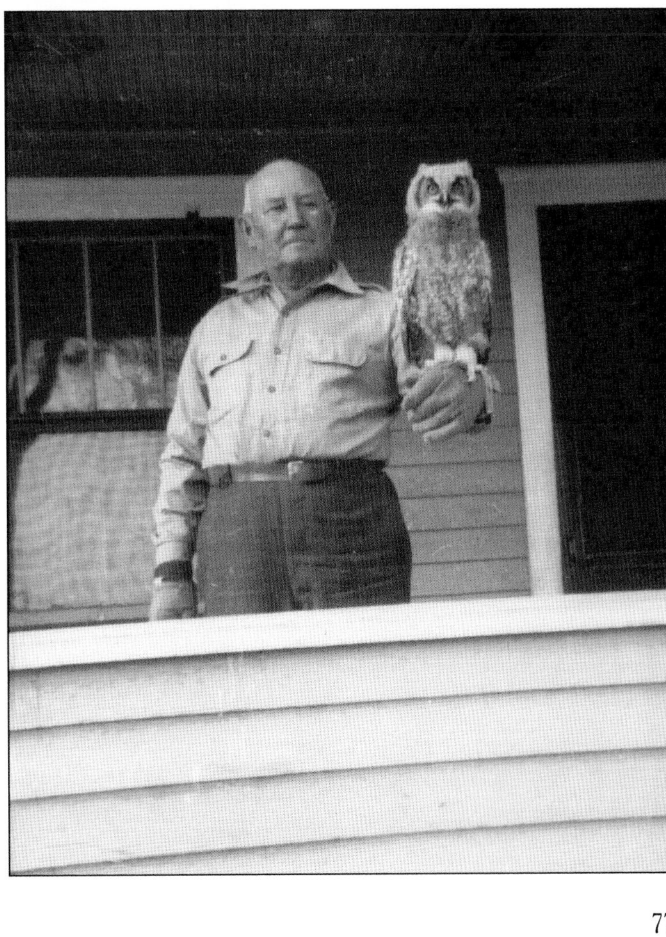

A great horned owl, common in the valley, perches on Herb Whalen's thickly gloved hand as he stands on the porch of the house he built on East Missouri Avenue, which is now owned by his granddaughter Elaine Koop MacKay. His brother-in-law Dudley Niles discovered the owl while haying in the meadow near Wilson Road south of town. The owl stayed at Whalen's home for one night. (DK.)

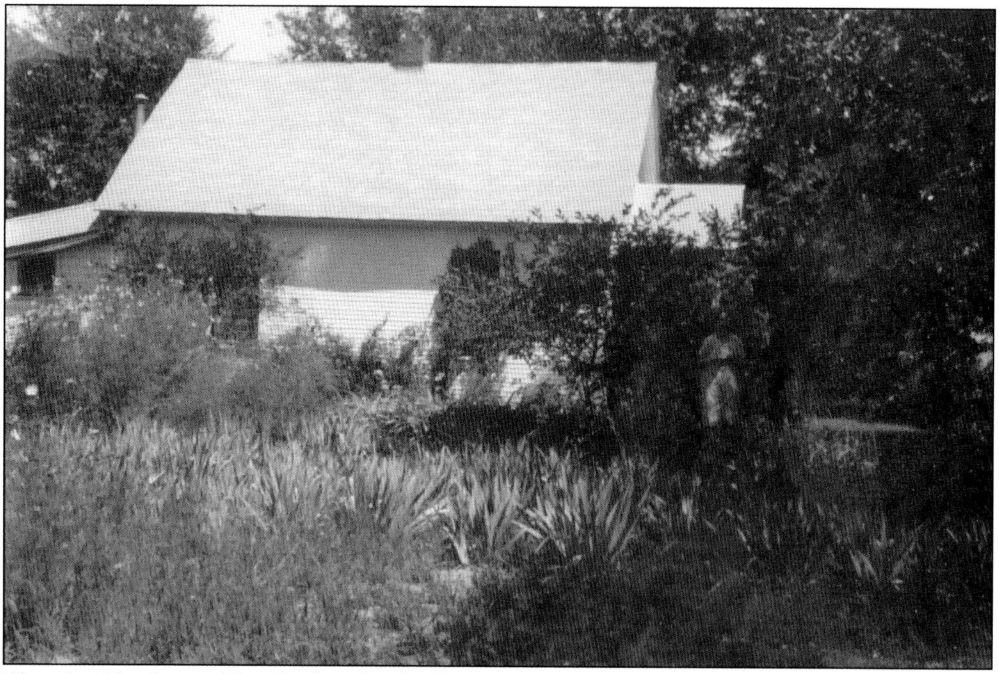

Blanche Charles and her husband, Charles Leroy Charles, moved to 215 East Ohio Avenue from Peaceful Valley after his stroke. Blanche raised chickens here and sold the eggs to Barney's Market, located in the old Fountain Trading Company building. In the 1950s, the houses sat on larger lots, providing room for animals and gardens. On the west side of the house, Charles grew colorful irises, cosmos, and lilies. (LT.)

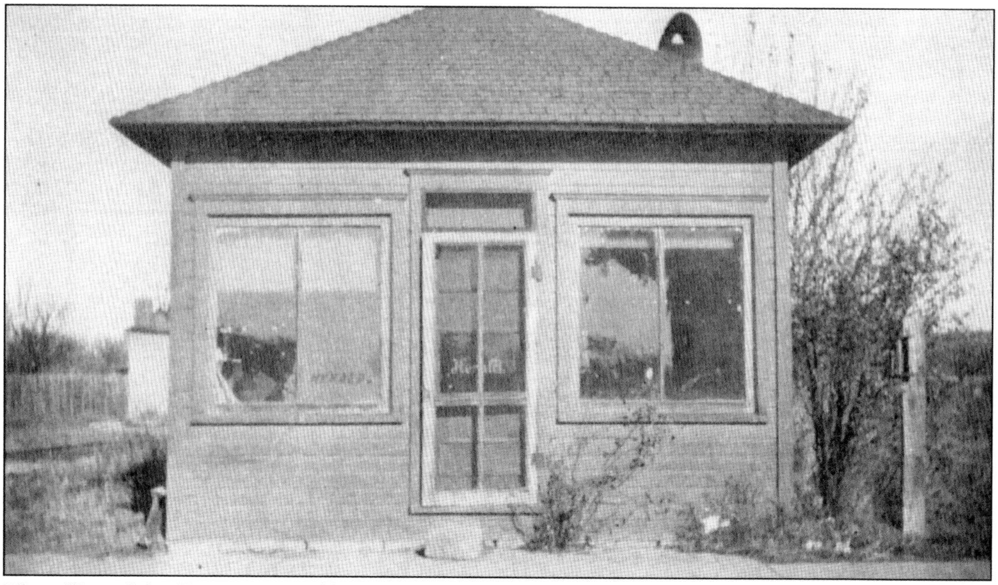

The office of the *Fountain Herald*, established in 1899 and situated on East Ohio Avenue, was also the home of its owners, Thomas and Nellie Pyles, who bought the paper in 1907. The publication ran for a few decades and carried news of Fountain's activities to subscribers all over the country. Across the street sits the office of the current hometown newspaper, the *Fountain Valley News*, established in 1958. (CC.)

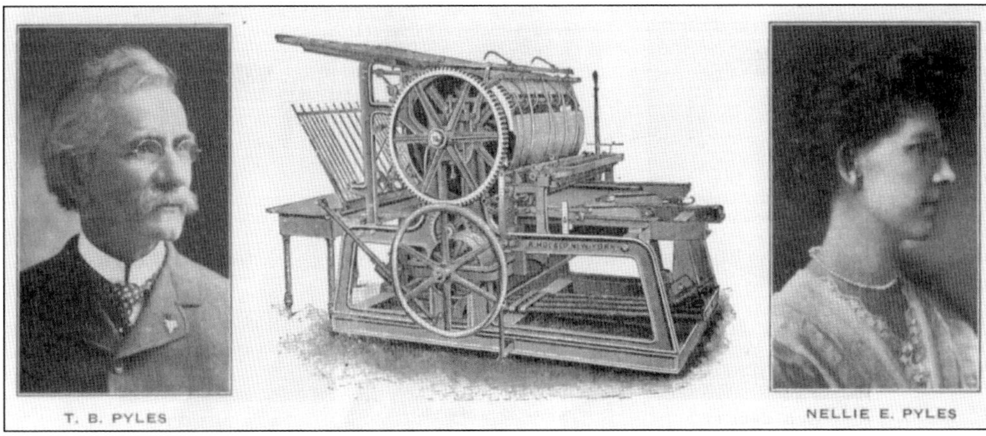

Experienced journalists Thomas and Nellie Pyles came to Fountain after publishing newspapers in Florissant and Colorado Springs. Under the Pyles family's ownership, the *Fountain Herald* was instrumental in acquiring the pipeline that brought water into town from the mountains to the west. They also helped in remedying the dangerous double railroad crossing north of town. In 1919, they backed plans to bring in electricity, a cheese factory, and a vegetable cannery. (CC.)

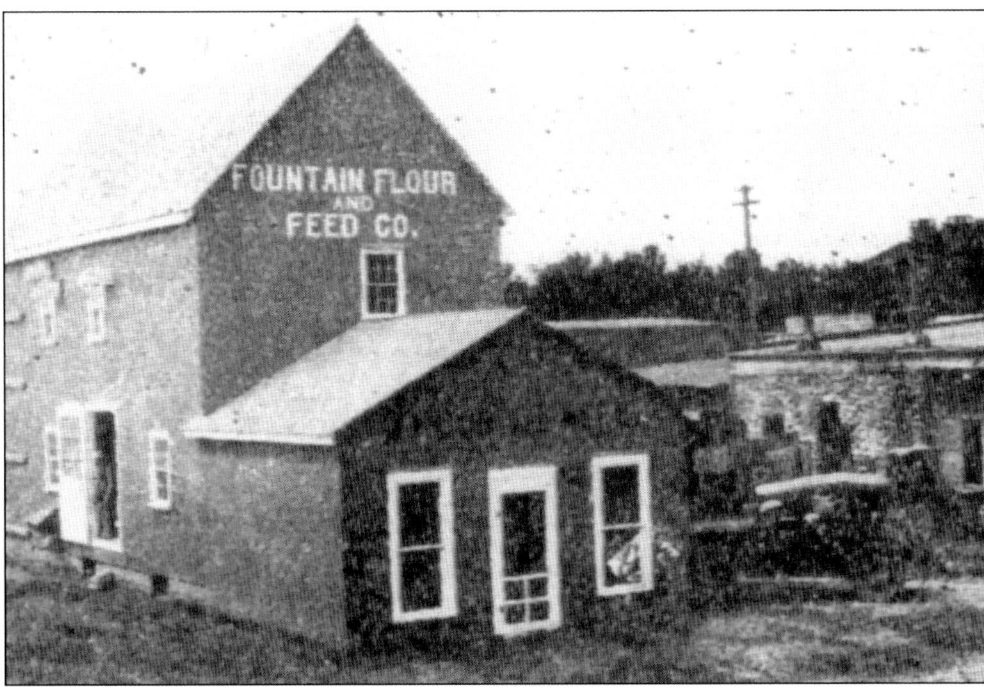

Located on the first block of East Ohio Avenue, Arthur Orcutt built this feed mill in 1932 and ground flour for area bakeries. Feed mills also provided stone-ground cornmeal and flour for home kitchens and processed feed for farm animals. The mill went through many owners before it was torn down to make way for other buildings. (FVM.)

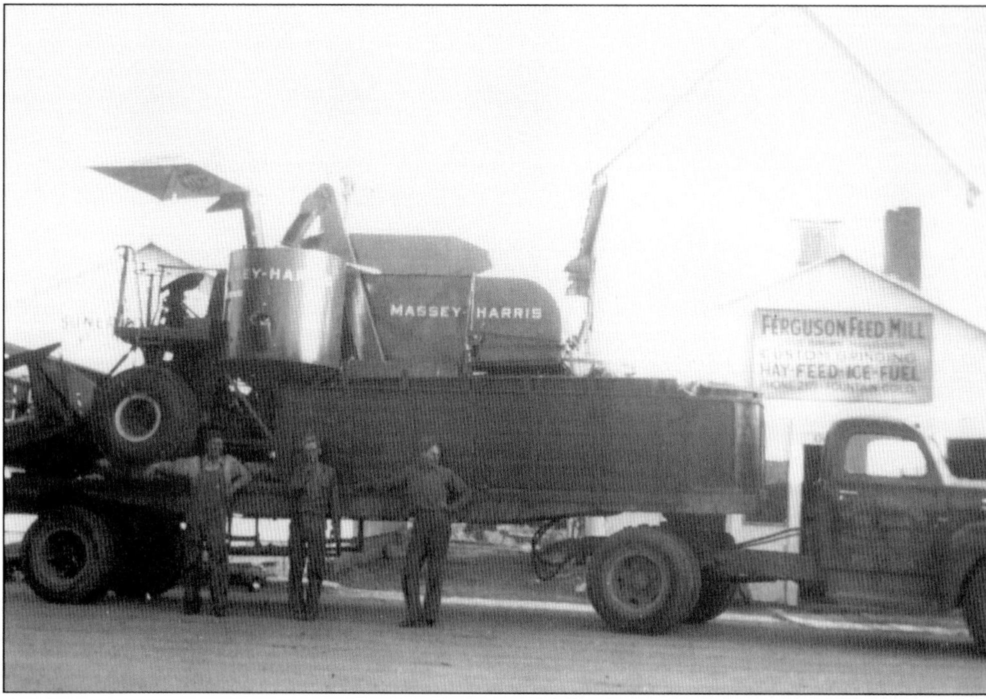

A Massey-Harris combine from the 1940s sits inside the bed of this company truck owned by Scott Ferguson, owner of the feed mill in the background on East Ohio Avenue. Farmers usually did not own such expensive machines but rather shared the cost of renting one and took turns using it. Ferguson was one of the many successive owners of this mill, which was originally built by Arthur Orcutt. (FVM.)

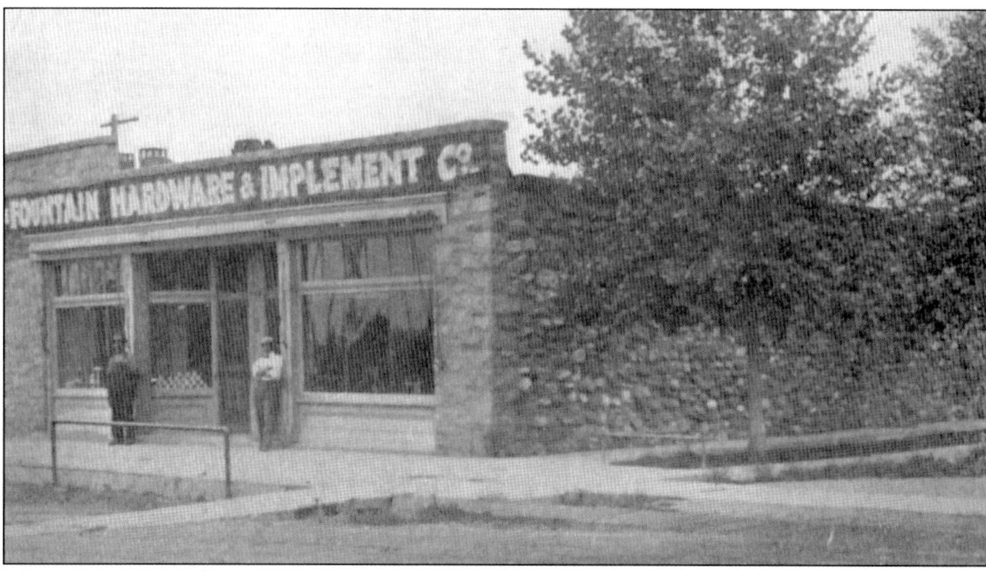

The Fountain Hardware & Implement Co., located at the main intersection in town, was built in 1906 of cobble rock, as were a few other structures in town. This busy store dealt in tools, building supplies, and housewares and was owned and managed by F.H. Monk, who also served as mayor in 1921. (CC.)

Evelyn Chiddix takes a break from her labors on South Main Street in the 1940s. The Square Deal Garage, owned by the Orcutt family, can be seen in the background. This space was later home to the town's fire department. At various times, the Exchange Grocery, the Fountaineer Drugstore, Crew's craft store, and Walt Fortman's hardware store occupied the building on the left. (FVM.)

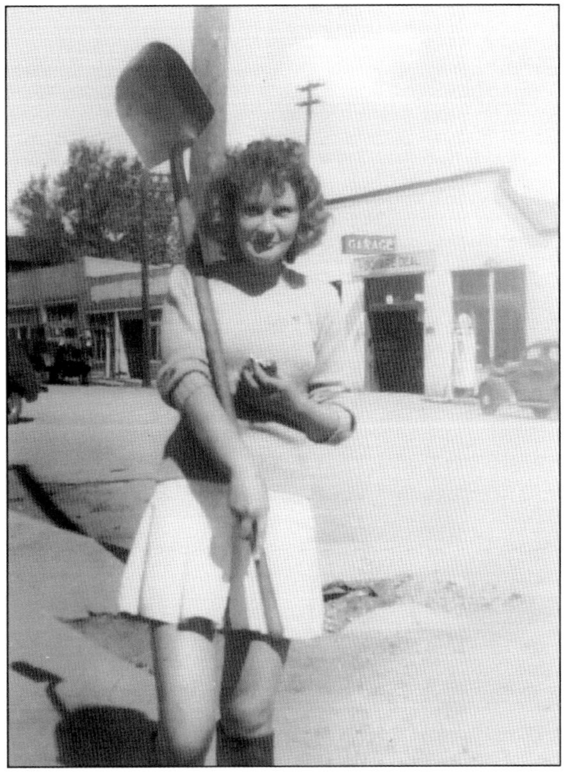

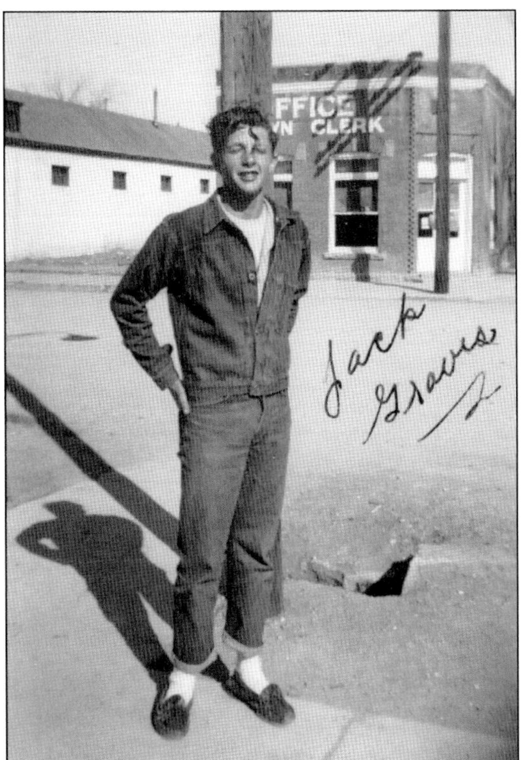

Jack Graves stands on the cement sidewalk beside South Main Street in the 1950s. The roads in town had not yet been paved. Across from him is the town clerk's office, which has since made way for the beautiful and modern new city building. (FVM.)

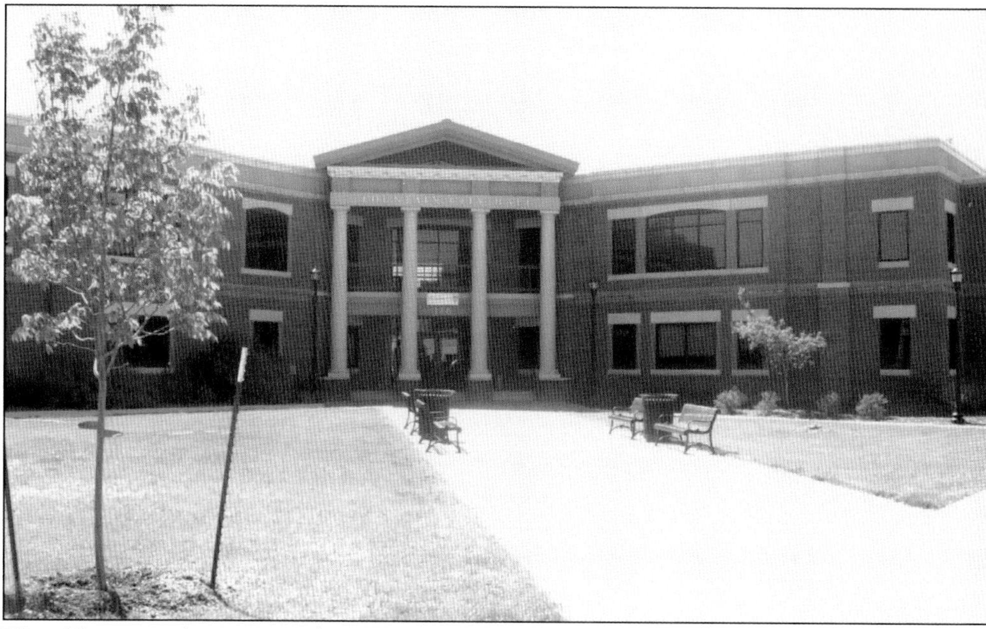

The old stores and garages on the east side of South Main Street have made room for the new city hall. The structure and the plaza in front now occupy most of the block. The spray fountain inside the plaza invites residents to cool off on hot summer days. Staying true to Fountain's agricultural beginnings, local farmers meet every week at the summer farmers' market in the plaza. (FVM.)

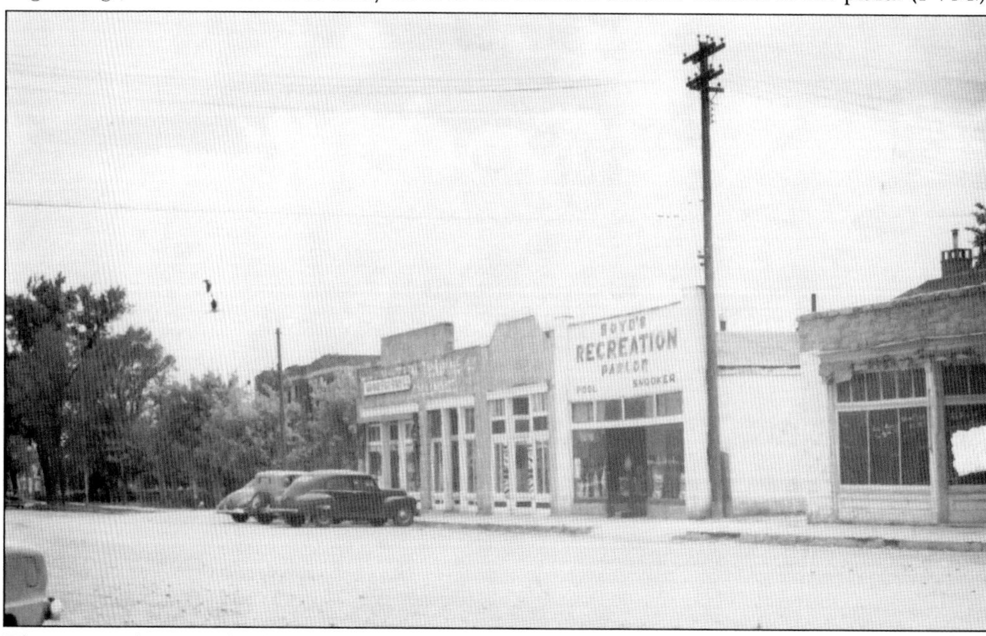

This 1940s photograph of South Main Street includes the high school, seen looming above the trees on the left. The Arapahoe Food Store has replaced the Fountain Trading Company. The barbershop occupies the space once used by a café, which would later house the post office. Boyd's Recreation Parlor operates from the old theater where, in the 1920s, people came to see movies, minstrel shows, magicians, knife throwers, sword acts, patent medicine men, and vendors selling wares. (FVM.)

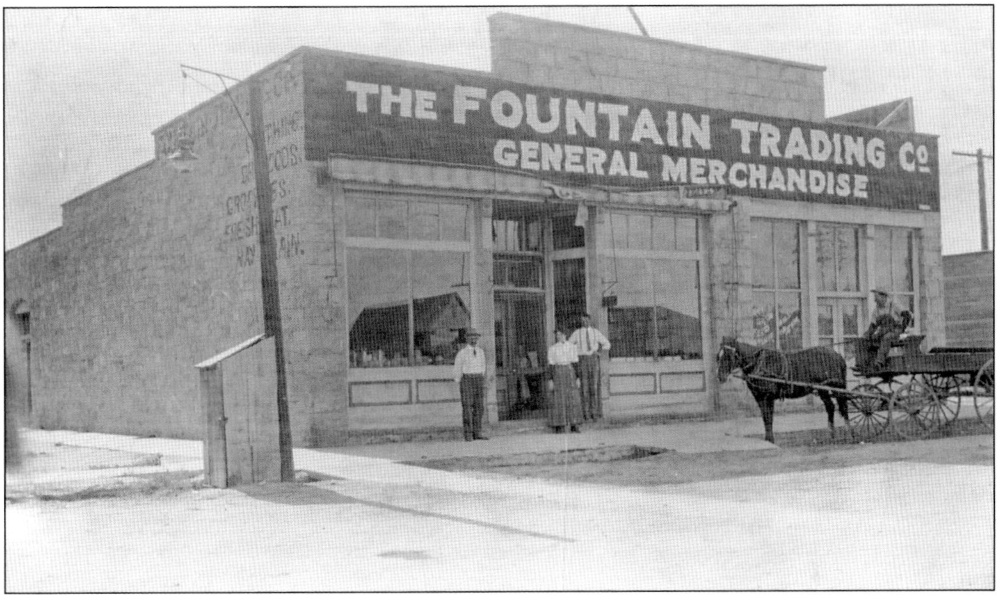

In this 1911 image of the Fountain Trading Company on South Main Street, Charley Frasier (left) stands with ? O'Riley and Jack Lindamood. The three are joined by William Torbit, sitting in the wagon. Sandstone blocks for this structure were quarried at Castle Rock and brought to Fountain by train. Remarkably, the advertising on the side of the building is still visible today. (NT.)

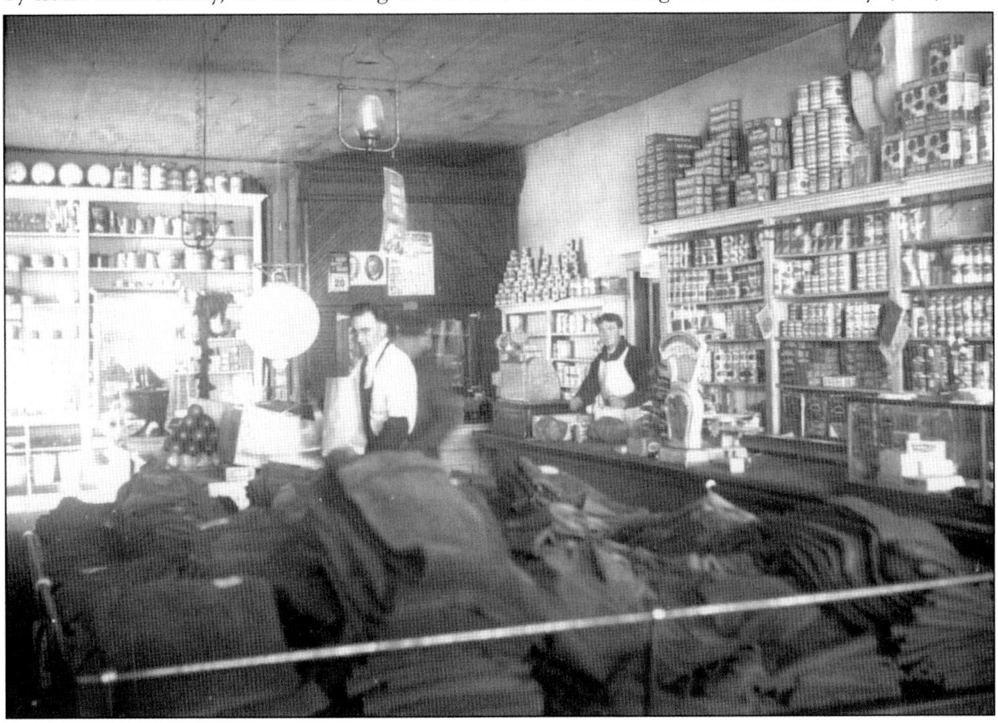

Inside the Fountain Trading Company, established in 1898, Charles Torbit, known by all as "Charlie," bags produce behind a bin of denim dungarees in 1916. Manager George Johnson stands beside the cash register and scale. Canned and boxed goods, crockery, and enamelware line the shelves in this well-stocked general store operated by Torbit's uncle F.E. Torbit. (NT.)

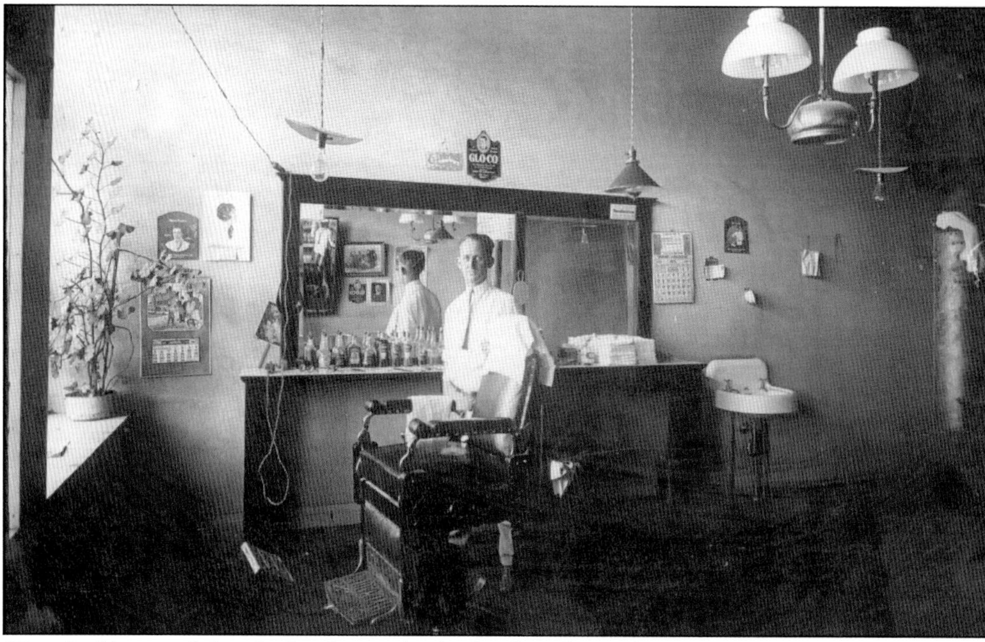

Clare Peebles stands beside the chair in his barbershop, located next door to the Fountain Trading Company, in 1925. A tall geranium enjoys the east window facing Main Street. Peebles's services included a shave for 20¢ and a haircut, shampoo, and massage for 40¢ each. This space later housed the post office. (DB.)

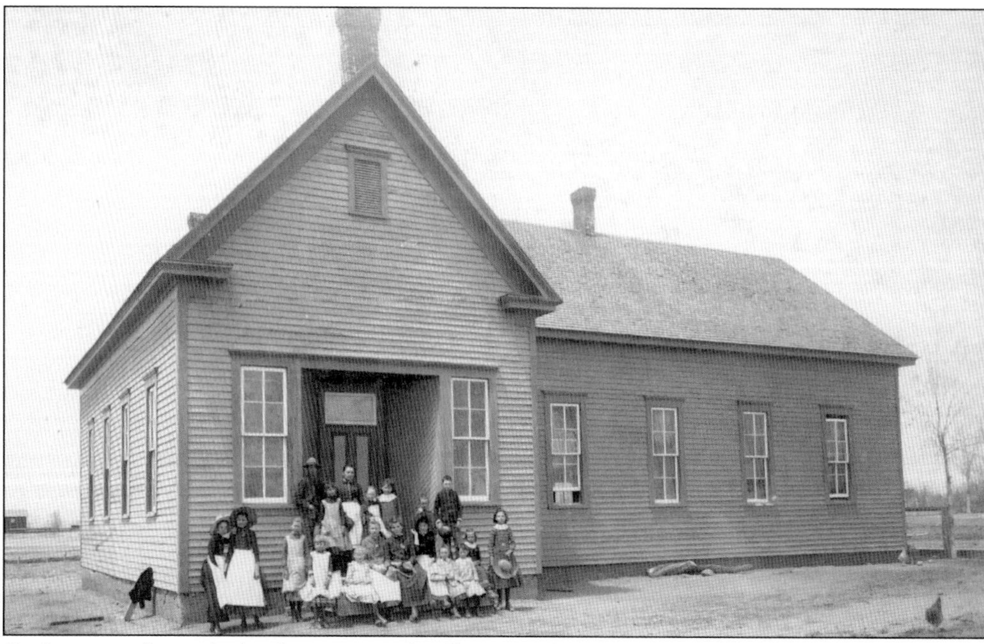

Students stand outside the three-room schoolhouse on Main Street in 1888. Located in the present school block, nine grades were taught to students who arrived each day on foot, by horseback, or in wagons. Notice the chickens in the foreground and at the corner of the building. When the wooden structure was dismantled in 1903, a piece of iron from the 1888 train explosion was found in the roof. (FVM.)

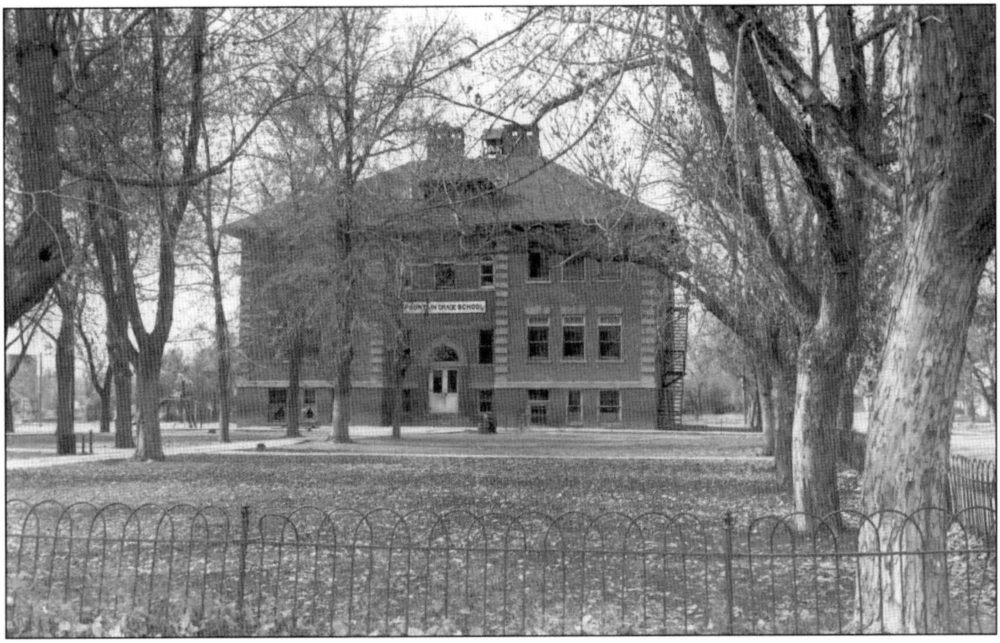

This beautiful redbrick building with eight rooms and 12 grades replaced the wooden school in 1903. Its first graduating class consisted of one scholar. The bell on the roof signaled lunch and recess, as well as the start and end of each school day, and was the delight of any child chosen to ring it. The building stood until 1971, when it was demolished. (FVM.)

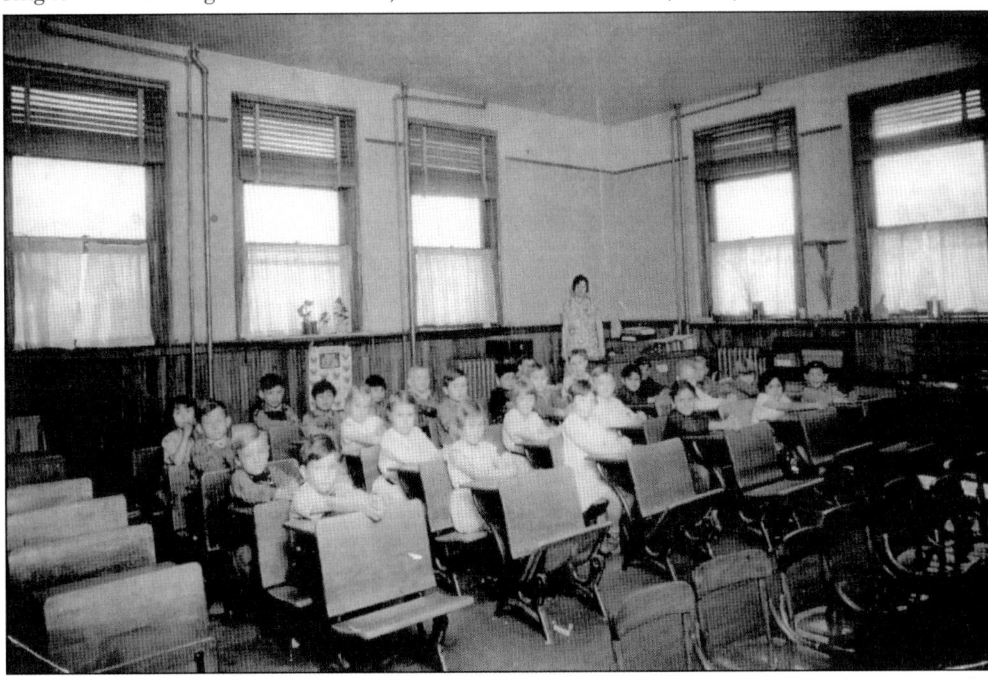

This Fountain Grade School teacher observes her students from the corner of her classroom in the 1920s. Her class of about 27 pupils appear well behaved as they sit at their own desks. The back of each fold-down seat was connected to the desktop behind it, forming one big unit. The large windows were dressed with curtains and blinds, and the room was heated by radiators. (FVM.)

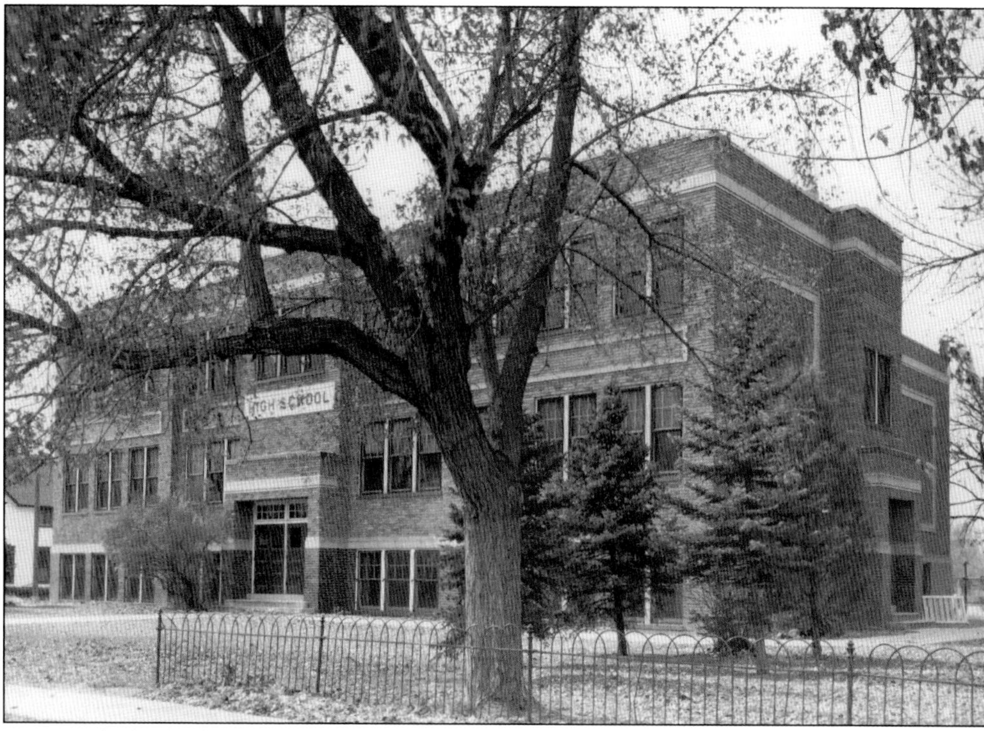

In 1924, the high school was built of brown brick next to the 1903 building, which then became the grade school. The high school boasted a fine auditorium, gymnasium, and a well-equipped home economics room. Five busses transported children from outlying farms and ranches. Fountain was proud to have 14 high school teachers, all with degrees or college credits. (FVM.)

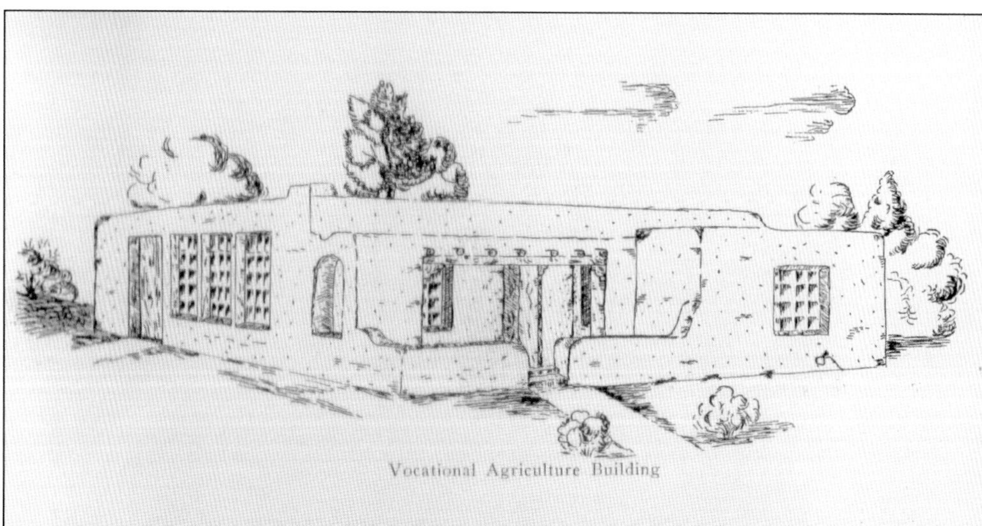

The school district purchased the adobe building that stood across Main Street for vocational and agricultural classes. It was constructed during a 1930s training program that provided individuals with marketable skills in building adobe homes. Typically, vocational and agricultural classes included animal science, crops, small engines, equipment operation, welding, maintenance, carpentry, wood shop, home economics, and art. (FVM.)

Both brick buildings on the school lot were demolished in the early 1970s and replaced with a newer building to serve the junior high grades. In 1987, Fountain-Fort Carson Junior High School was renamed in honor of Fountain native Jose Aragon, who posthumously received the Bronze Star for his heroic actions during a tragic air-base accident that led to his death, making him the first Colorado airman to die in Vietnam. (FFCSD.)

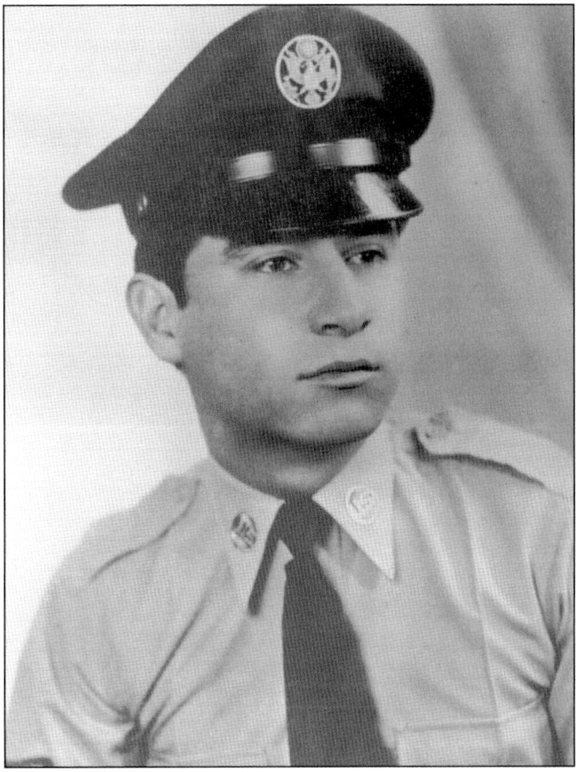

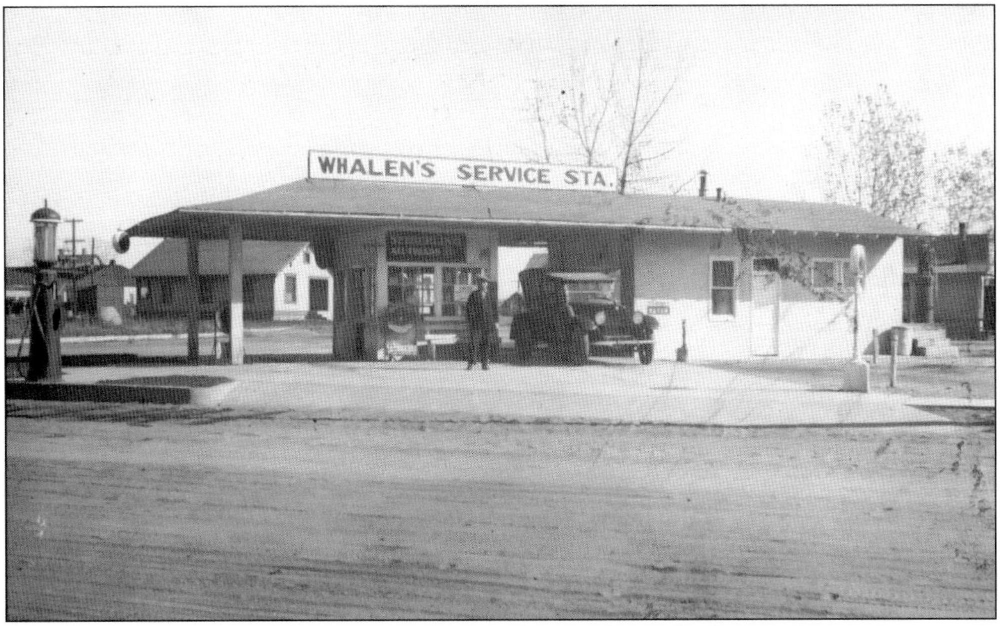

Herb Whalen stands with his Ford Model T Runabout in front of Whalen's Service Station, one of several such businesses in town. It was conveniently located on the southeast corner of Missouri Avenue and South Main Street. Fountain might well have been the last chance for autos to fill up before heading to Pueblo in the 1920s. This filling station sold Conoco gasoline and provided mountain water to local residents and motorists passing through. (DK.)

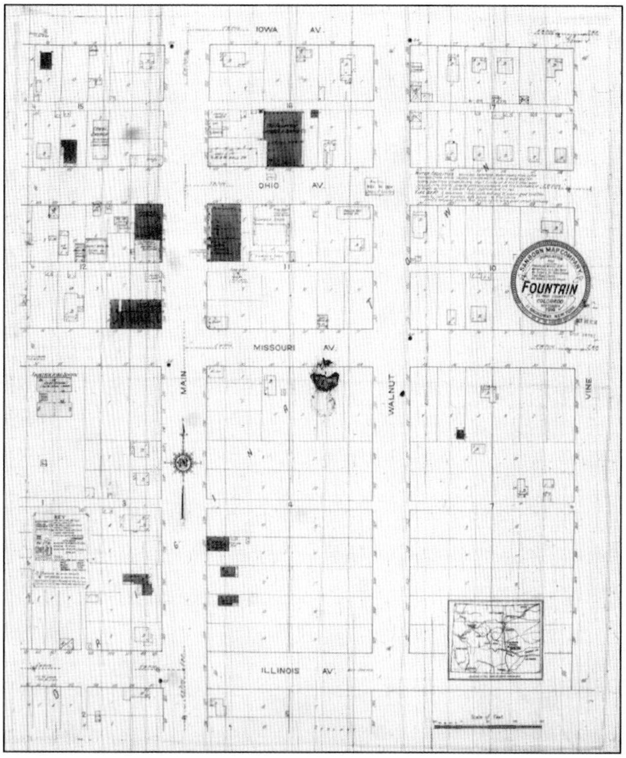

This 1914 Sanborn Fire Insurance map shows a portion of the original town. Created to estimate fire insurance liabilities, great detail about a town and its buildings was recorded. Some notable buildings include the Congregational church, the Woodmen of the World Hall, the Fountain Lumber and Supply Company, and the Fountain High School. (PPLD.)

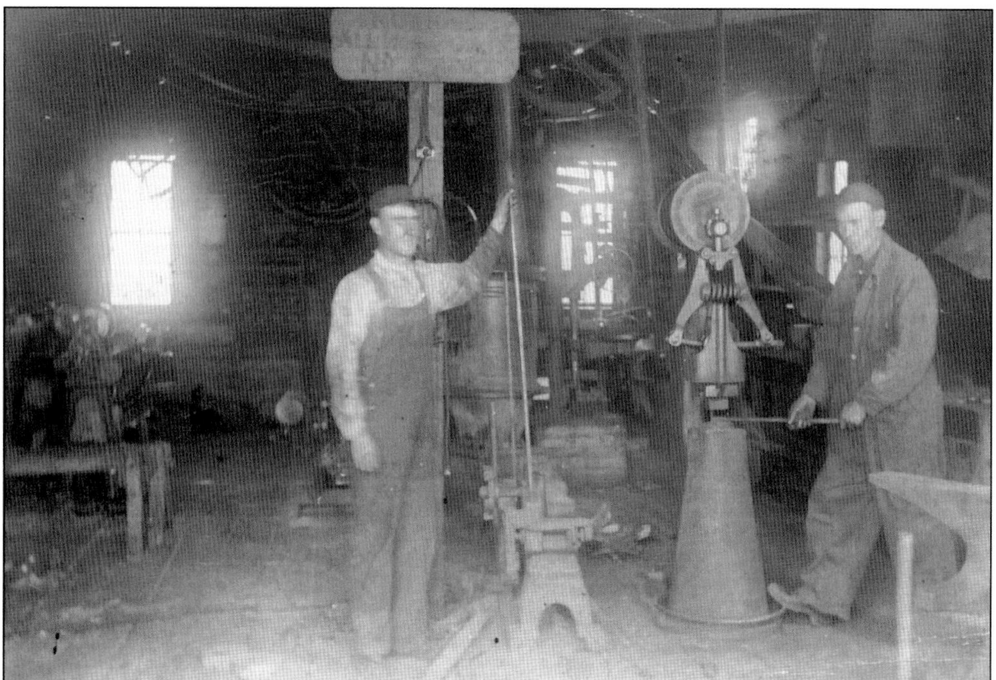

These men, one of whom could be George Marshall, stand ready to hammer and bend metal. Marshall operated a blacksmith and welding shop, such as the one pictured here, which features a drill press, lathe, and hammer, all belt driven. (DB.)

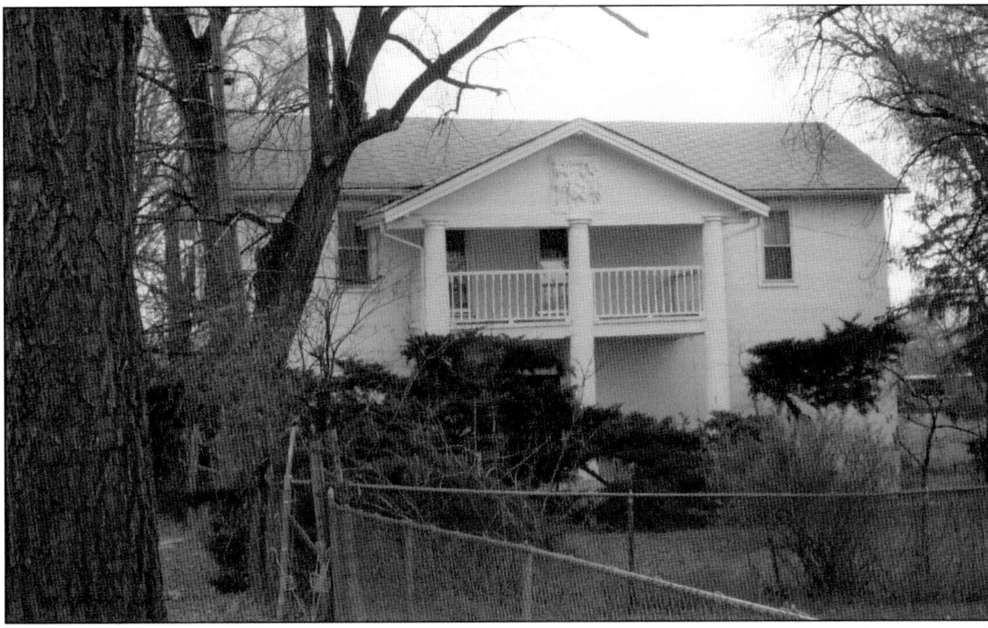

Once the location of Fountain's first post office (and also rumored to be haunted), this stately home on South Main Street was built originally as a one-story residence. The second story was later added with columns and an inlaid sculpture near the roof. Its thick walls and deep foundation are credited with saving it from destruction in the 1888 train explosion. It later became an antique store known as the Ark. (ATH.)

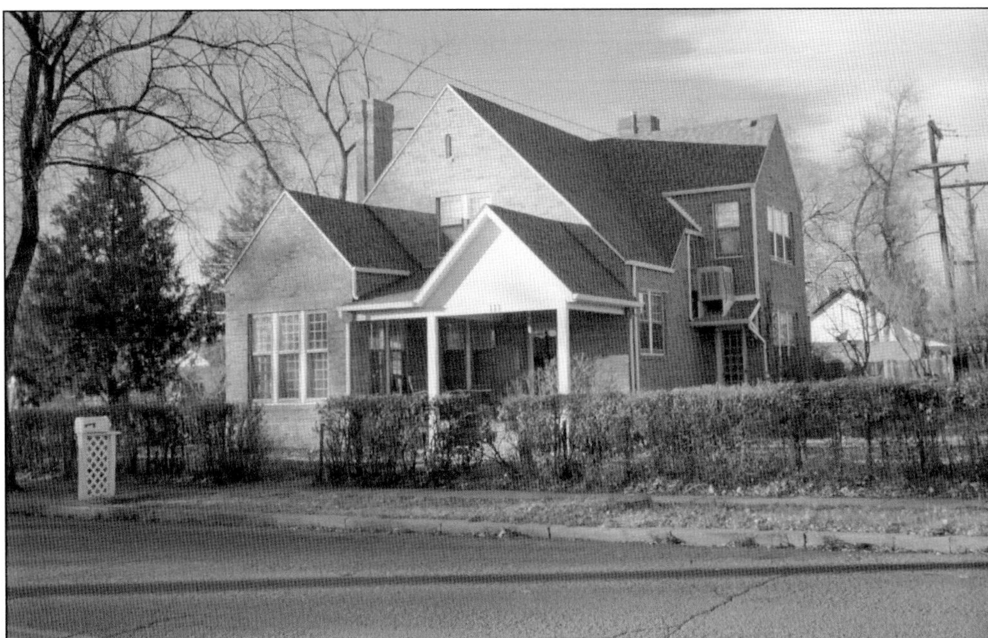

Uncharacteristic of other homes in Fountain, this mansion was built in 1925 by Rose Torbit after the death of her husband, F.E. Torbit. Located behind the Fountain Trading Company on West Missouri Avenue, this home's ornate furnishings included fireplace tiles made by Colorado City's famed potter Artus Van Briggle. The home was later purchased by Joseph Janitell. (ATH.)

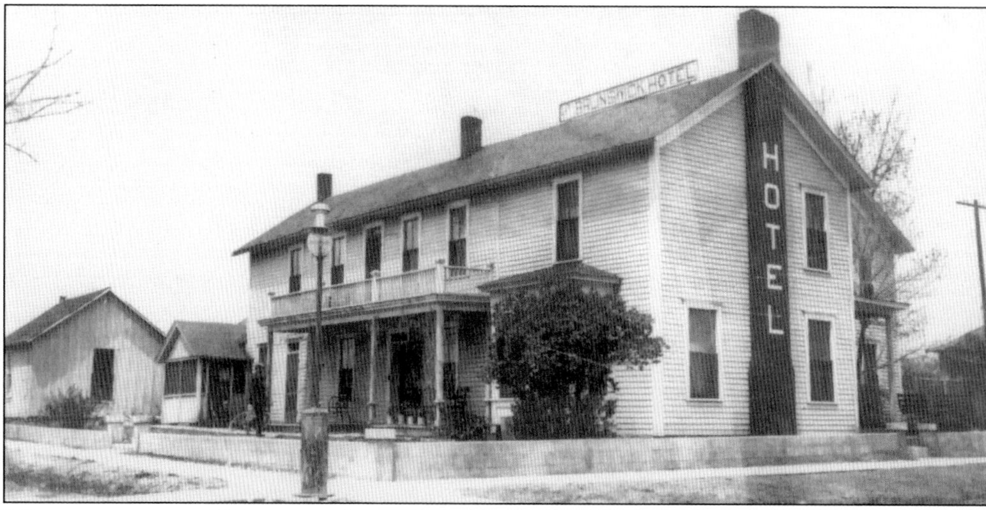

When visitors got off the train, they only had to walk a block to the Brunswick Hotel on West Missouri Avenue. Said to have been built by Henry Link, the hotel functioned under several owners and names before being converted into an apartment building. This structure survived a fire in the late 1930s and was finally torn down about 1960. (NT.)

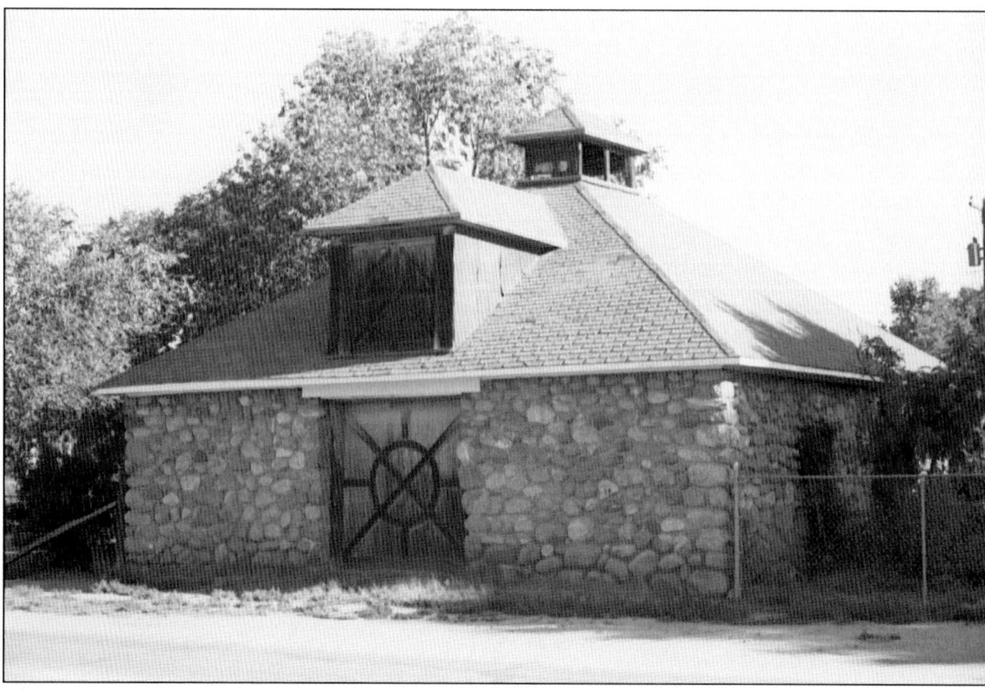

The livery on West Missouri Avenue is said to have been built by Henry Link. It has remained a constant sentinel for at least 100 years. There are a few other rock structures in Fountain. Historians say that the rock for the livery came from eastern Colorado. It is certain, however, that travelers put their horses in stalls here before retiring at the Brunswick Hotel next door. (PPLD.)

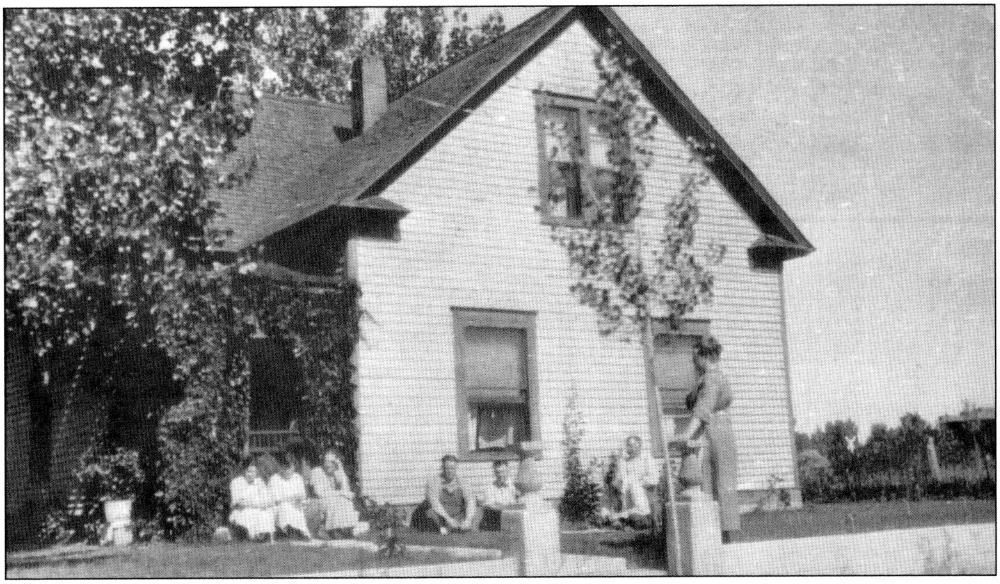

Annie Love stands outside her shaded home while her family gathers around. Still on South Race Street today, the home had previously been used as the parsonage for the Baptist church when it was located next door prior to 1913. The Love family first settled on a ranch south of Fountain on the Denver-to-Pueblo Road in 1901. By 1920, the family lived in town, and the farm was leased to sharecroppers. (FVM.)

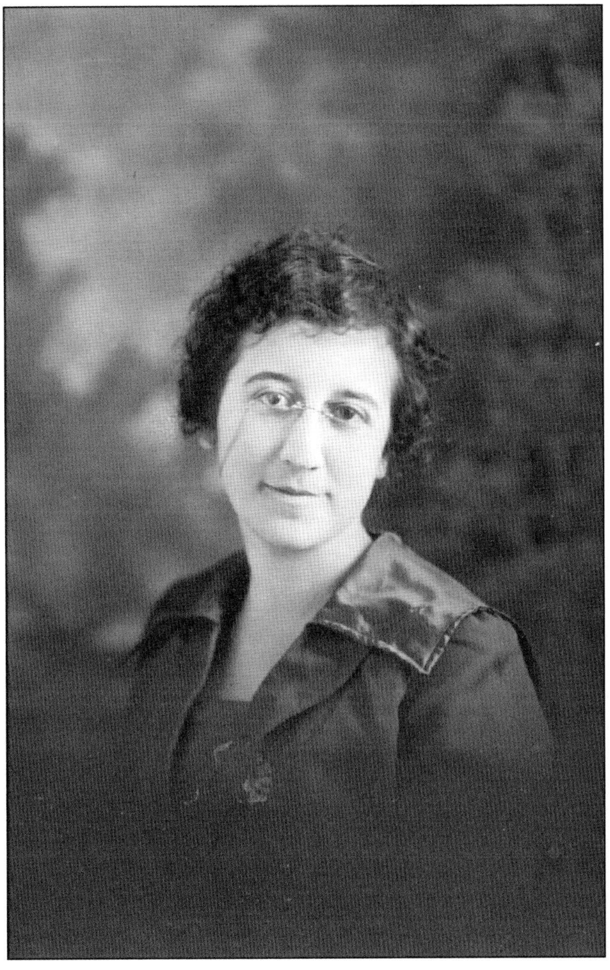

Marguerite Spicer lived on Race Street in 1920. She was the daughter of Hovena Spicer and granddaughter of Fountain pioneer Barbara Lock, both known for their remarkable strength and independence. As a teenager, Spicer listened to her grandmother's stories and became the family and town historian. She compiled scrapbooks of photographs, news clippings, stories, and genealogical information on Fountain families. This collection has become a treasure to subsequent historians. (RW.)

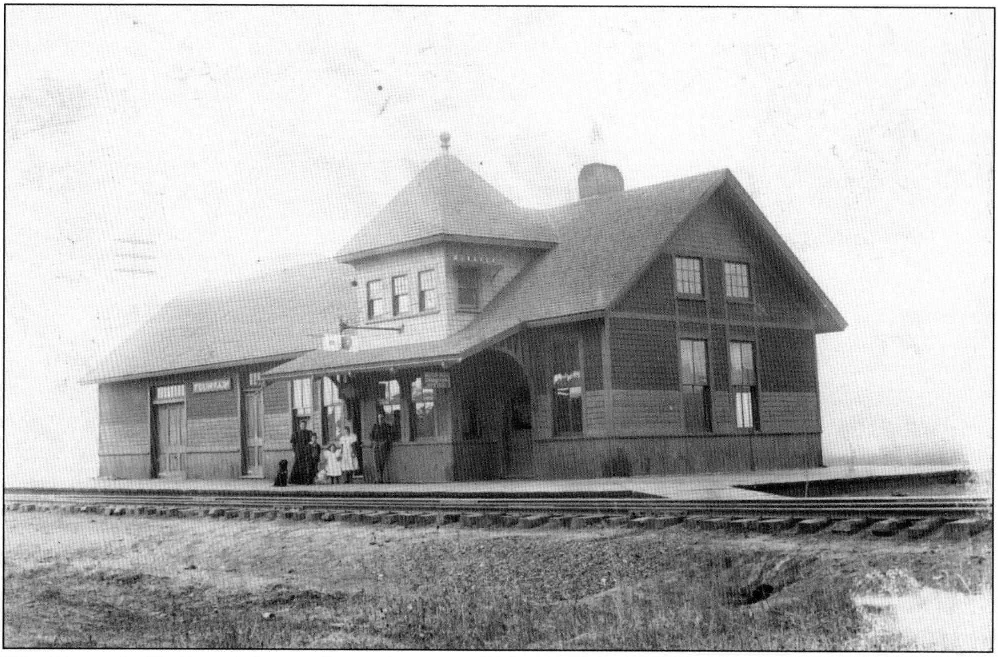

The Santa Fe Railroad depot, shown here in 1882, sat along the tracks on the west side of town near Illinois Avenue. Several years later, a detached section of cars quietly slipped away from the Colorado Springs depot, gathering speed on its gradual descent into Fountain, where it collided with an engine and ignited into a tremendous explosion. (DB.)

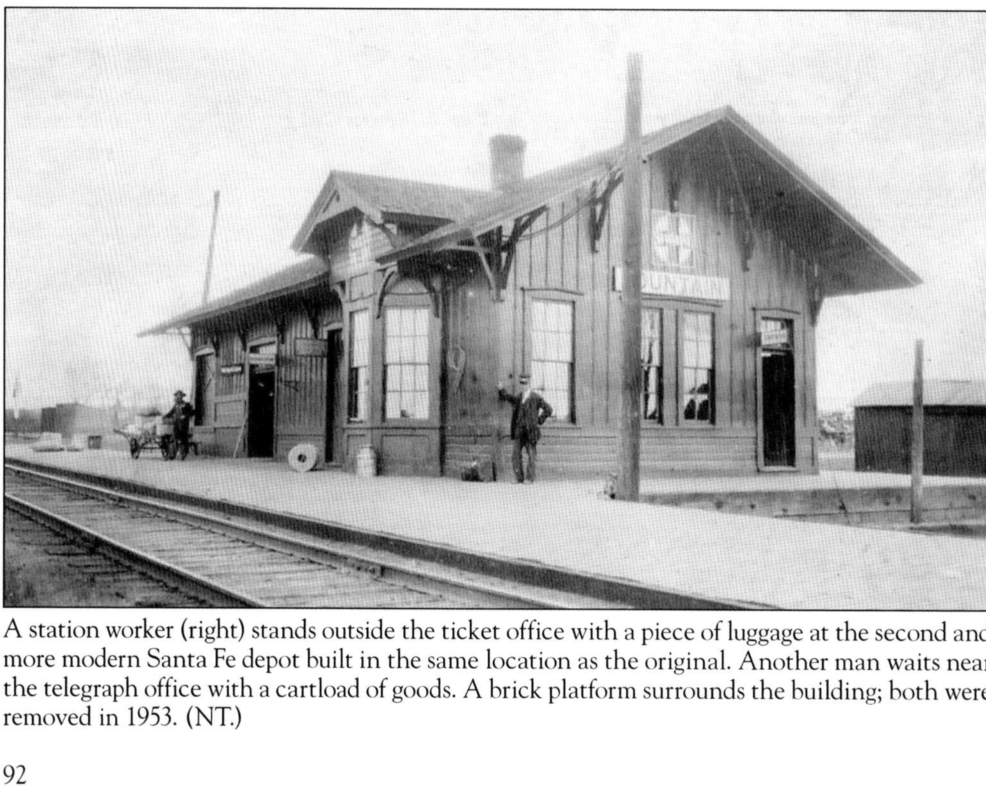

A station worker (right) stands outside the ticket office with a piece of luggage at the second and more modern Santa Fe depot built in the same location as the original. Another man waits near the telegraph office with a cartload of goods. A brick platform surrounds the building; both were removed in 1953. (NT.)

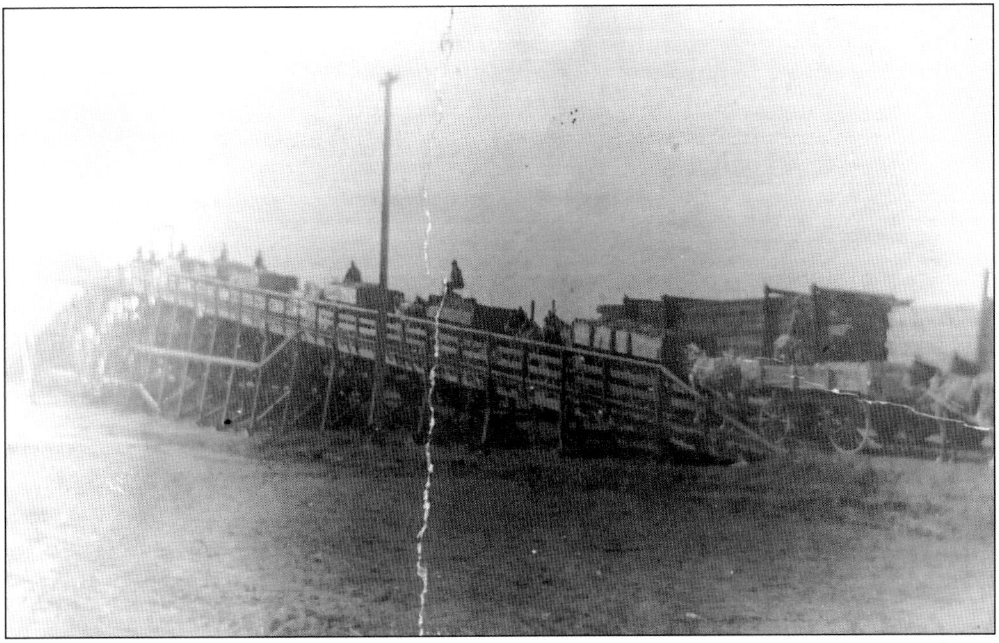

Horses pull wagonloads of sugar beets from surrounding farms up the ramp of this beet dump, located near the Santa Fe depot in Fountain. Wagon beds were made with collapsible sides for loading and hauling sugar beets. In the beet field, one side was lowered to allow beets to be tossed into the wagon and then secured back in place for the trip to the beet dump. (FVM.)

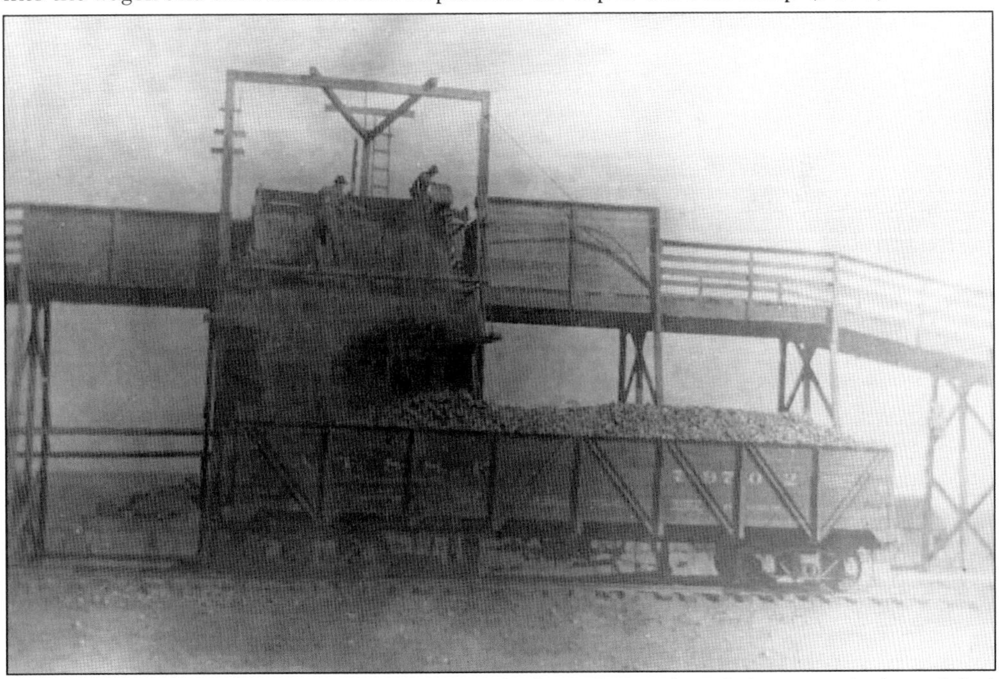

At the top of the ramp, the side of the wagon bed was lowered, and the entire bed was lifted by pulley to dump the beets into a railcar below. With the bed lowered back to the wagon, the horses then pulled it down the ramp on the other side. Farmers stopped growing sugar beets when transporting them became too costly. (DB.)

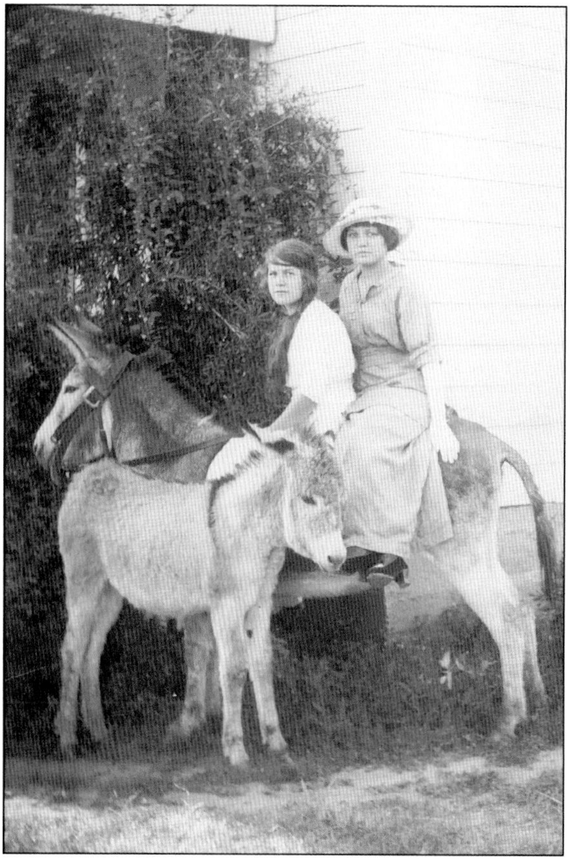

Sisters Daisy (left) and Coral Toothman sit astride a donkey in this 1914 photograph that was probably taken outside their home on Illinois Avenue, west of Santa Fe Avenue. Photographers traveled with a donkey or pony into residential neighborhoods, looking for parents who would pay to have their children photographed with the animals. (NT.)

An open house for the new Fountain High School, located on Santa Fe Avenue, was held in April 1954. L.A. Toothman installed the wood floor in the gym, which is still in use 70 years later. This school became a community effort, as much of the labor was donated by volunteers who worked on the school after the paid contractors left each day. (FVM.)

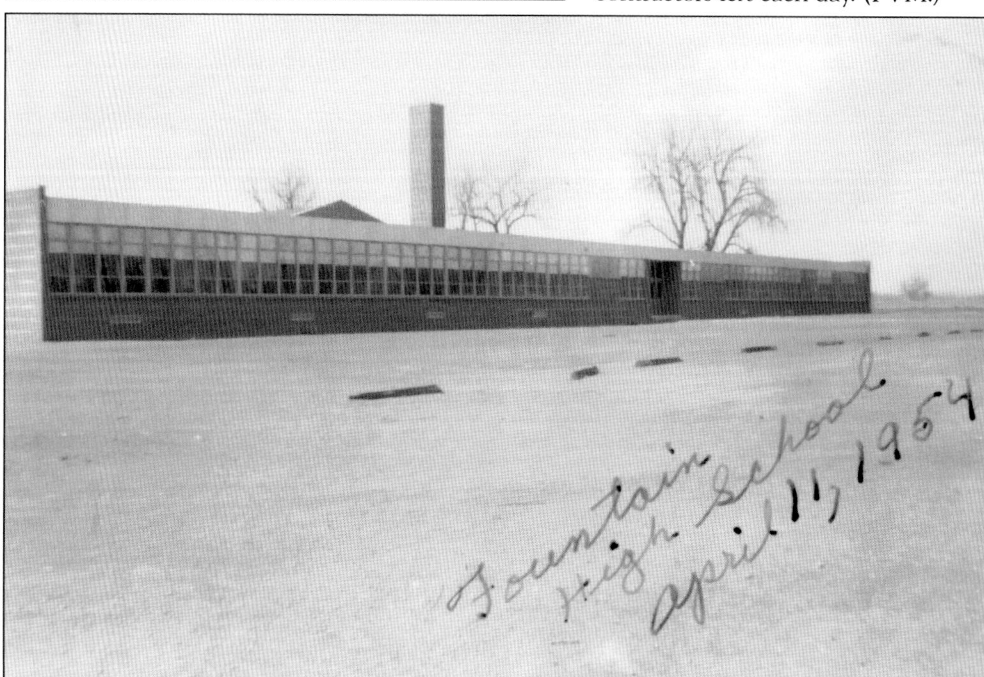

Evelyn and Clare Peebles operated Peebles' Lunch Room in 1930, which featured sandwiches and cold drinks. Situated on Santa Fe Avenue, the new Highway 85, it was in the perfect location to catch hungry and thirsty motorists passing through on their way to Pueblo or Denver. The building now serves as a residence. (DB.)

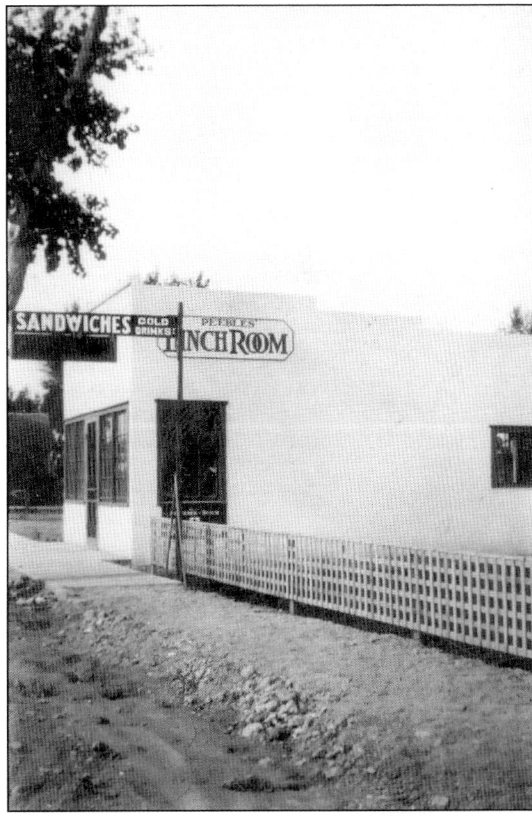

Evelyn Peebles stands next to her husband, Clare, at her clean lunch counter in the 1930s. She advertised homemade chili for 10¢. Her menu included milk toast for 15¢, pie à la mode for 15¢, hamburger steak for 40¢, and sweet milk and pop for 5¢ each. The presence of the Budweiser sign behind the counter likely dates this photograph to the mid-1930s after Prohibition ended. (DB.)

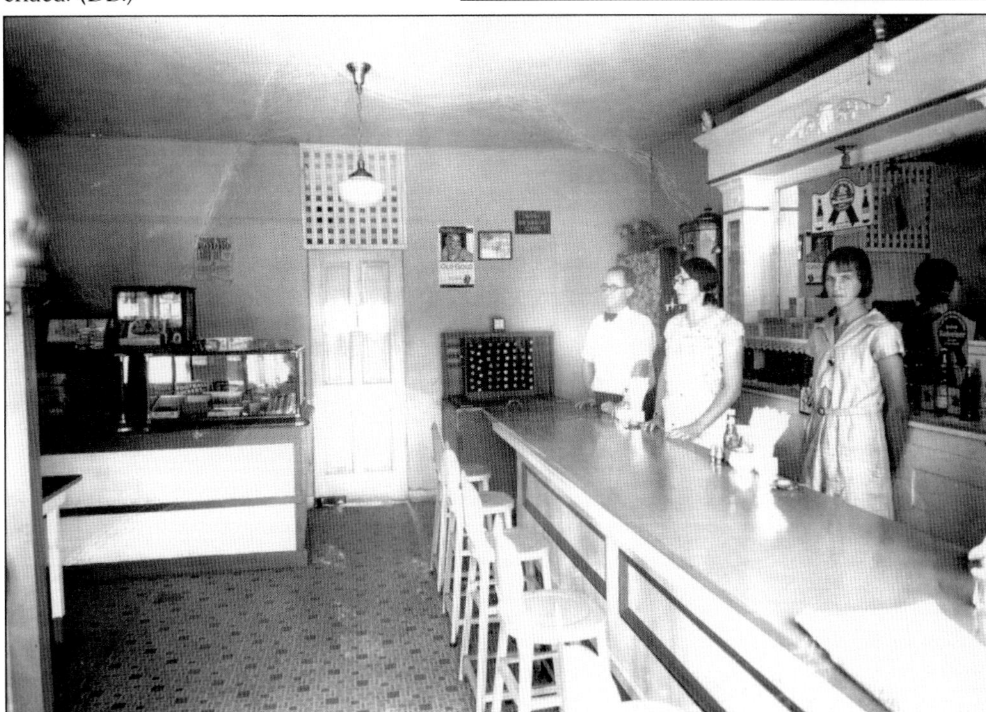

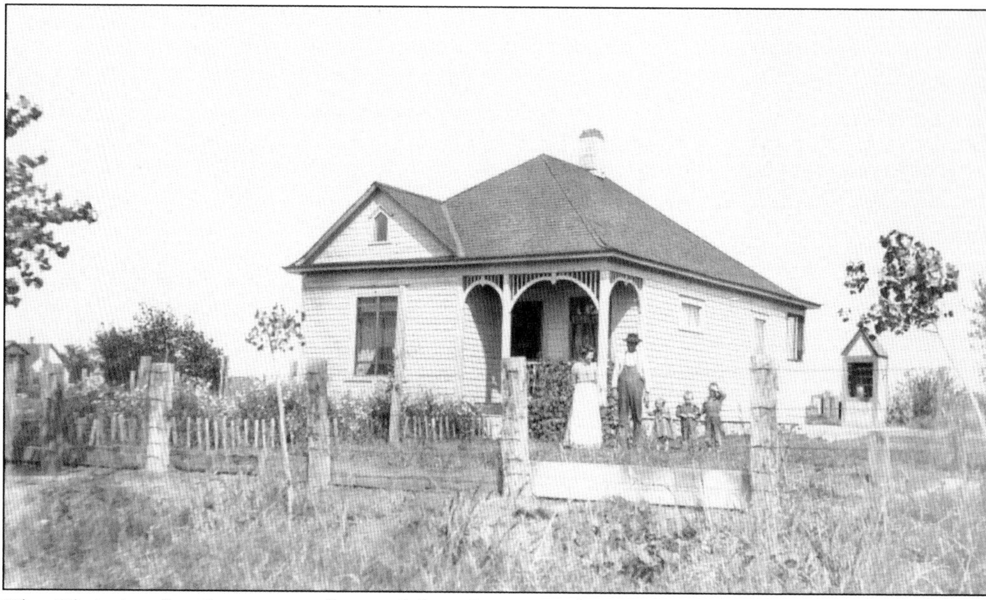

The Christian family poses in front of their home in this 1903 photograph. From left to right are Mamie, Lee, Elizabeth, Robert, and Michael. This house still stands at the corner of Illinois Avenue and Santa Fe Avenue. Quite a few homes west of the Santa Fe tracks were occupied by members of the Christian family. (DB.)

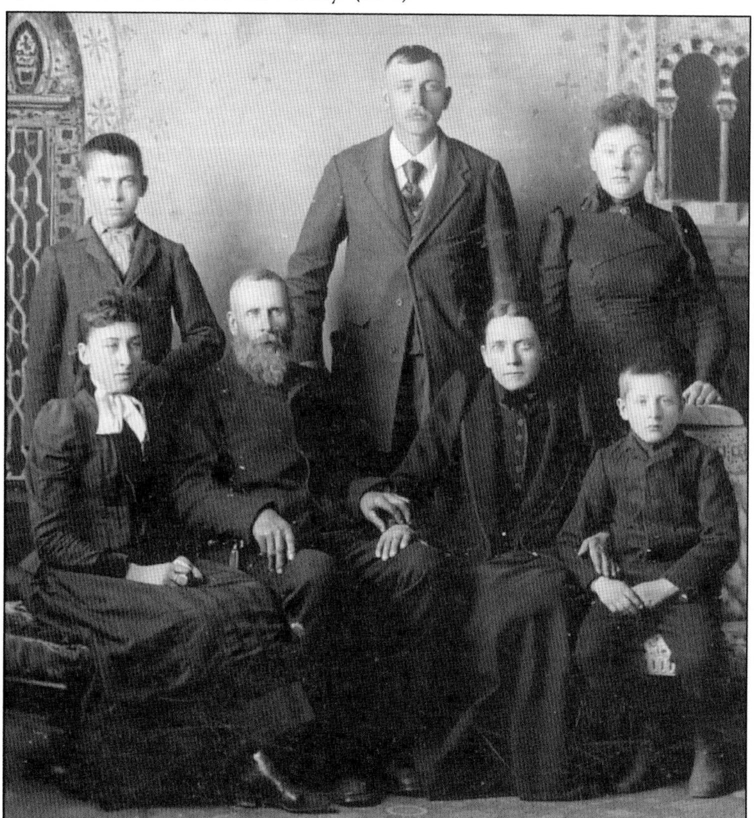

William Christian, a Civil War veteran from the state of Tennessee, moved his family to Colorado in 1891 after living in Missouri for a short time. The Christian family from left to right are (first row) Catherine, William, Lovica, and William; (second row) Lorn, Lee, and Annie. Descendants of William Christian still live in Fountain today. (DB.)

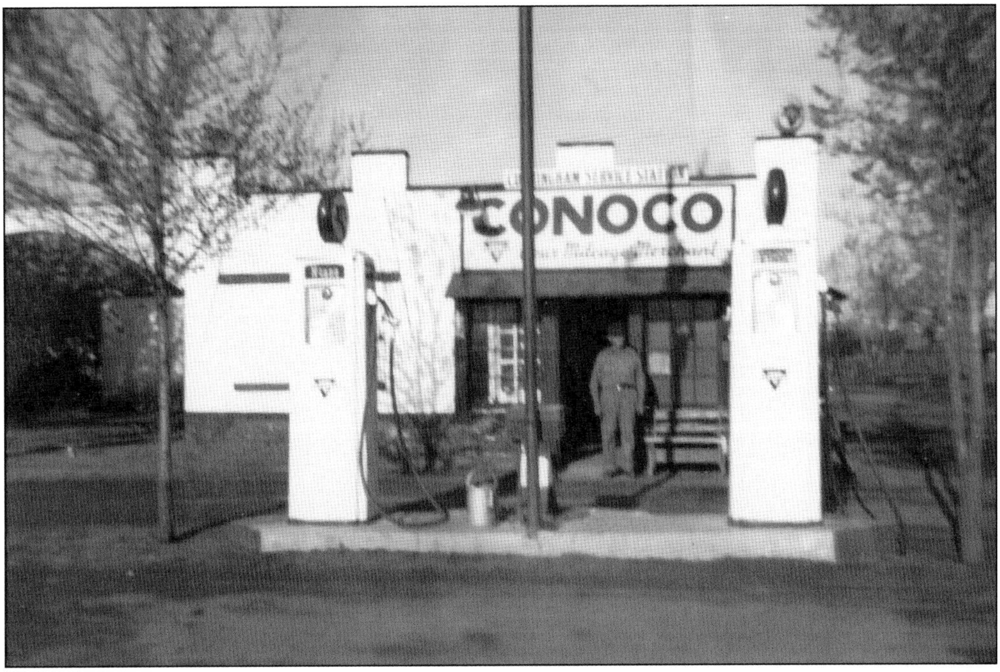

Grandpa Cunningham stands in front of the Cunningham Service Station on South Santa Fe Avenue, which became part of the new Highway 85. Bypassing the Denver-to-Pueblo Road on Main Street, it was the new main business street in town. Filling stations offered their customers full service by filling the car's tank with gas, checking the fluids, and washing the windshield. (FVM.)

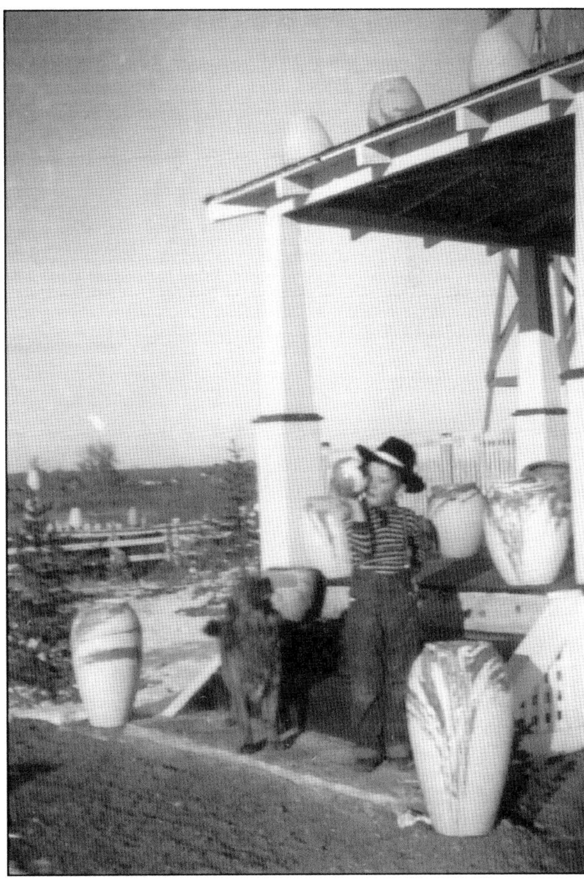

Young Jimmy Chancellor and his dog stand among the many pieces of pottery made by hand at his father's Rocky Mountain Pottery Company. John Chancellor and a few employees worked with a mixture of finely ground gravel, sand, and cement to daily turn out scores of yard ornaments to include lambs, birdbaths, and brightly painted planters. (FVM.)

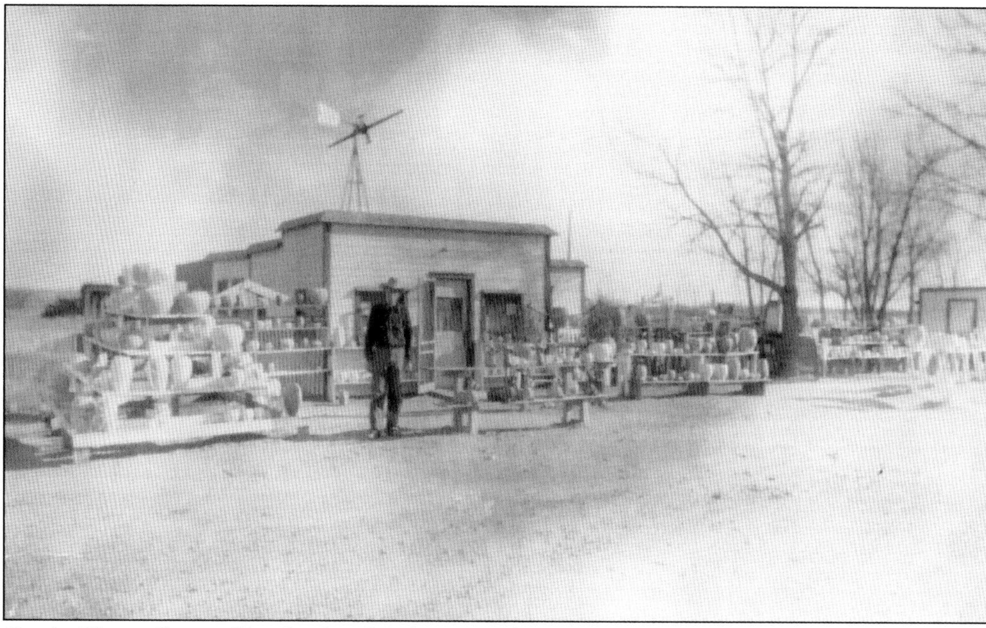

Cecile Chancellor and her husband, John, moved to Colorado with their infant son in 1934 so she could be treated for tuberculosis. When John lost his job with a lumber company, he used his potter skills to start his own business in an abandoned filling station at the south end of town. Items from the Rocky Mountain Pottery Company were shipped all over the western United States and adorned the yards of many Fountain homes. (JC.)

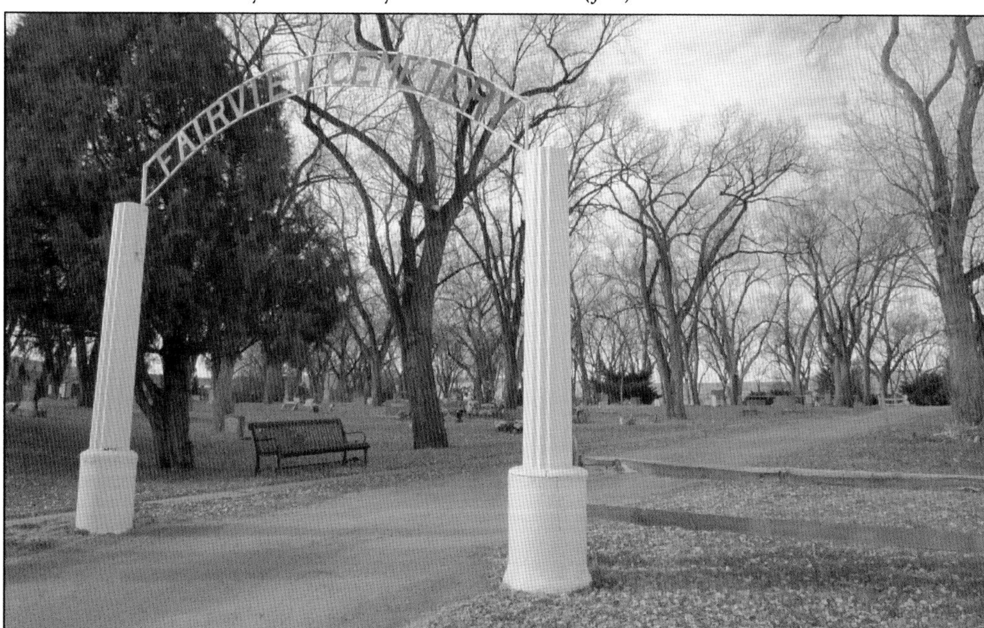

Historic Fairview Cemetery is tucked away on the southwest side of town across the river. Donated to the town by Mary Imes, it is now the final resting place of many of Fountain's residents, past and present. A visitor will find many familiar families and historical names represented here on a quiet walk among the trees and monuments. (ATH.)

Five

Coming Together

Citizens of Fountain have a long history of coming together as a community, as the following photographs show. In decades past, times were slower and more relaxed; people had more opportunities to chat with neighbors and visit with friends. There were numerous clubs and organizations in which to participate. Groups of teenagers spent time together in the mountains, where entire families also went for picnics.

As people did not venture too far from home, many marriages took place among high school sweethearts, thus uniting two families into a bigger one. Eventually, there were many large extended families in town. A family reunion tended to be a large gathering at the home of the patriarch. Indeed, quite a few Fountainites are descended from several early residents.

Even without the family relationships, citizens bonded together as fellow townsmen, where everyone knew everyone. Neighbors willingly served in local and state governments to better their community. The whole town turned out for school programs and club presentations, as well as rodeos, parades, traveling tent shows, Christmas festivities, and the annual fall festival. The whole town rallied around the families of soldiers fighting in wars overseas. The whole town mourned when the 1918 flu epidemic took some of their neighbors. The whole town came together in times of disaster, whether it was after a flood, tornado, blizzard, or train explosion.

That spirit of community involvement is still prevalent today, even though the population and physical area of the town have increased immensely. Just as in times past, the citizens of Fountain do not hesitate to get politically, civically, and voluntarily involved in their community. Some noted civic leaders are remembered in the names of local roads, schools, community centers, and parks. Fountainites still come together for town events. They come together in patriotic support of military troops, both past and present. They come together in various efforts of charitable aid. They come together on civic teams to improve the community. And, they still look forward to Labor Day, when the town comes together for the annual Fountain Fall Festival.

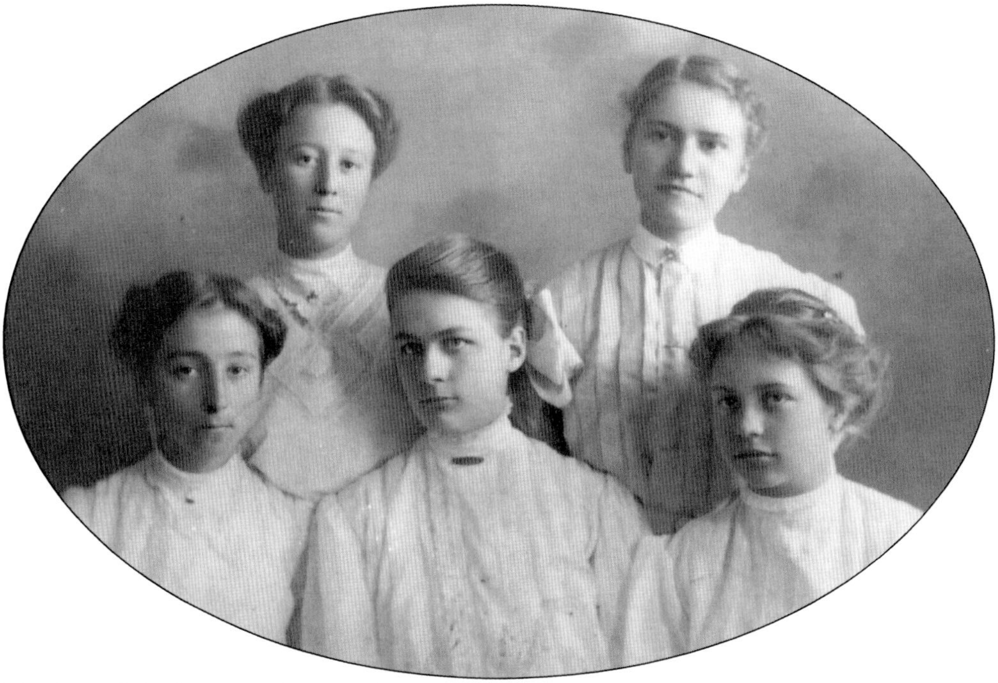

Members of the fourth graduating class of Fountain High School pose in their crisp, white lace and pleats for this class picture in 1907. From left to right are (first row) Rita Spicer, Florence Avison, and Gladys Phillips; (second row) Geraldine Spicer and Gertrude Walkup. (MB.)

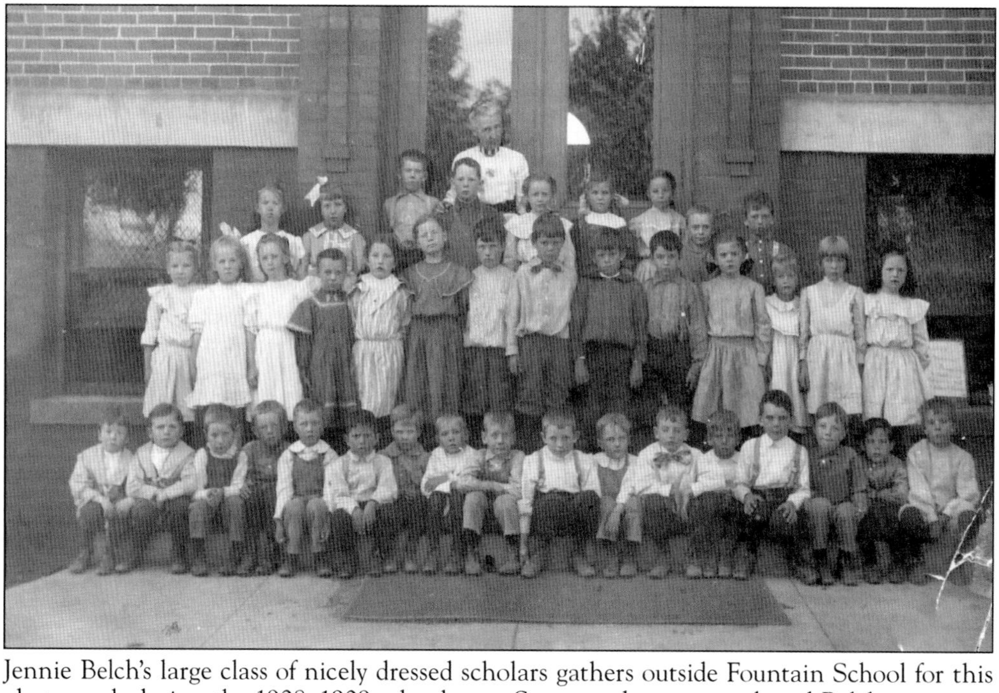

Jennie Belch's large class of nicely dressed scholars gathers outside Fountain School for this photograph during the 1908–1909 school year. Some students remembered Belch as a stern teacher, but others remembered that she rewarded her students with a dime when they learned to count to 100. (NT.)

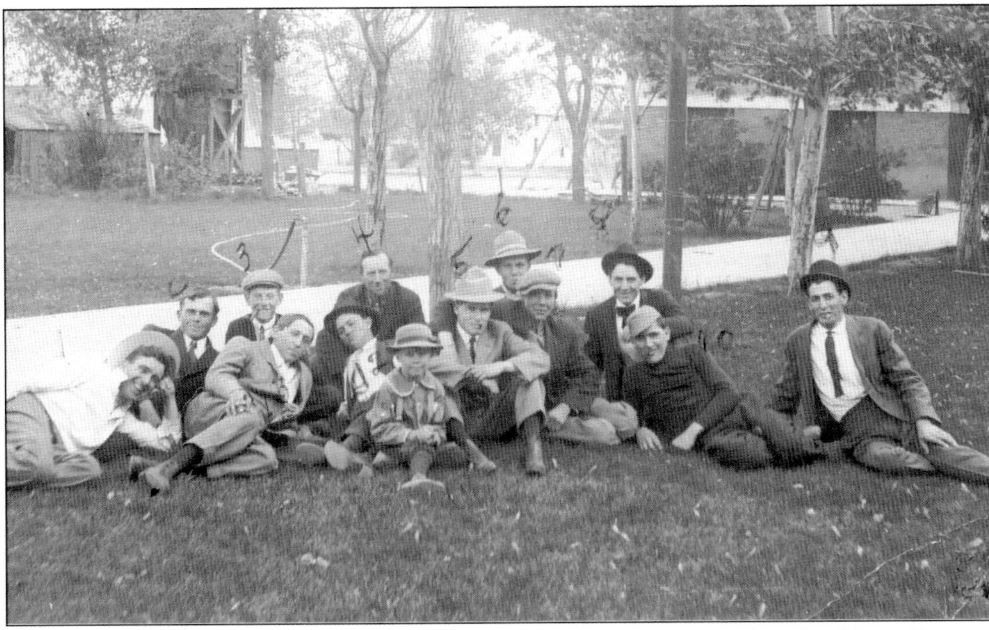

In 1910, these men and boys dressed in their Sunday best congregate on the school lawn. Pictured are Harry Galbraith (1), Hi Colbert (2), Harvey Miller (3), Gary Simmons (4), Truman Gore (5), Wesley Benedict (6), Dick Fugit (7), ? Considine (8), Walter Considine (9), Charley Torbit (10), Glenn Dillie (11), Frank Townsend (12), and John Sullivan (13). (NT.)

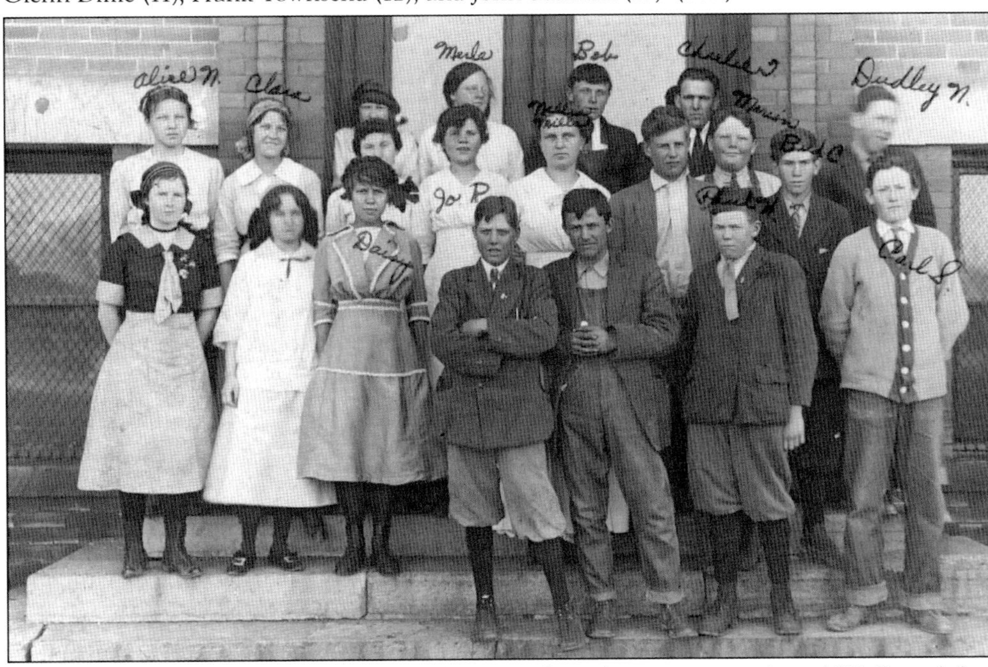

Fountain School's seventh and eighth graders pose for a class picture in about 1911. From left to right are (first row) Joan West, Marjorie Benedict, Daisy Torbit, Herbert Virden, Walter Gore, Arleigh White, and Carl Smith; (second row) Alice Nuce, Clara Eichel, Nora Gibbie, Josephine Rhinehart, Nellie Mills, Hascol Barnes, Marion Love, Bud Child, and Dudley Niles; (third row) Cora Virden, Merle Love, Bob Christian, and Charlie Torbit. (NT.)

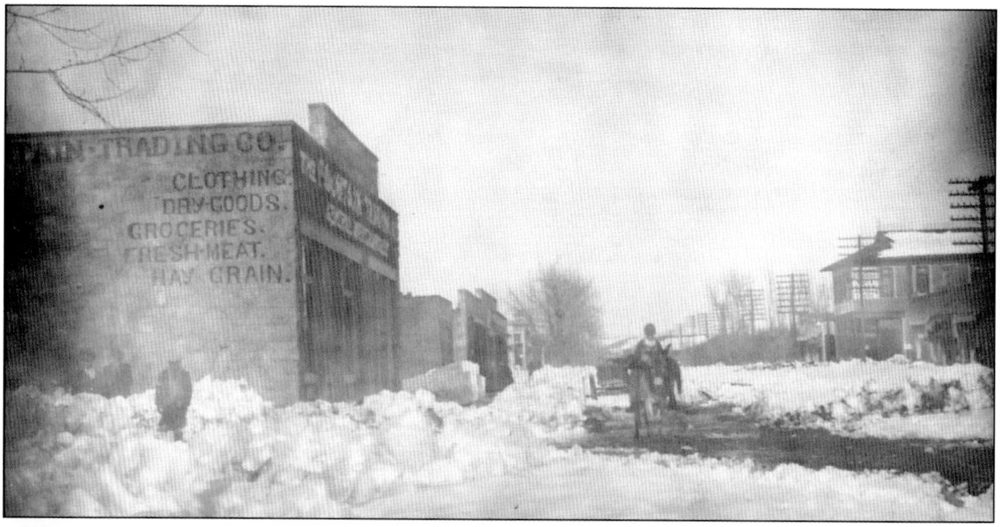

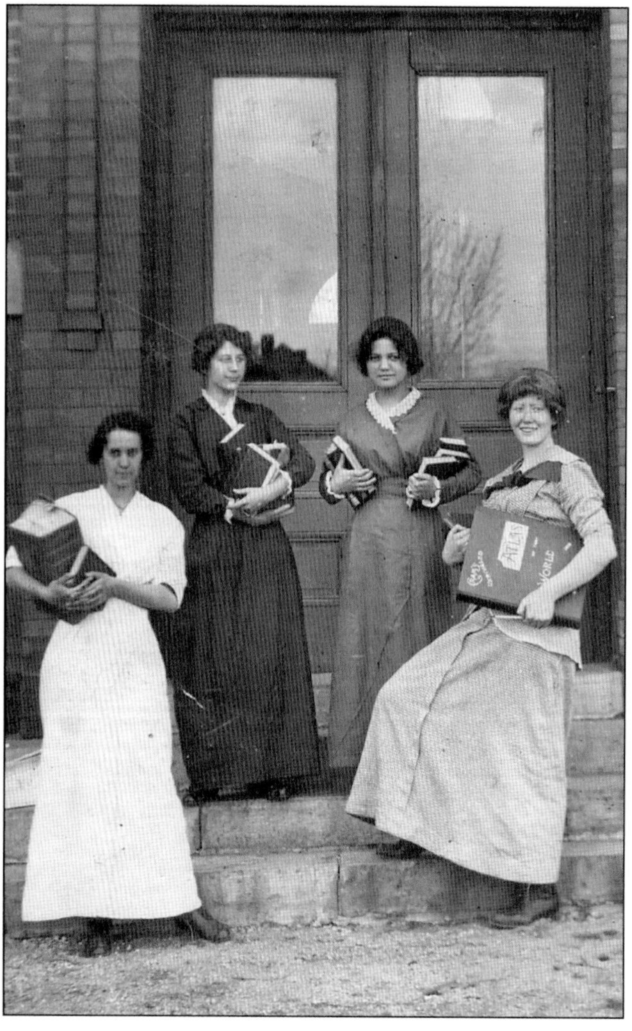

A donkey and rider make their way south along muddy Main Street in the wake of the Big Snow of 1913. Three feet of snow accumulated across the entire state over three days in December that year. At that time, snow removal consisted of men and shovels; they threw the heavy, wet mass into wagons and hauled it away from town, where it was then shoveled back out of the wagons. (NT.)

Coral Toothman stands (back right) outside the Fountain School building about 1914. She was about 18 years old when she posed here with her studious friends, laden with reference materials and textbooks. The typical subjects taught at the high-school level were English, history, science, math, and Latin. (NT.)

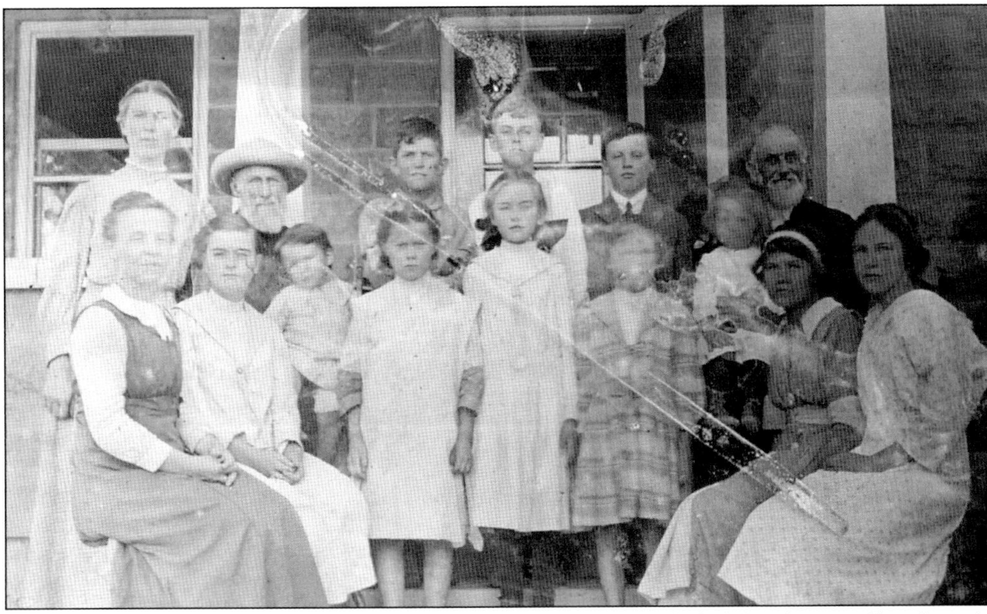

At Robert Loomis's 11th birthday party in 1914, his guests included family as well as friends. From left to right are (first row) ? Loomis, Edith Jones, Bernice ?, Helen Jones, unidentified, Daisy Toothman, and Mary Loomis; (second row) Rose ?, ? Loomis, unidentified, R.B. Toothman, Harry Jones, Robert Loomis, Clarissa Toothman, and J.F. Garret.

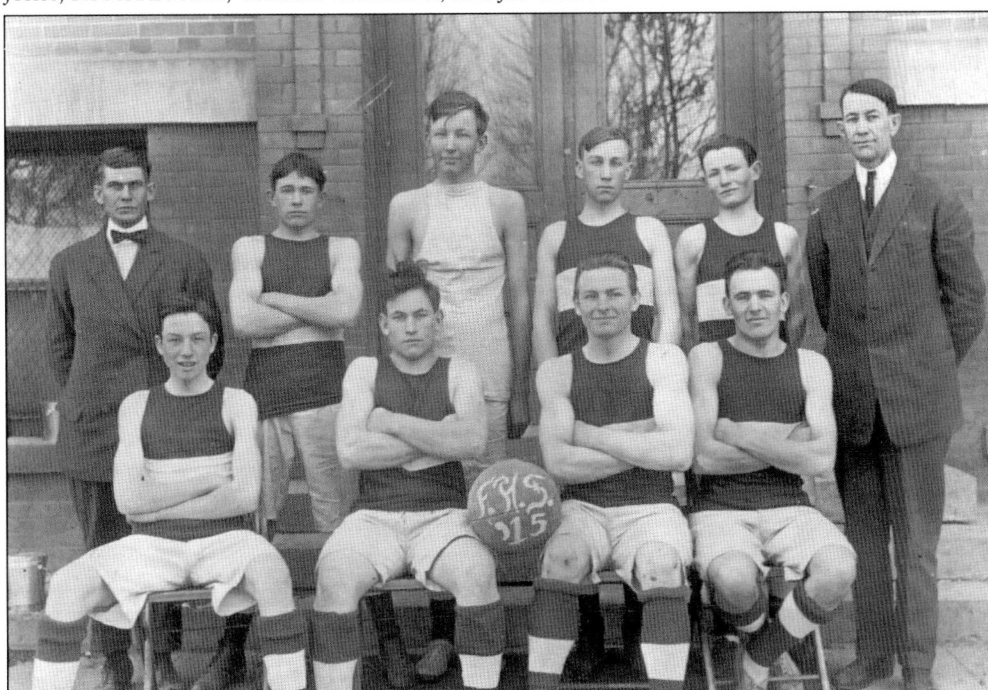

The capable Fountain High School basketball team poses for this picture in 1915 outside the school building. From left to right are (first row) Harold Hoover, Alva Gibbe, Elton Love, and Charles Torbit; (second row) coach Charles Riddoch, Paul White, Harry Nuce, Lester Wilson, Carl Smith, and Superintendent Alps. (NT.)

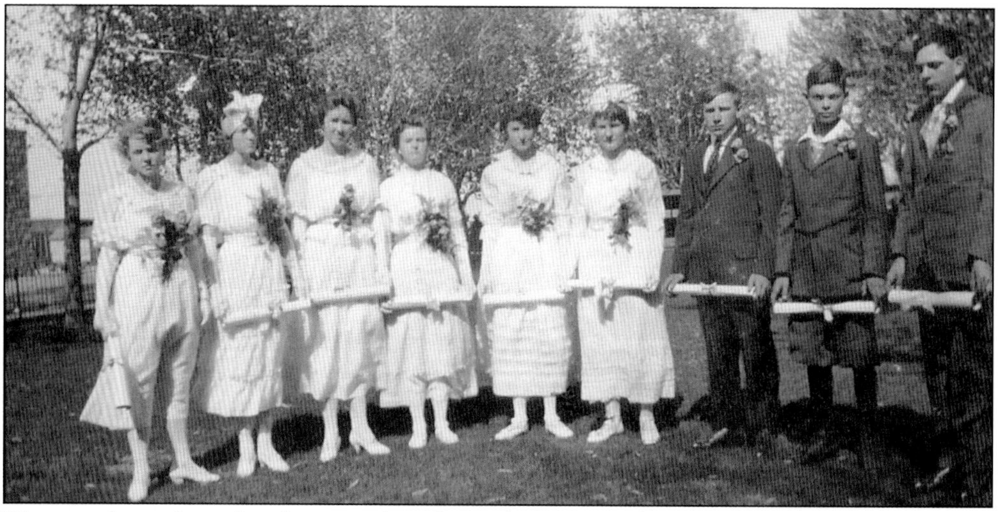

These students, dressed in their very best for graduation, stand on the school lawn in 1916 while holding their eighth-grade diplomas bound in ribbon. Graduation exercises usually consisted of music by school musicians, an invocation, musical solos, and a speech by the superintendent or another school official. The graduation often coincided with a school field day, both of which were attended by most townspeople. (NT.)

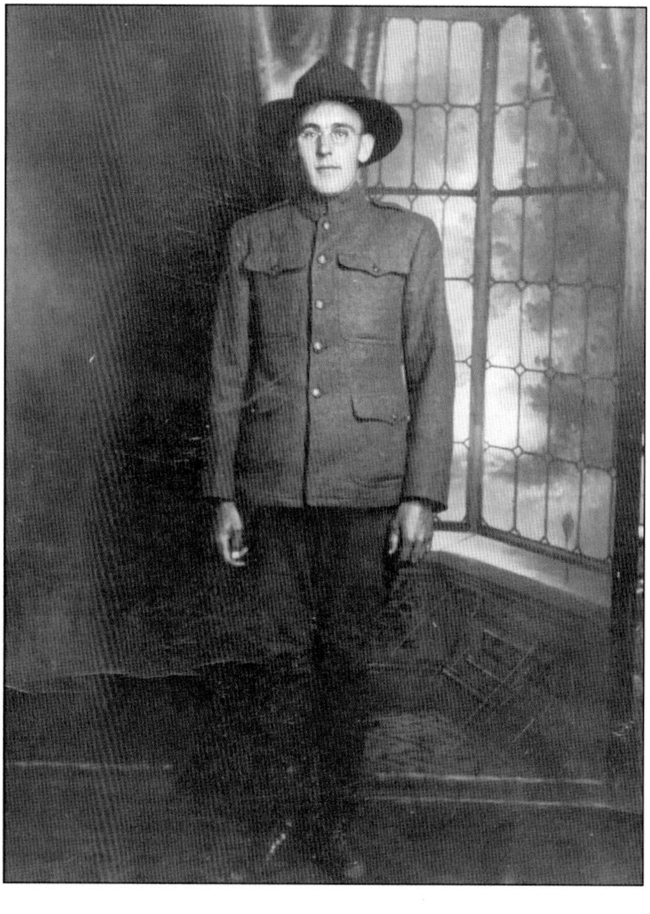

Charlie Torbit served in the Great War in 1917. He and his Fountain Valley comrades numbered about 60. Torbit registered with a physical description of blue eyes and auburn hair. Fountain was well represented in all the wars, including World War II, the Korean and Vietnam conflicts, and the more recent wars in Iraq and Afghanistan. (NT.)

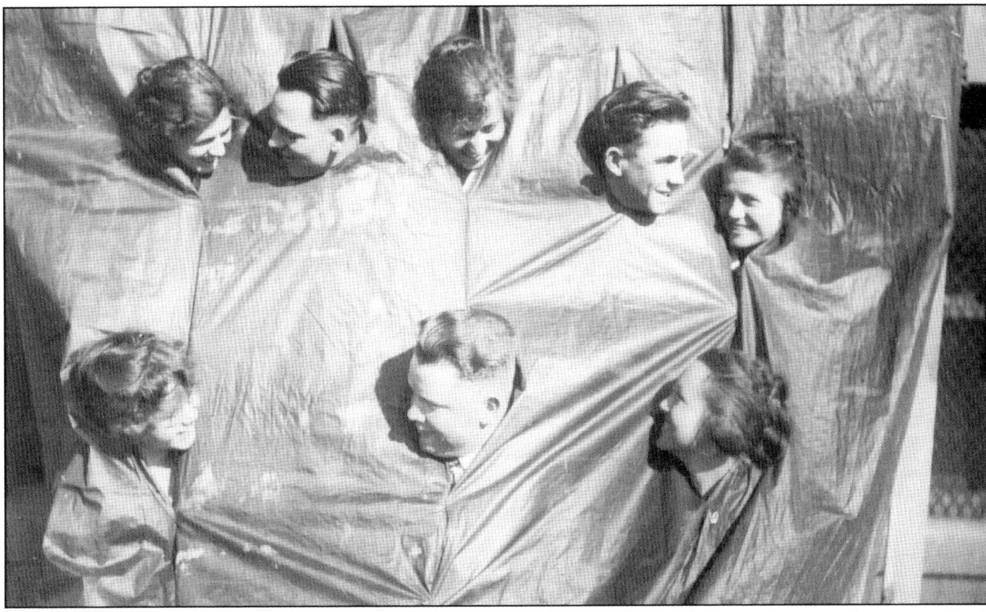

Daisy Toothman (upper right) and her schoolmates enjoy themselves as they perform in a high school play around 1918. Toothman and most of her friends grew up in Fountain and attended all grades of school together. The whole town was probably invited to attend this play as they often attended other such school programs and events in support of their youth. (NT.)

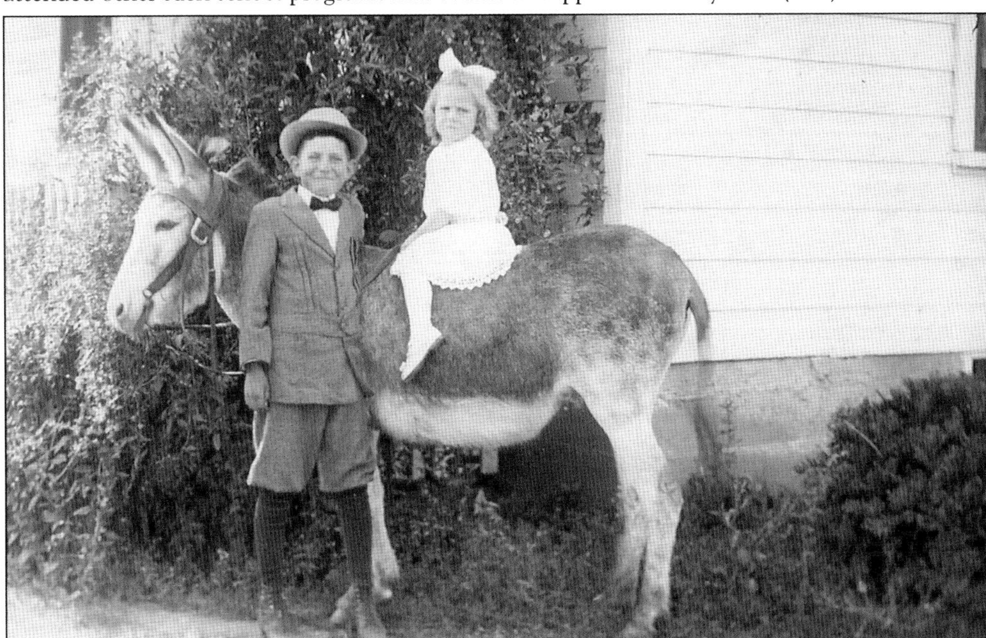

In 1914, R.B. Toothman (left) stands next to his little sister Clarissa, known to everyone as "Toots," as she sits astride a donkey. Both children fell ill with the flu in 1918, and R.B. did not survive. Because the funeral homes and hearses in Colorado Springs were too crowded and busy, the family kept Toothman's casket in the home and used a horse-drawn hearse to transport him to the cemetery. (NT.)

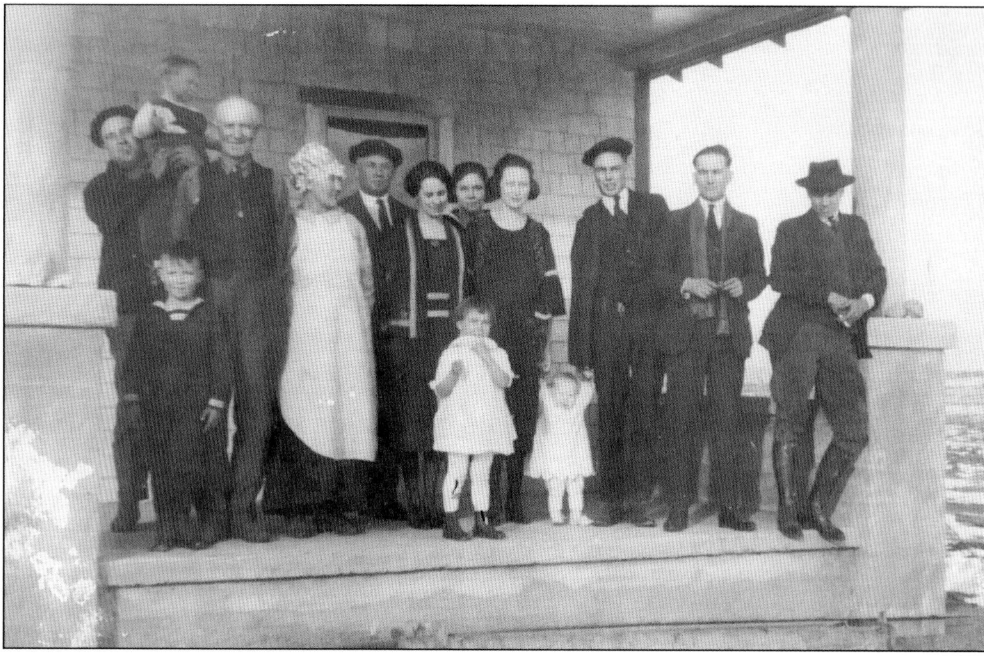

The Whalen family gathers for a holiday celebration at the family home on Link Road in about 1920. The kids standing from left to right are (front row) William Whalen and two unidentified children. The rest of the family members in the photograph are, from left to right, (second row) W.E. Whalen, May "Tubby" Clopton, William Whalen, Lucy Whalen, A. Clark, Vivian Clark, Meril Clark, Cy Vaughn, and Top Clopton; (third row) Herb Whalen and Louella Whalen. (DK.)

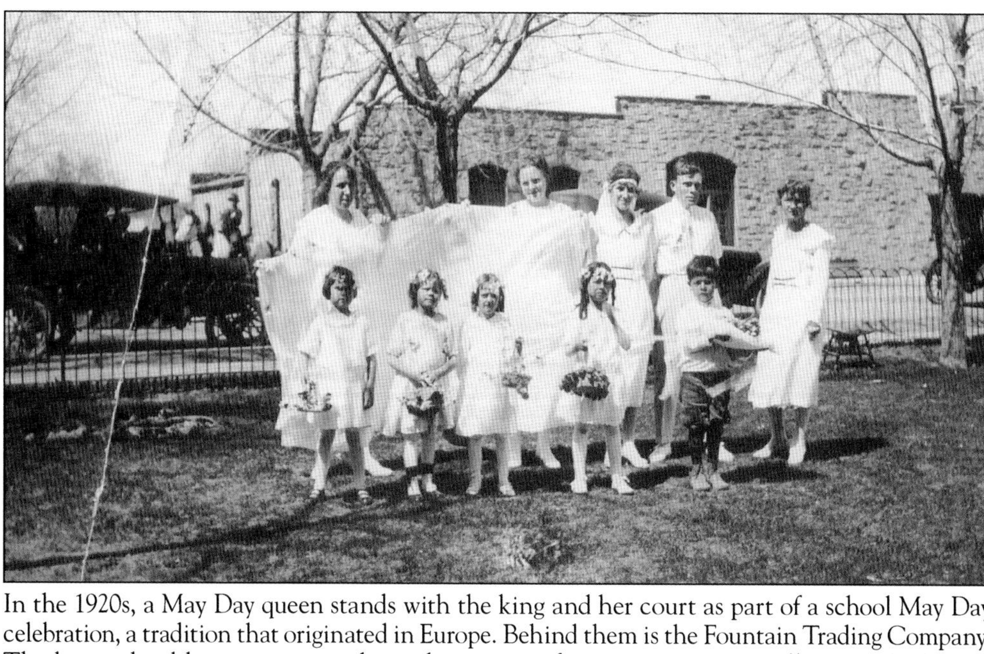

In the 1920s, a May Day queen stands with the king and her court as part of a school May Day celebration, a tradition that originated in Europe. Behind them is the Fountain Trading Company. The large school lawn was a popular gathering spot for groups, as many tall trees, which were planted when the school was built in 1903, shaded it. (NT.)

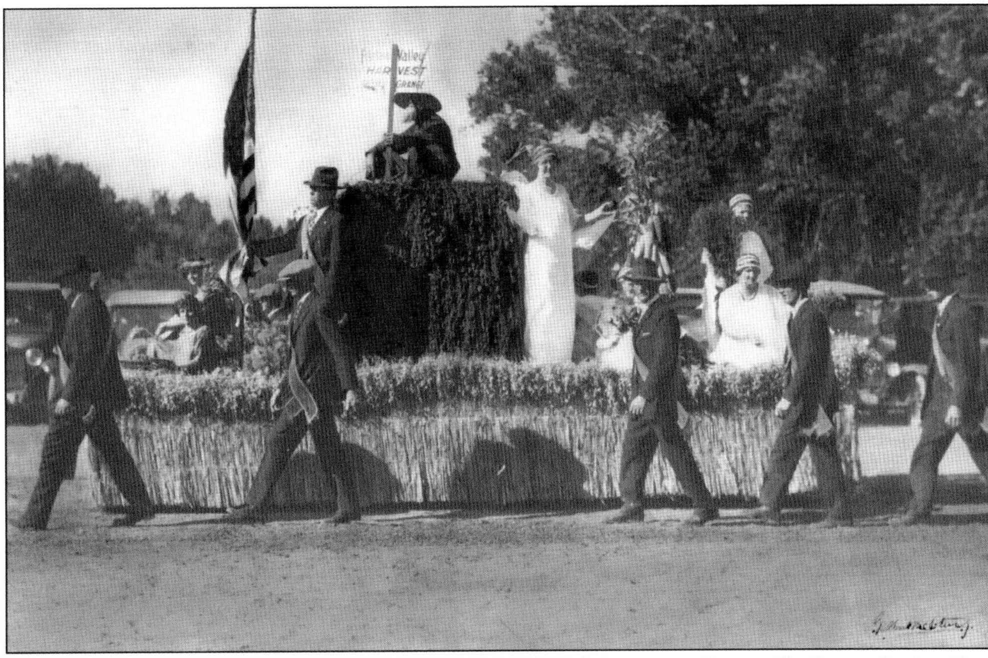

Officers of the local Fountain Valley Grange wear their banners as they walk alongside this float prepared for the first chamber parade in 1920. Representing local farmers and ranchers, the theme of the float is "Harvest." Ladies of the Grange in their flowing white dresses greet the crowd from a simulated cornfield. (FVM.)

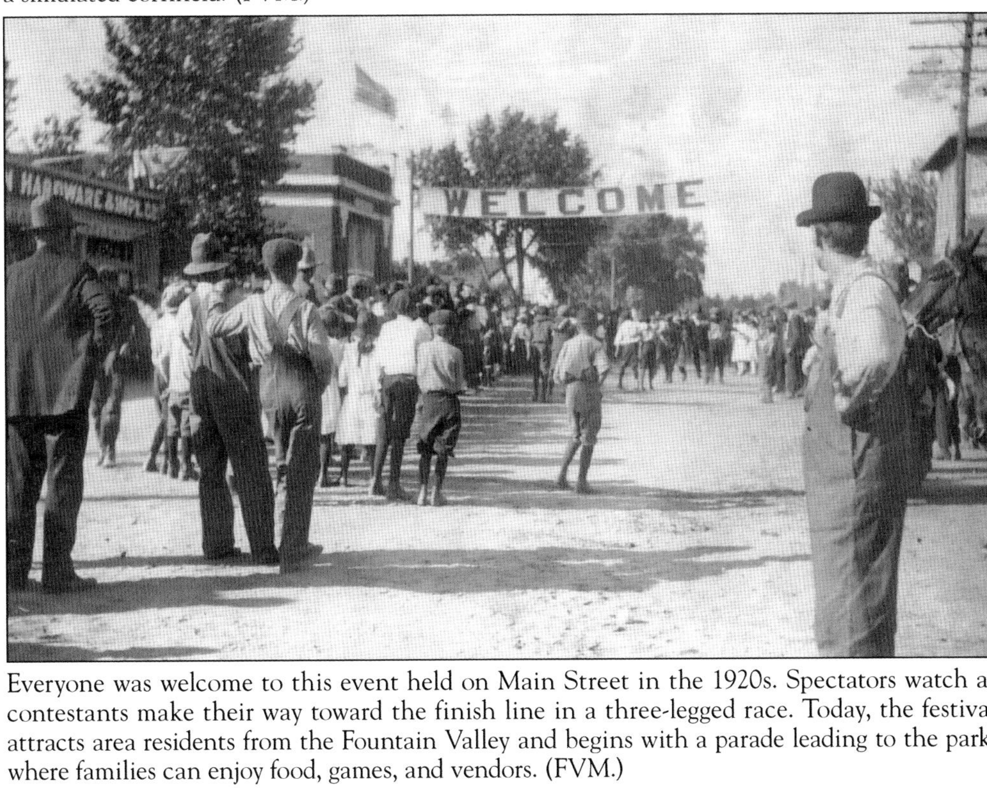

Everyone was welcome to this event held on Main Street in the 1920s. Spectators watch as contestants make their way toward the finish line in a three-legged race. Today, the festival attracts area residents from the Fountain Valley and begins with a parade leading to the park, where families can enjoy food, games, and vendors. (FVM.)

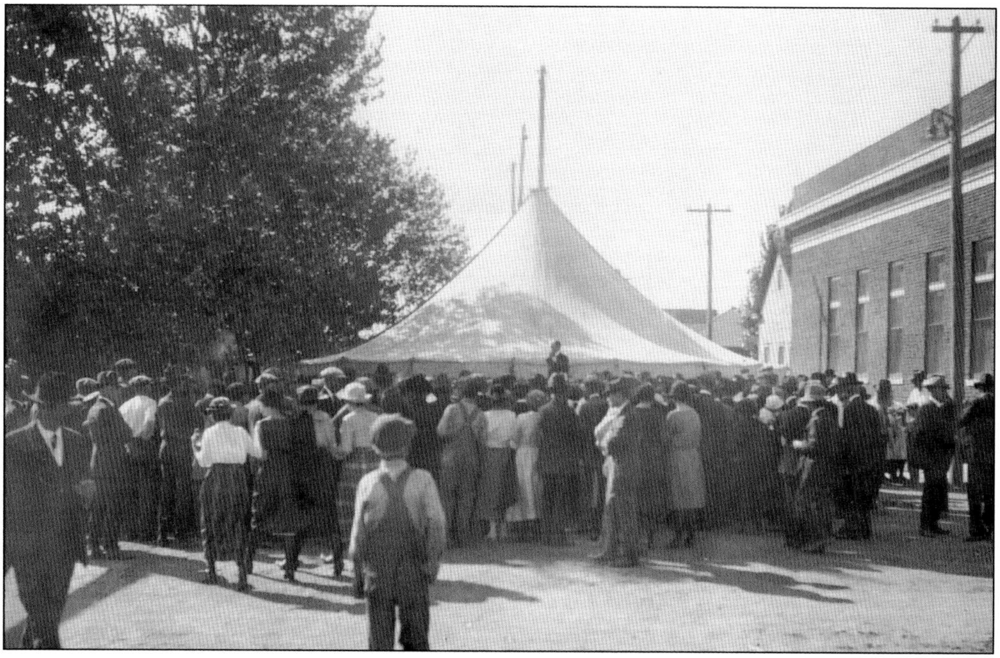

Spectators gather on a sunny day at this big tent staked on Ohio Avenue next to the bank and Congregational church. Chatauqua lectures were common in the mid-1920s. Likewise, tent shows were a popular form of entertainment, offering minstrel shows, vaudeville, drama, comedy, and musicals. The lectures and shows traveled through rural America by covered wagon. (NT.)

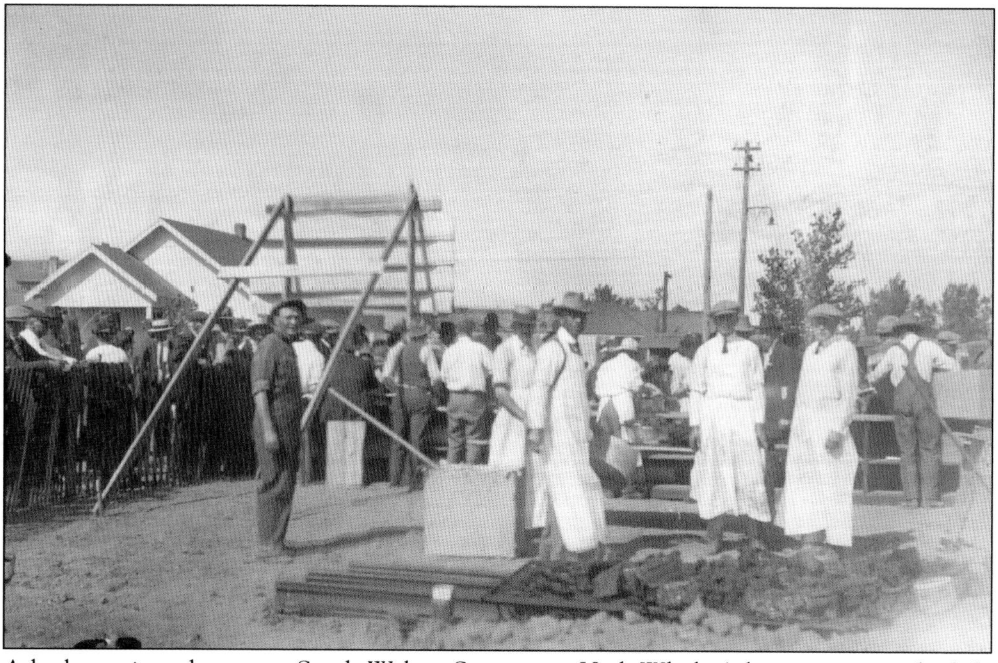

A barbecue is underway on South Walnut Street near Herb Whalen's house, seen on the left. Aproned men tend the coals in the foreground and dish out food in the serving line to the rear. An outdoor barbecue like this, where the whole town was invited, would have occurred at events such as the fall festival. (NT.)

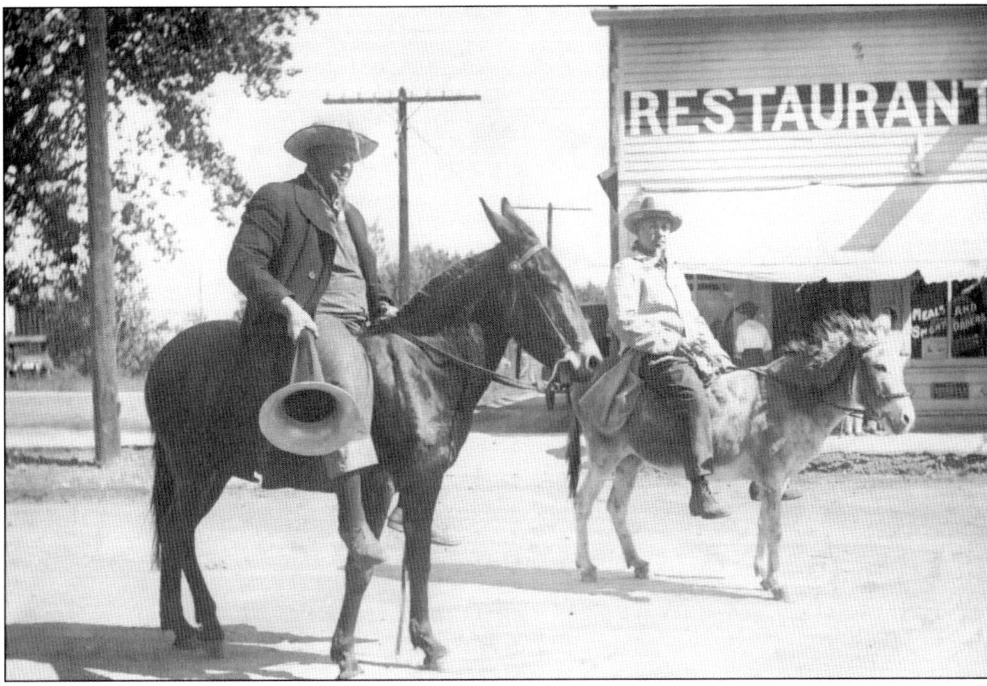

This scene is probably that of a parade in which Marion Love, holding a megaphone, and Herb Whalen, holding a pistol, make their way down the street in 1922. The men seem to be wearing historical costumes, including long, flowing goatees, suggesting they may have been participants in a Colorado Day parade. The restaurant in the back, specializing in meals and short orders, appears to be open for business. (DK.)

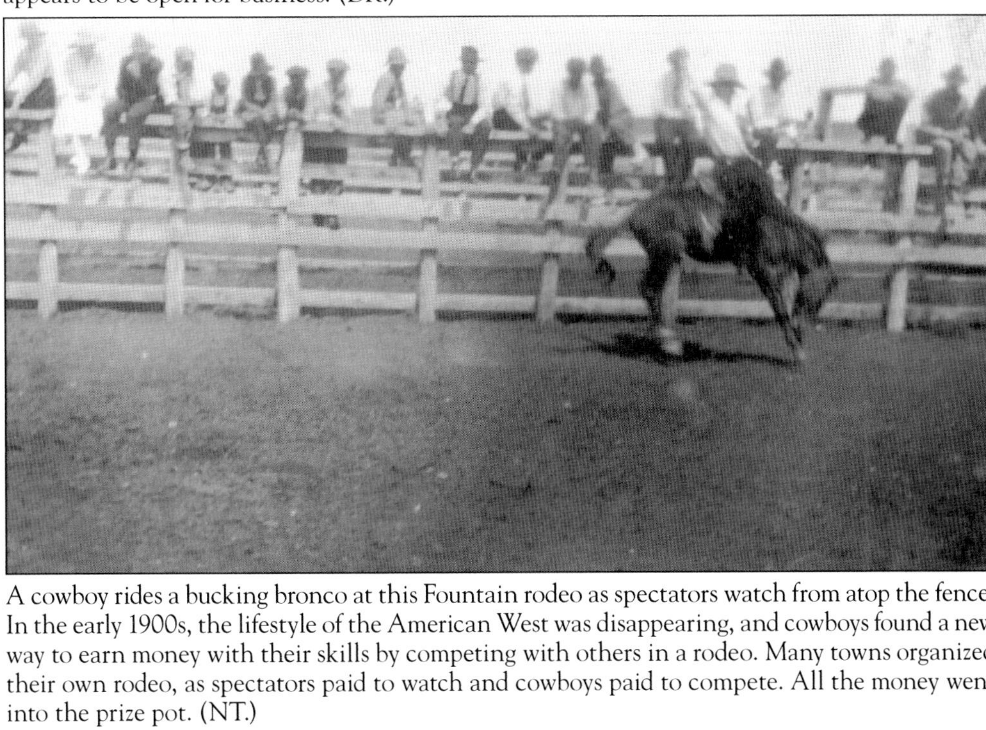

A cowboy rides a bucking bronco at this Fountain rodeo as spectators watch from atop the fence. In the early 1900s, the lifestyle of the American West was disappearing, and cowboys found a new way to earn money with their skills by competing with others in a rodeo. Many towns organized their own rodeo, as spectators paid to watch and cowboys paid to compete. All the money went into the prize pot. (NT.)

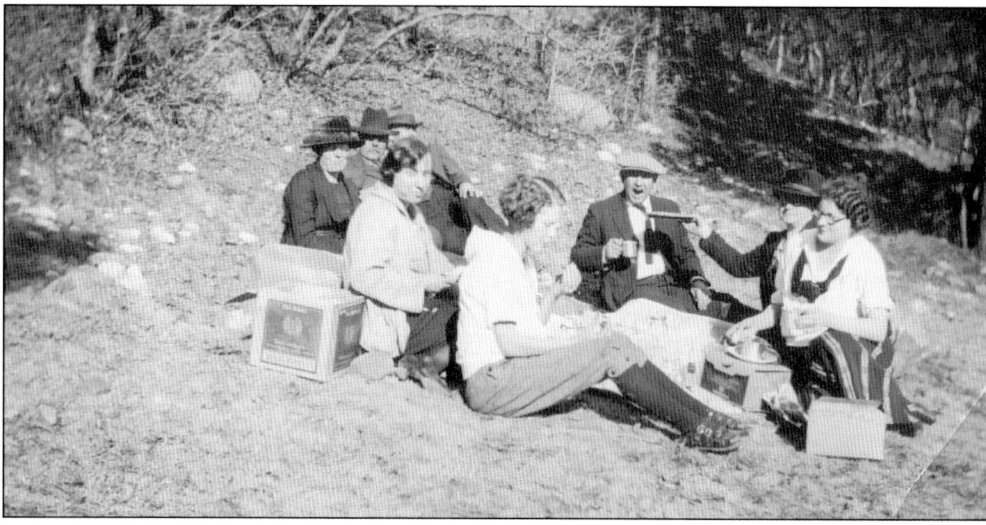

One of the prettiest and most popular picnicking spots was located in Rock Creek Canon, situated beside a flowing stream in the mountains about nine miles west of town on a good county road. Relatives celebrating the 1925 birthday of Bob Love are, from left to right, Mamie Christian, Lee Christian, Bob Love, Eloise Whalen, Grace Love, Herb Whalen, Annie Love, and Merle Love. (DK.)

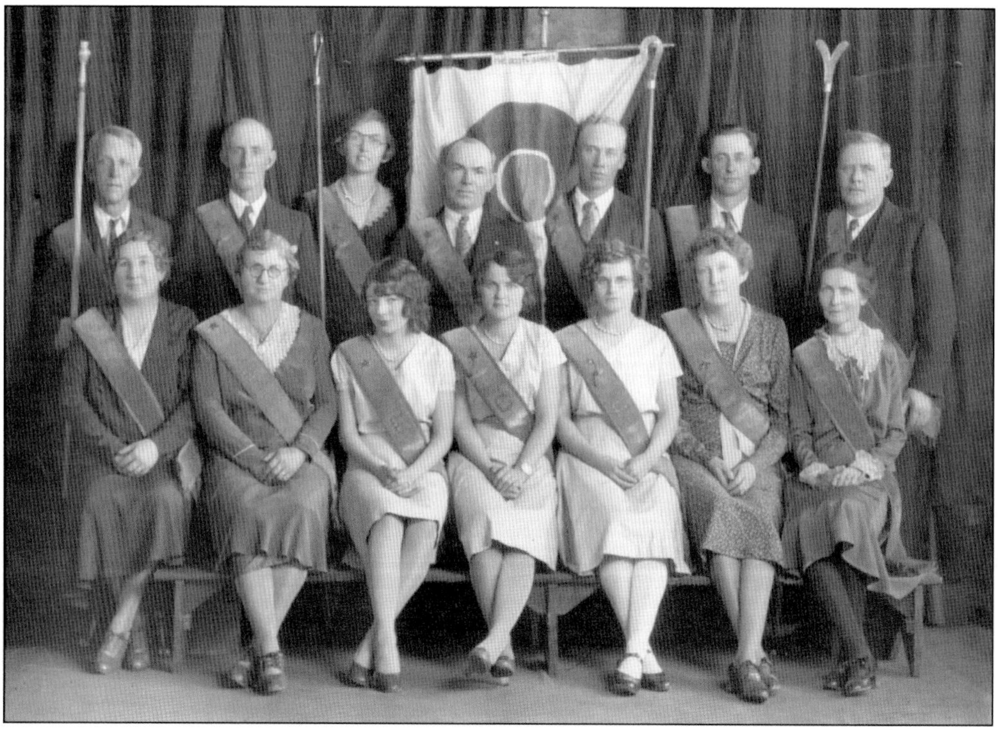

Officers of the Fountain Valley Grange No. 253 degree team pose with banners and staffs. Farmers and ranchers belonging to this fraternal organization met for educational events and social gatherings. From left to right are (first row) Lottie Wilson, Cora Jones, Elva Colbert, Mattie Oaks, Elma Althouse, Florence Harris, and ? Sinton; (second row) Hayes Jones, Earl Hughes, Prudence Mick, Sam Siep, R.I. Althouse, George Oaks, and Alfred Story. (FVM.)

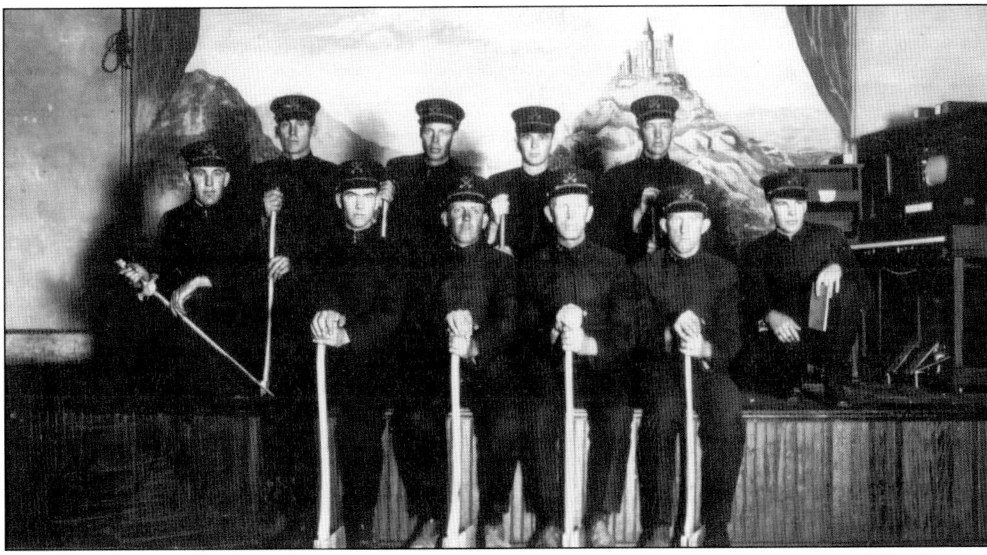

Charlie Torbit (left) and John Torbit (right) kneel at the ends of the stage as Fountain's Woodmen of the World Camp No. 231 poses for this photograph at the Woodmen Hall in 1928. The Woodmen of the World was an insurance organization that provided financial security for its members and their families. Other lodges in Fountain included the Royal Neighbors of America, Neighbors of Woodcraft, and Modern Woodmen of America. (NT.)

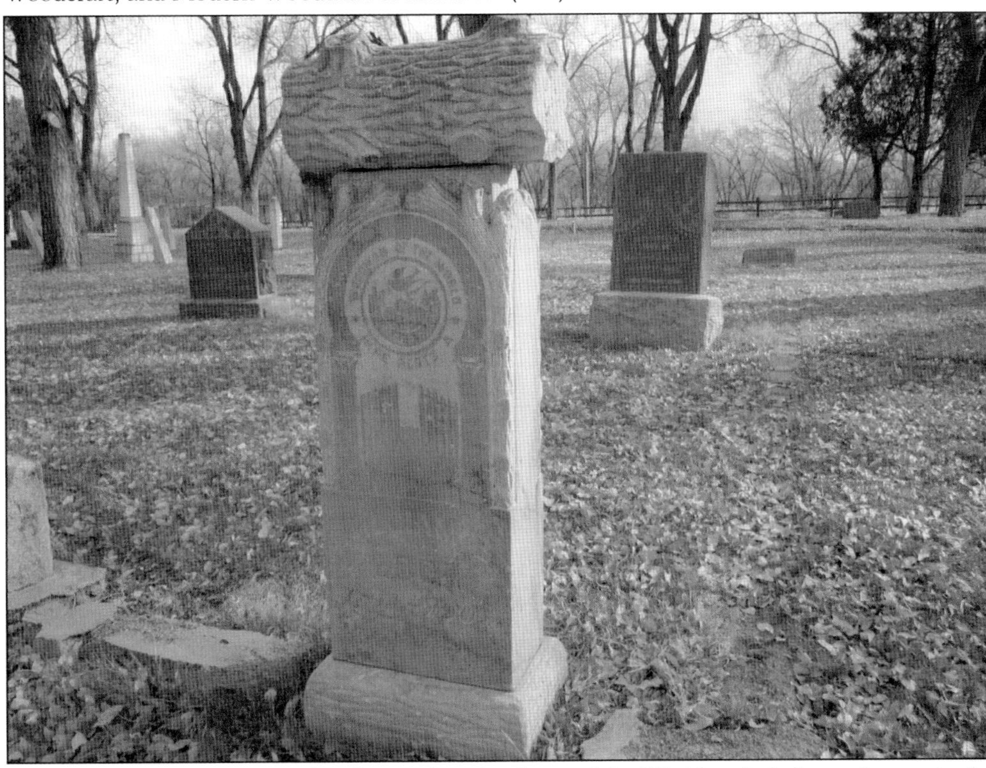

Prior to 1930, benefits of membership in the Woodmen of the World included a tombstone in the shape of a tree stump or log. This monument in Fountain's Fairview Cemetery marks the resting place of William "Mark" Bismark Lock. (ATH.)

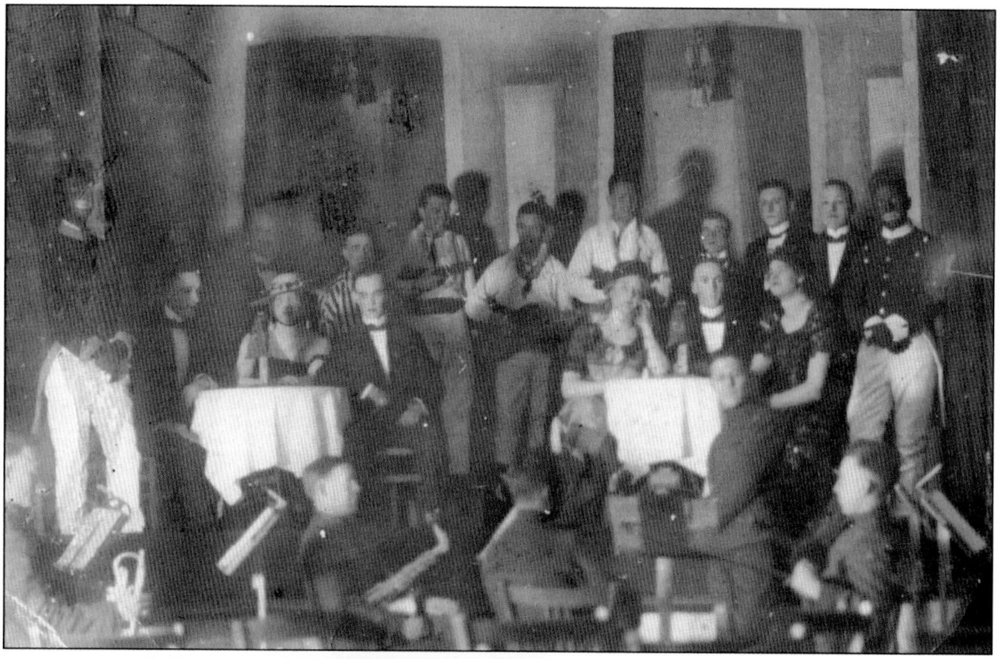

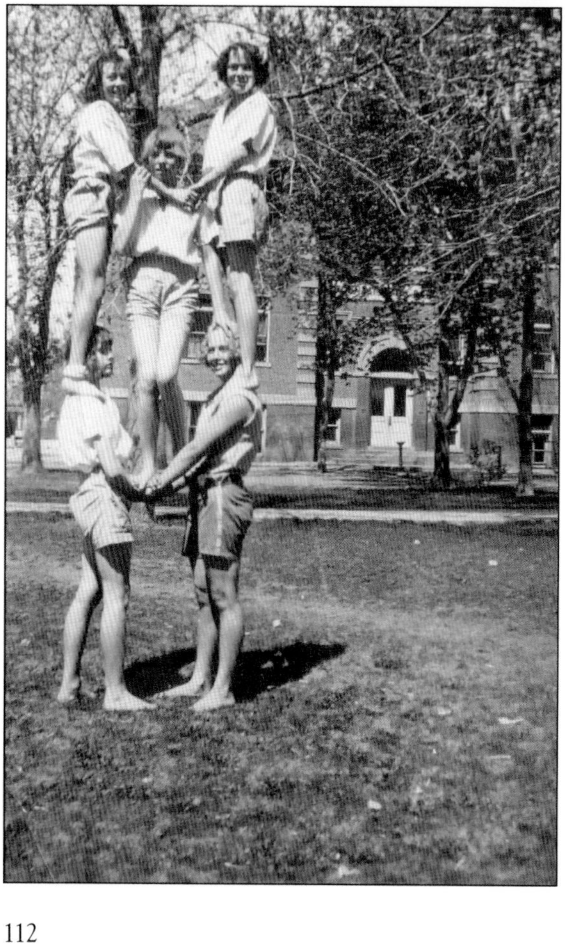

Harold Orcutt and Herb Whalen appear in blackface in this musical minstrel show, which was probably performed at the Woodmen Hall or the theater, once located on South Main Street. Several different clubs and organizations in town presented this popular form of entertainment consisting of comic skits, variety acts, dancing, and music. (NT.)

Jessie Page (top left) displays trust in her schoolmates as they form a human ladder on the front lawn of the grade school in the early 1930s. Her father, Floyd Page, worked on the road crew that built the new Highway 85. The family moved up the road as it progressed; therefore, Jessie did not stay in Fountain very long. (FVM.)

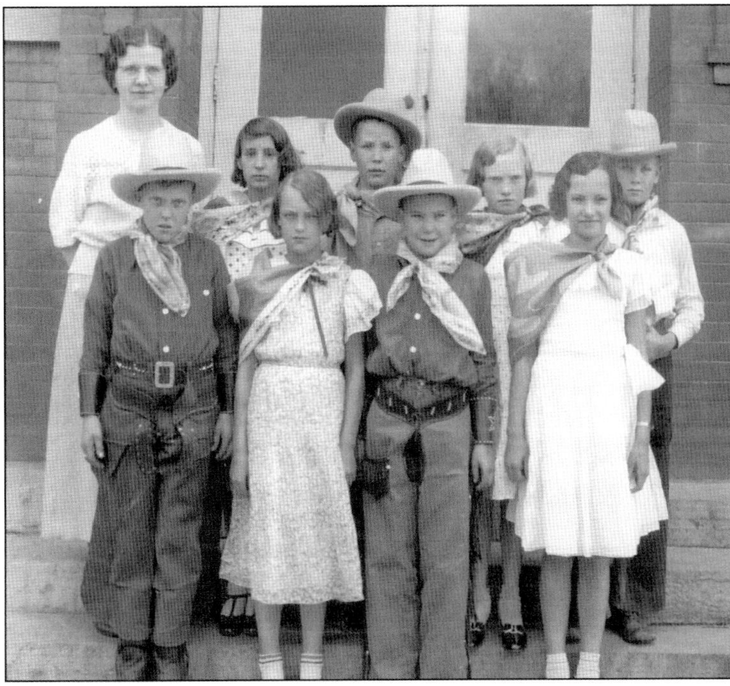

These cowboys and cowgirls stand outside the Fountain Grade School in 1934. Bud Torbit's costume was probably created by his mother, Daisy, as she often sewed for her children and their friends for special activities. From left to right are (first row) Walter Aldridge, Alma Spradling, Bud Torbit, and Maxie Keys; (second row) Katherine Hilgendorf, Jim Askers, and two unidentified children. (NT.)

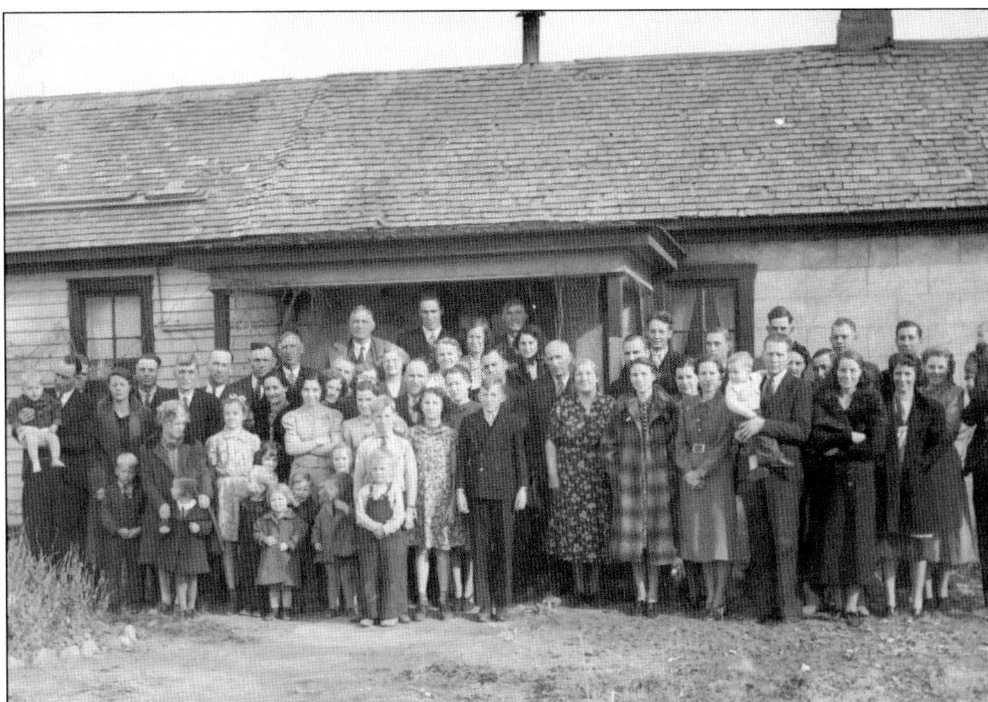

The Wilson family gathers for a reunion in 1935. The five Wilson brothers arrived in the valley after 1900. While Seward Wilson settled on a farm north of Fountain, brothers Morris, Orestas, John, and Joseph each took up acreage south of town. As their families grew, these reunions became large gatherings. Quite a few Fountain residents today claim lineage to one of these five brothers. (MB.)

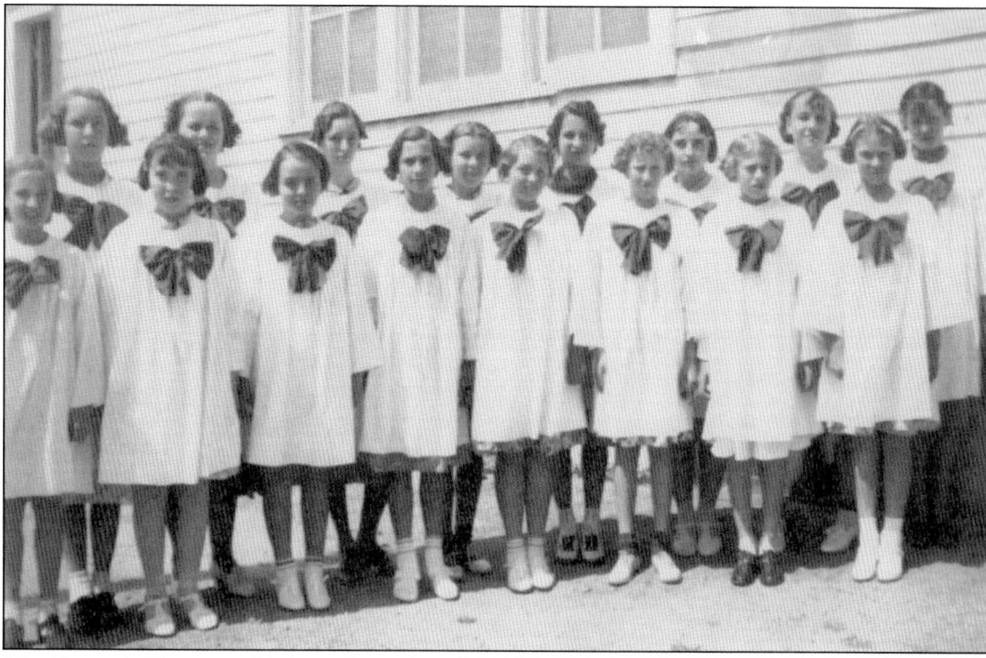

The Fountain Baptist girls' choir, dressed in their choir robes, gathers for this photograph in 1940. From left to right are (first row) Betty Sappington, Adelpha Adams, Bobby Christian, Muriel Sample, Margaret Christian, Betty Miller, Eileen Childs, and Nettie Foster; (second row) Twila Sawyer, Basetta Perriman, Rachel Sayers, Jeanie Wisdom, Phyllis Wilson, Mildred Adams, Ruth Perriman, and Katherine Hughes. (MC.)

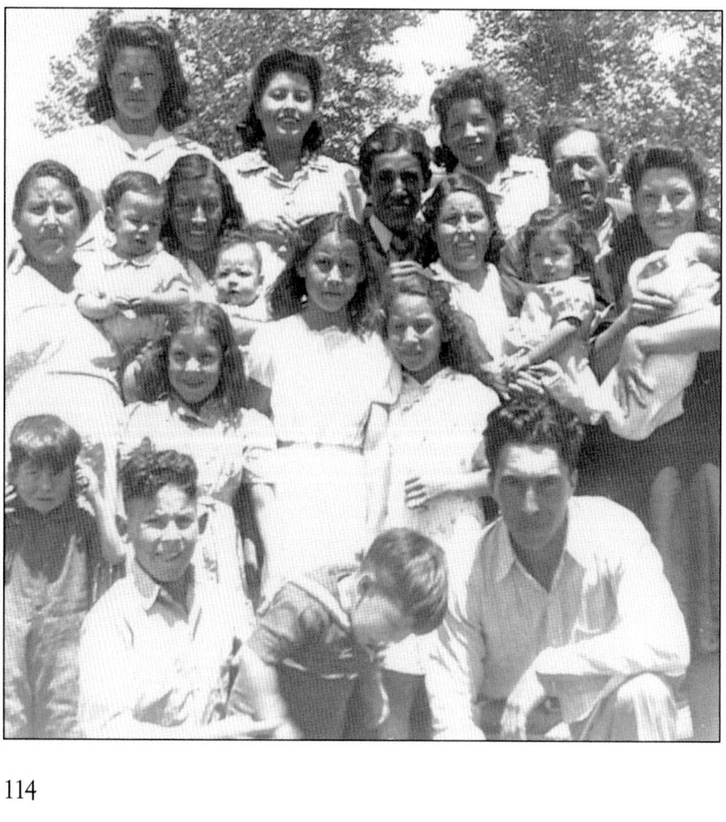

The Rivera family gathers for a reunion in 1942 at the Love ranch south of Fountain. From left to right are (first row) Damian Rivera, Floyd Martinez, and Moises Martinez; (second row) Avenico Rivera, Margaret Rivera, Virginia Rivera, and Bernice Rivera; (third row) Arcelina Rivera, Moises Martinez, Lucy Tafoya, Jesusa Tafoya, Albino Vasquez, Teresa Vasquez, Trinidad Vasquez, Juan Rivera, Genoveva Martinez, and Maria Martinez; (fourth row) Ida Rivera, Emma Rivera, and Macedonia Rivera. (MM.)

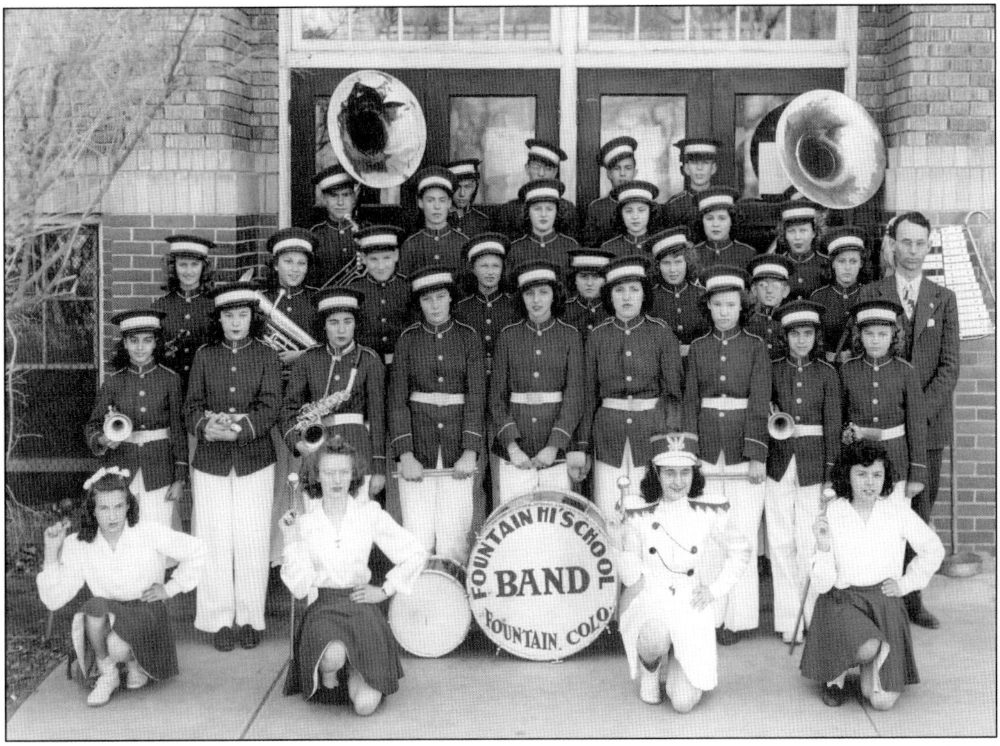

Outside the Fountain High School building, Donna Whalen (second from left in the second row) holds her baritone horn among musicians in the high school band during the 1946–1947 school year. Influenced by the Marine military uniform, the band wore white pants and red jackets and marched in Fountain's many parades. (DK.)

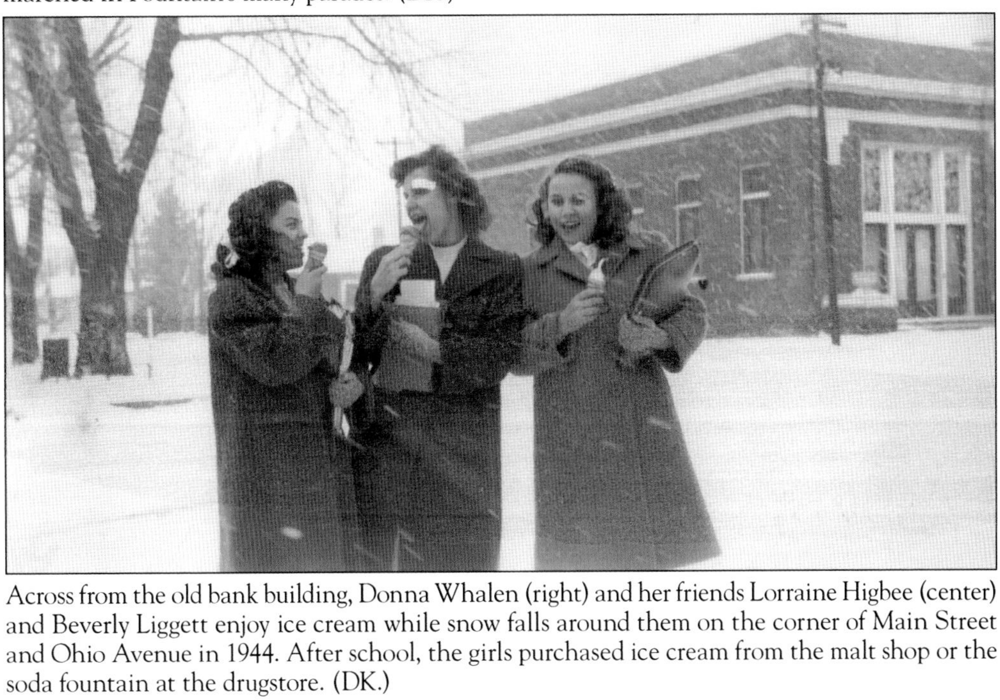
Across from the old bank building, Donna Whalen (right) and her friends Lorraine Higbee (center) and Beverly Liggett enjoy ice cream while snow falls around them on the corner of Main Street and Ohio Avenue in 1944. After school, the girls purchased ice cream from the malt shop or the soda fountain at the drugstore. (DK.)

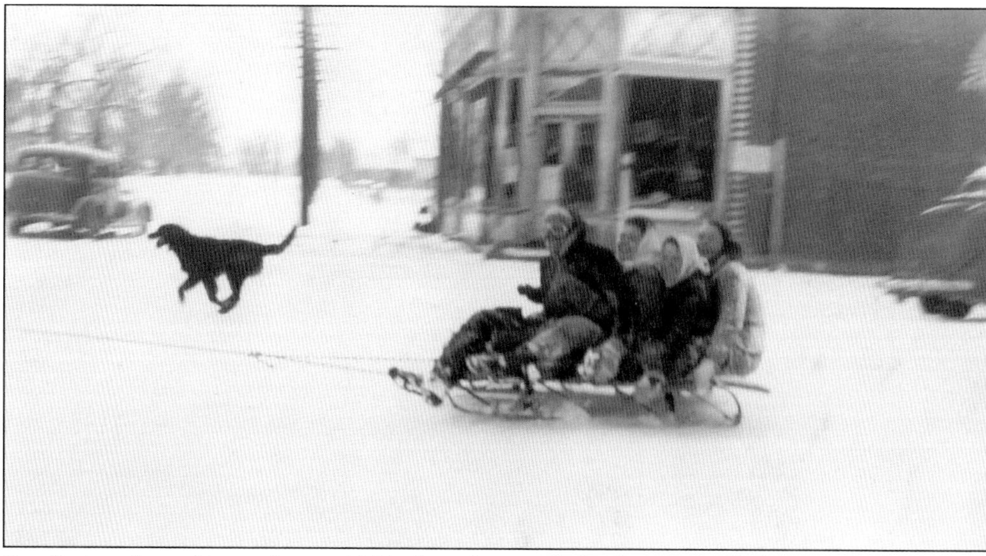

Bundled up for cold weather in 1944, these happy sled riders are pulled west on Main Street past the Woodmen Hall. A frisky dog races with them in the fresh snow. Wet snow makes great snowmen and snowballs, but dry snow is a good foundation for sledding. (DK.)

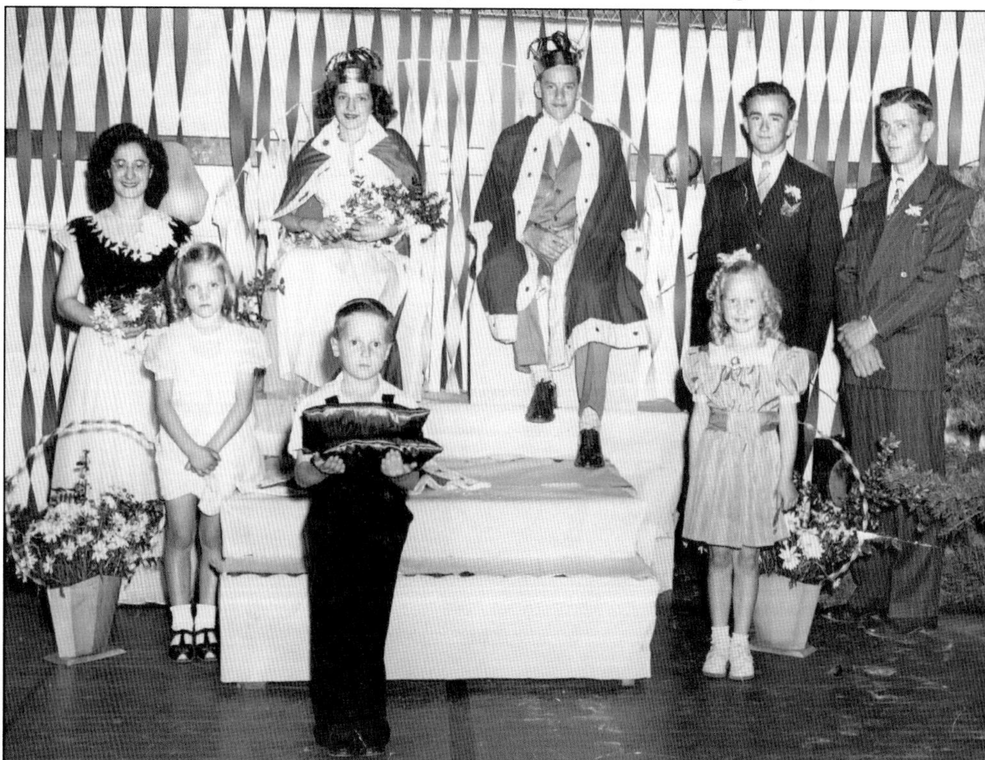

The Fountain High School homecoming king and queen of 1947 gather with their court. Fountain School alumni were invited to participate in homecoming activities, which included a parade, a ball game, and the election of the king and queen. There may also have been a barbecue and carnival games as well as a dance—an event that the whole town would have attended. (FVM.)

This float proceeds north on Main Street in what was probably a Colorado Day parade in the 1940s. The Ark antique store and residence peeks from the background. The sign on the float reads, "Fountaine qui Bouille—1691 A.D." The characters on the float standing among native plants and rocks represent the first people in the region: Indians, Spanish priests, and Mexican peasants. (FVM.)

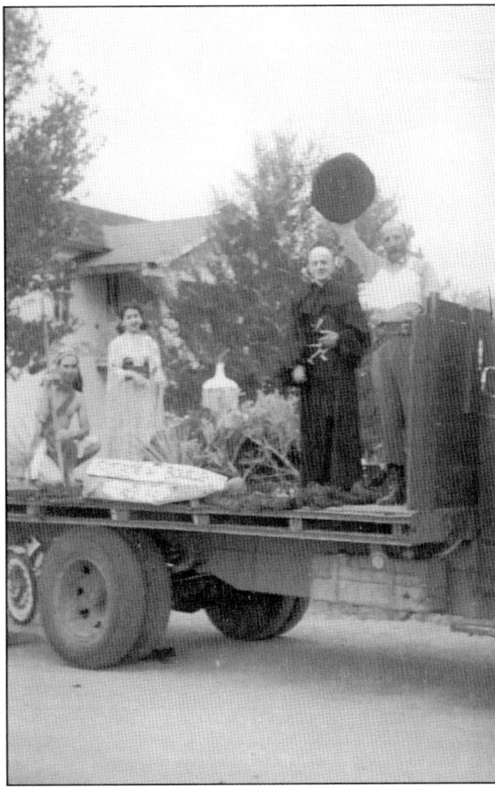

This float, created by the Home Demonstration Club, rolls by in a 1948 parade, promoting the message of harmony in the home. The organization provided a social outlet, as members taught other women how to get past the economic effects of the Depression and the war. They taught women how to garden, raise poultry, preserve food, prepare nutritious meals, sew clothing, and clean house, making them frugal homemakers. (FVM.)

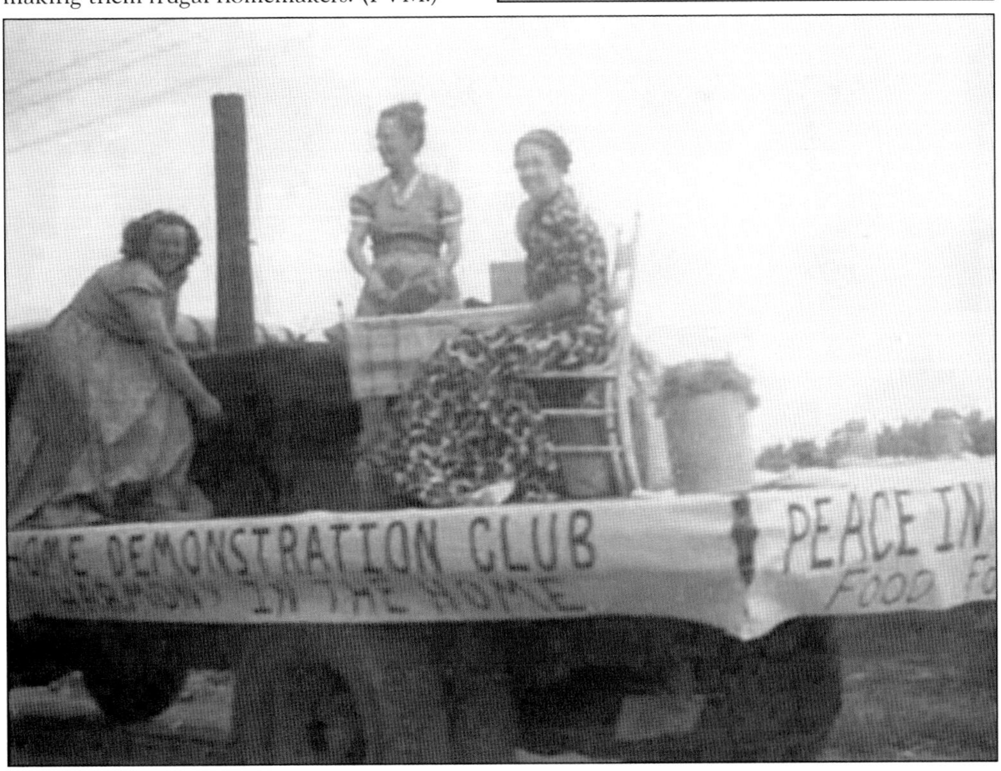

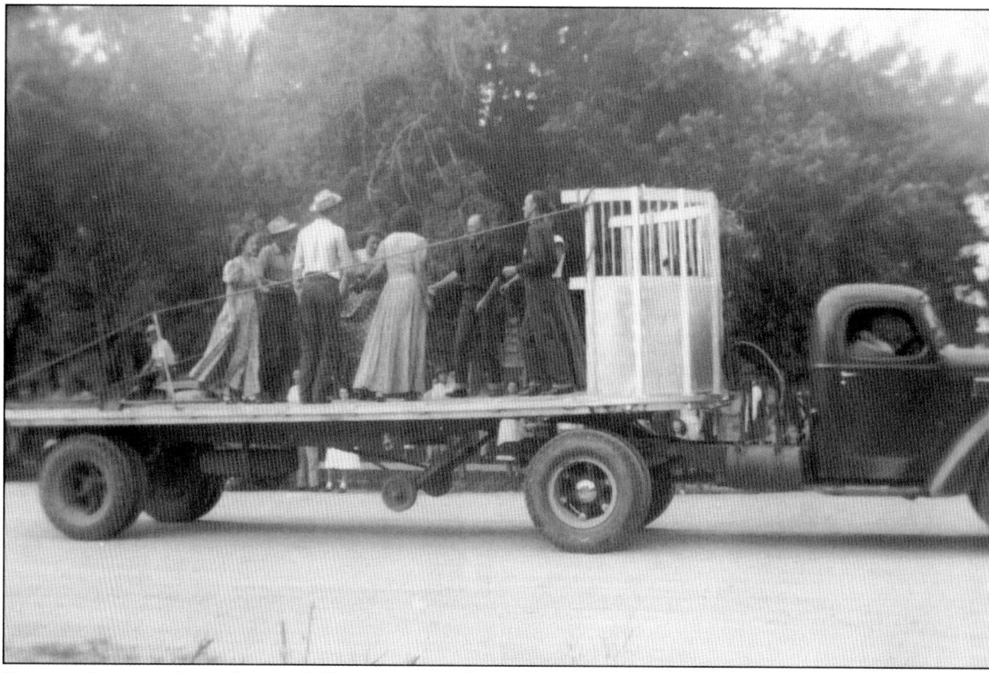

Square dancers do-si-do carefully on the back of this truck heading north on Main Street in a 1940s Colorado Day parade. August 1 was designated a state holiday in remembrance of Colorado's admittance into the Union in 1876, but the special day was discarded when Martin Luther King Jr. Day became a state holiday. (FVM.)

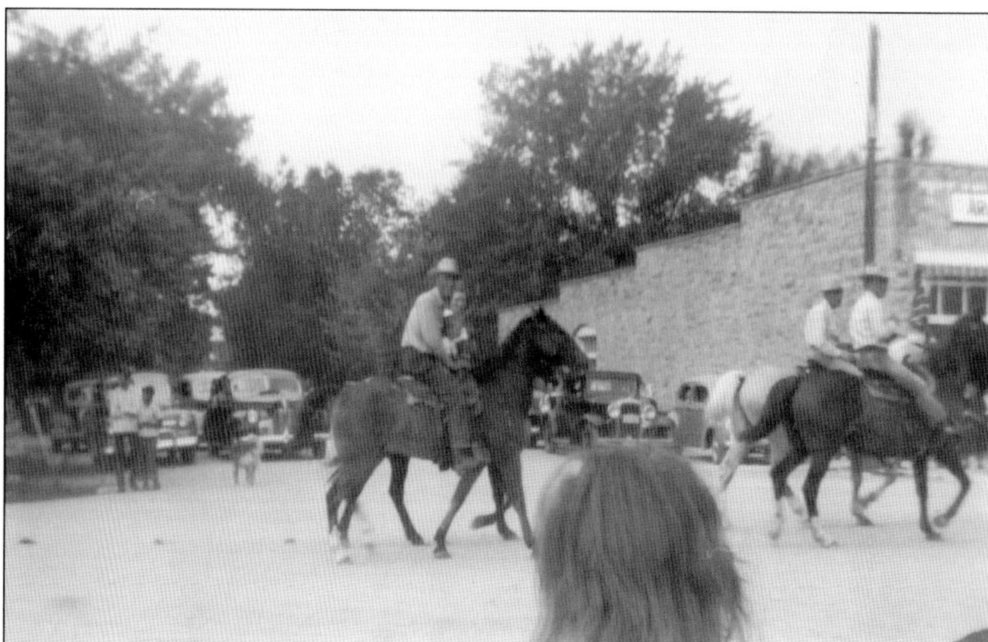

They say everyone loves a parade, and Fountain has had its fair share. In this 1940s Colorado Day parade, a group of horses and riders head north on Main Street past the Arapahoe Market. Spectators parked their cars on Missouri Avenue between the school and the store. (FVM.)

Bonificio "Bonnie" Cordova rides a donkey in a 1948 parade probably commemorating Colorado Day. Dressed in a brightly colored costume, he represents his ancestors and Mexico's prior ownership of and influence on the southwestern portion of the United States, including the Fountain Valley. The Ark stands in the background. (FVM.)

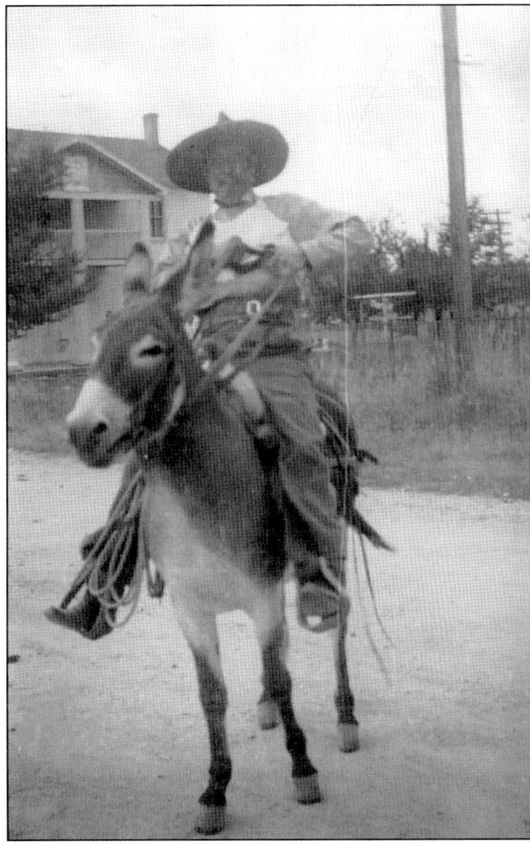

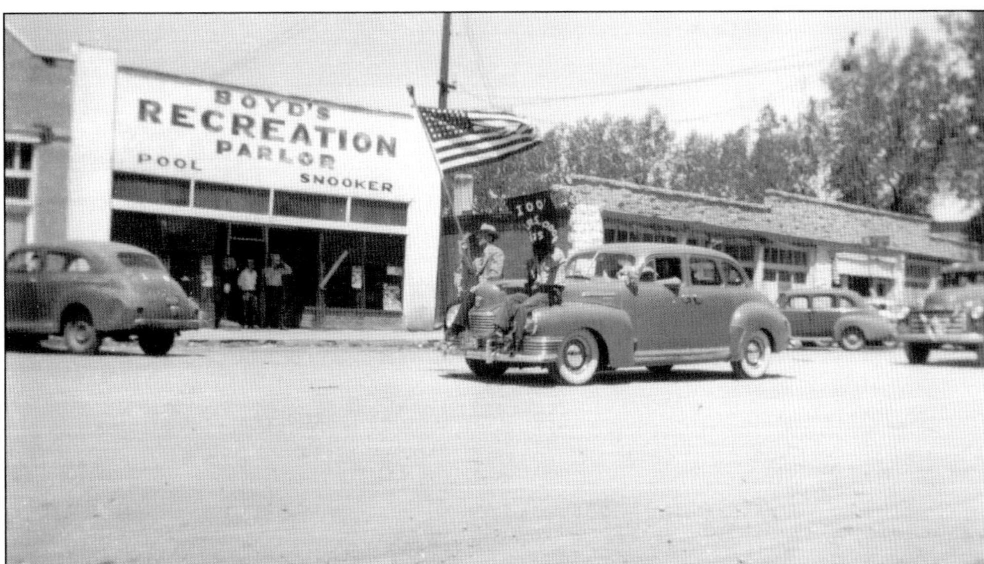

Two men from the Rogers Lodge of the Odd Fellows No. 175 ride the fenders of this car as it drives south on Main Street in a Memorial Day parade in the 1940s. The cemetery at the south edge of town marked the end of the parade route. Boyd's Recreation Parlor replaced the old theater in the 1940s, and movies were then shown in the Woodmen Hall. (DK.)

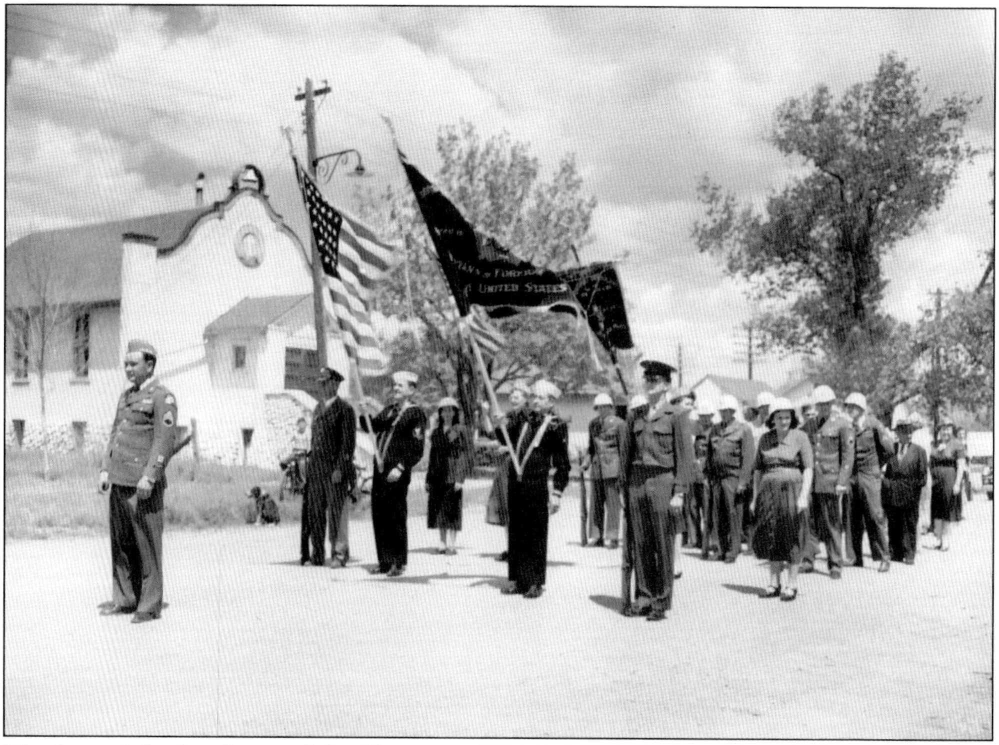

Members of the local post of the Veterans of Foreign Wars prepare to march in a Memorial Day parade in the 1940s. Behind them is the First Methodist Church with its rock skirting and Spanish Mission–style architecture. Built in 1912, the congregation met here until 1969, when it moved to a new building on Highway 85. The unique facade has been removed, and the building is now a Masonic lodge. (FVM.)

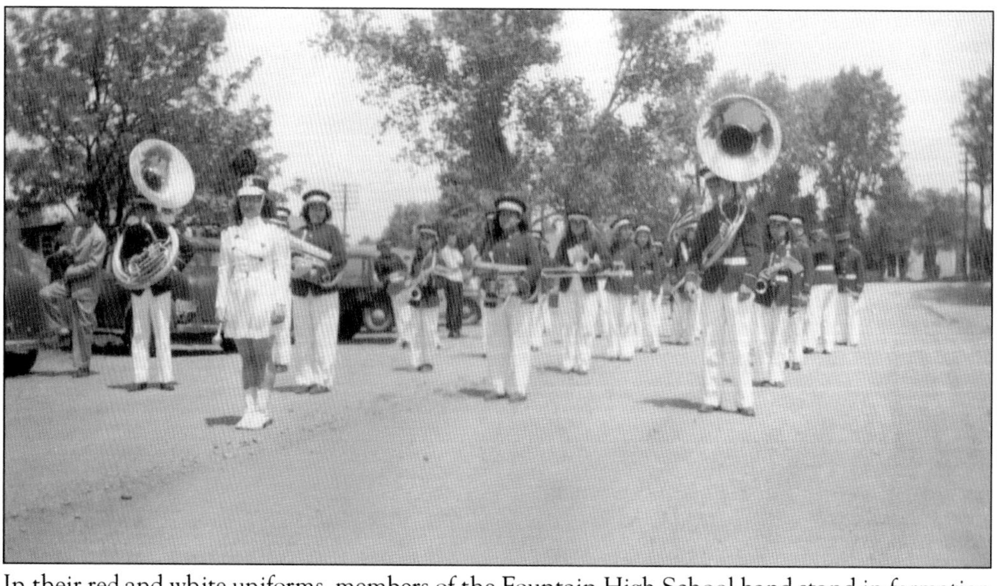

In their red and white uniforms, members of the Fountain High School band stand in formation at the north end of Main Street as they prepare to march in a Memorial Day parade in the mid-1940s. (FVM.)

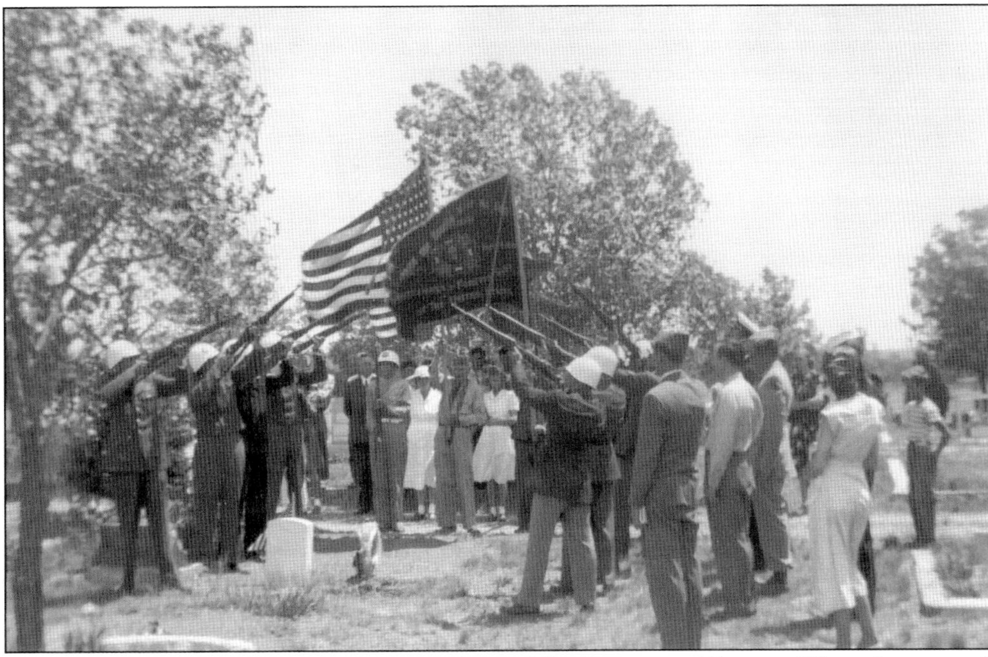

On this Memorial Day in the 1940s, members of the Veterans of Foreign Wars, the women's auxiliary, and observers gather around what appears to be a recent grave marked by a serviceman's monument at the Fairview Cemetery in Fountain. Alongside the country's flag flies the banner of the Fontaine Qui Bouille Post No. 6461. This post still functions today. (FVM.)

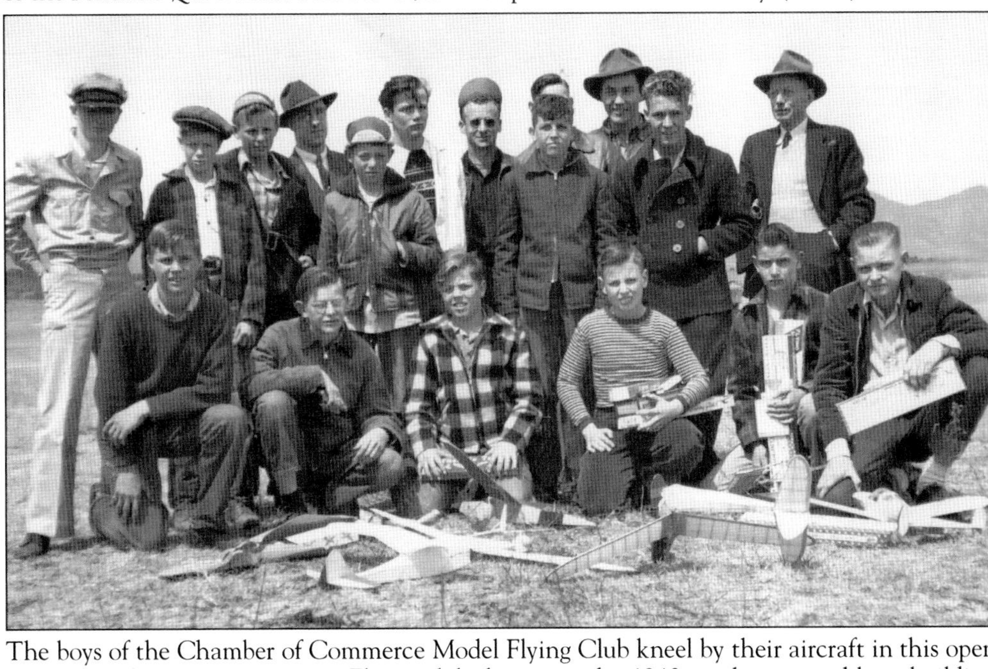

The boys of the Chamber of Commerce Model Flying Club kneel by their aircraft in this open field somewhere near Fountain. Flying clubs began in the 1940s with men and boys building and then entering their aircraft in competitions. The boys kneeling in the front row from left to right are Darrell Powell, Ronald Frauenhoff, Morris Singleton, Danny Martin, Eldon Ermel, and Jamie Chiddix. (FVM.)

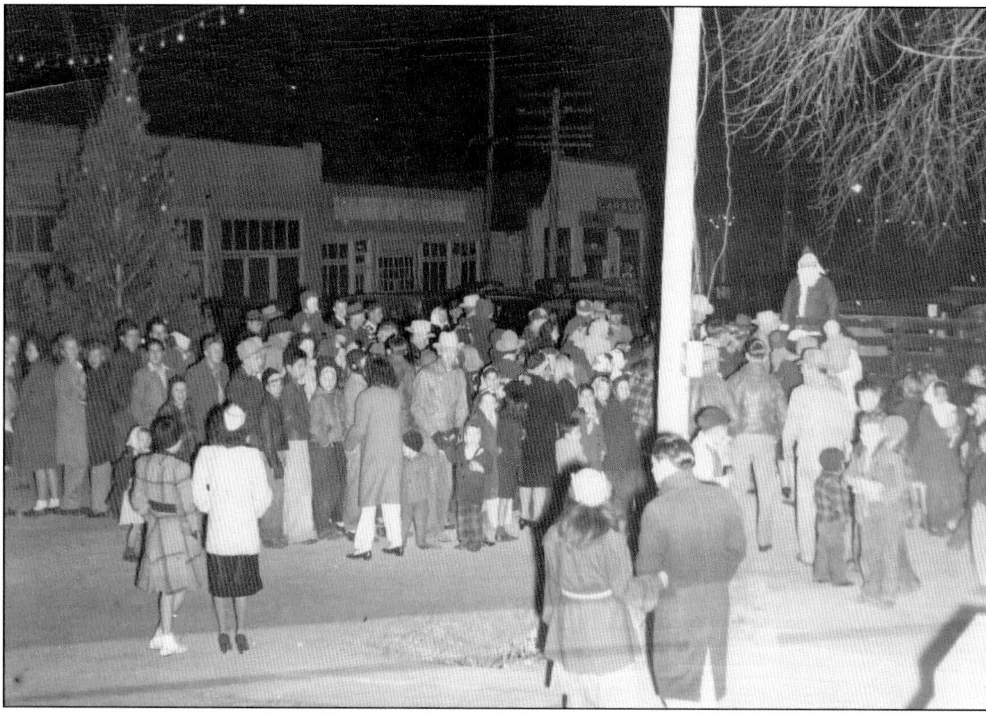

On this cold December evening sometime in the 1940s, the town congregates on South Main Street to visit with Santa Claus. The Square Deal Garage can be seen in the background on the other side of the street. Today, children still are delighted to see Santa Claus, and the town celebrates the season with the annual Cowboy Christmas at city hall. (FVM.)

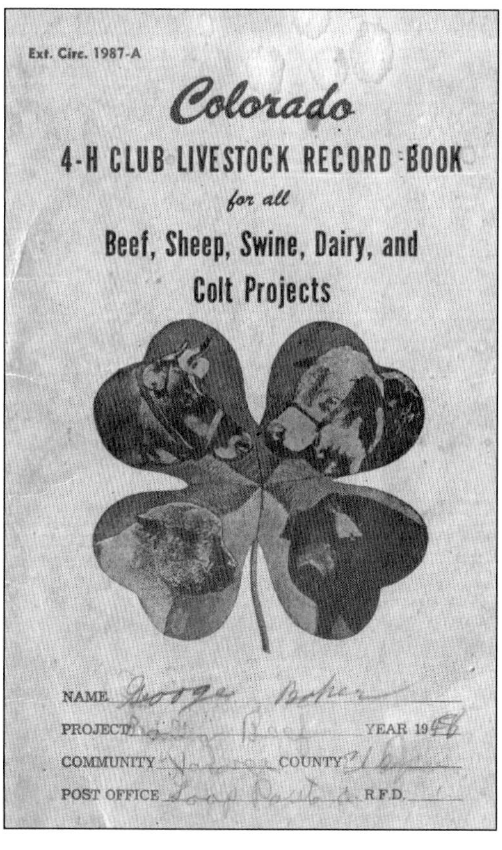

This livestock record book helped George Baker of the Hanover Producers 4-H Club keep track of his beef project in 1948. He raised a purebred Shorthorn and named her San-Juan Susanna. Baker was expected to groom and present her at stock shows. He also learned how to properly care for his heifer and keep records on her feeding costs and his profit when she was sold. (MB.)

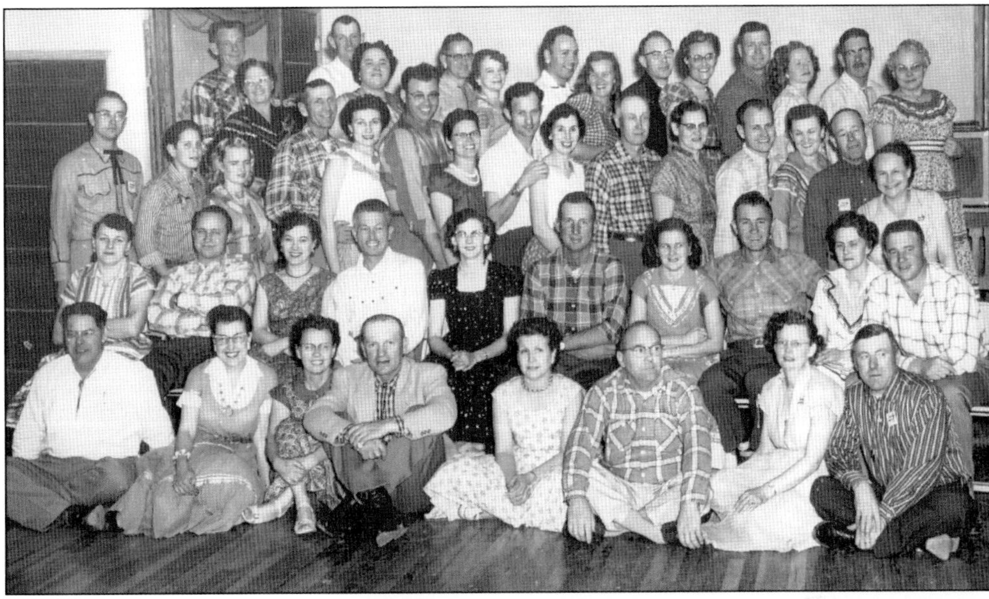

Pictured at the Community Hall is Fountain's Square Dance Club in the 1950s. Florence and John Metcalf are the second couple from the left in the first row. The next couple to the right is Eula and Walt Forman, and the third couple from the left in the second row is Mary and Wendell Sample. Square dancing, an American folk dance evolving from European traditional dances, provided a social outlet for husbands and wives. (FVM.)

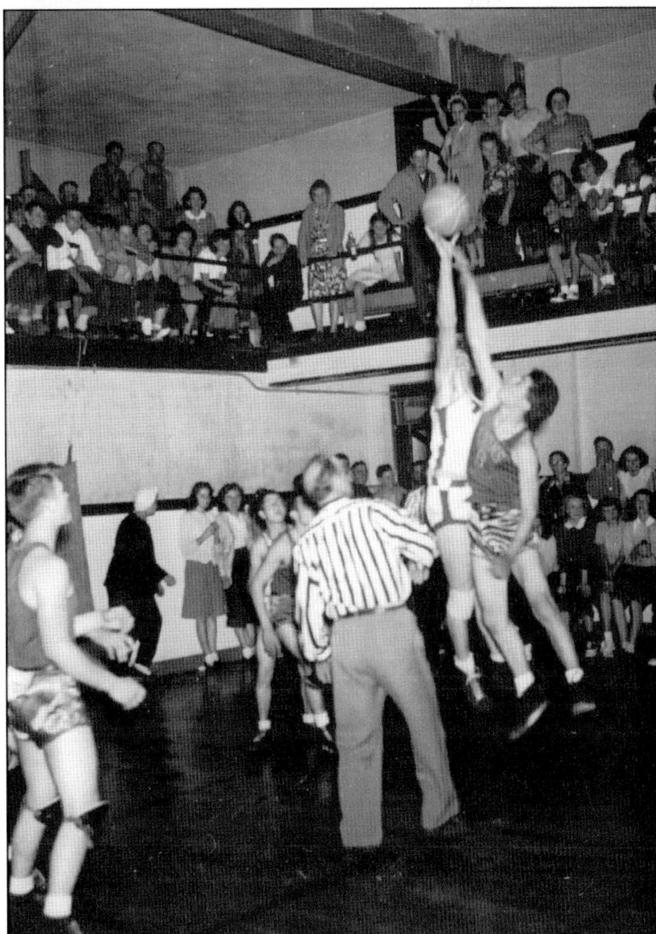

A Fountain High School basketball player keeps the ball away from his opponent during an exciting game in the 1950s. High school basketball was very popular in small towns, commonly attracting the town's support. Team players often became hometown heroes. (FVM.)

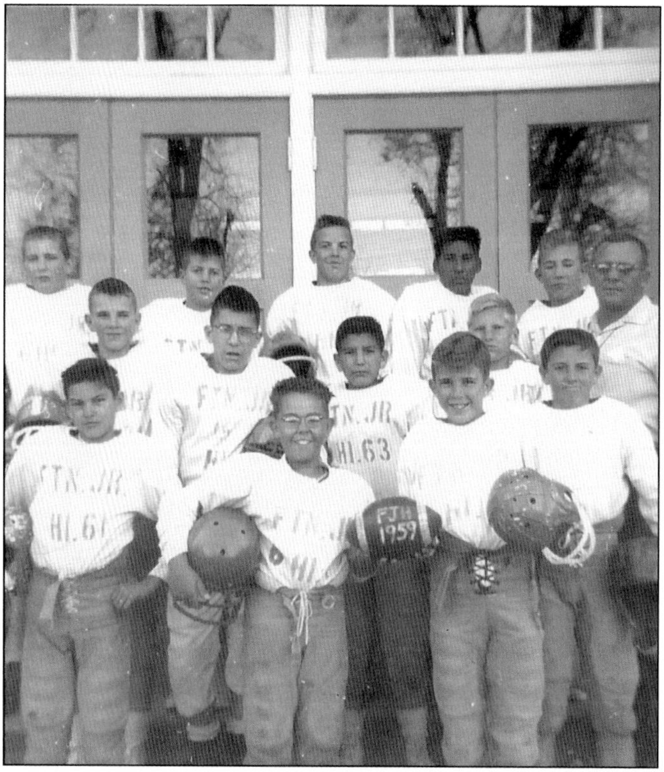

The Fountain Junior High School football team poses with Coach Campbell for this picture in 1959. Members of the team include Johnny Orcutt (second from left in the first row), Joey Martinez (second from left in second row), and David Arellano (fourth from left in the third row). (BA.)

Fountain High School's class of 1961 consisted of 52 seniors. Some of the children of Fort Carson soldiers attended Fountain schools and brought with them an ethnic diversity not yet experienced by the town. The elementary school built in Countryside subdivision, south of Fountain, is named for Orvey Jordahl, the high school principal pictured here. (MM.)

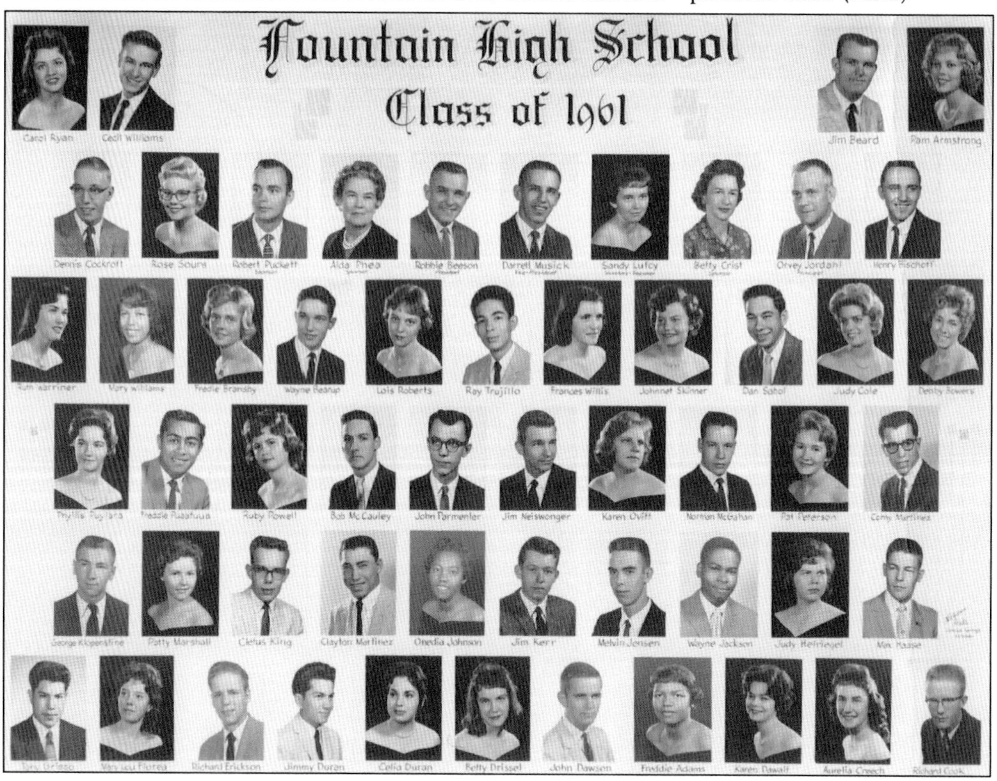

Children gather for an event on the grounds of the grade school in the 1960s. The school bell in the foreground was salvaged from the grade school when it was scheduled for demolition and placed on a plinth near the corner of Main Street and Missouri Avenue. It now hangs in the atrium of Aragon Elementary, the current school building in the block. (FVM.)

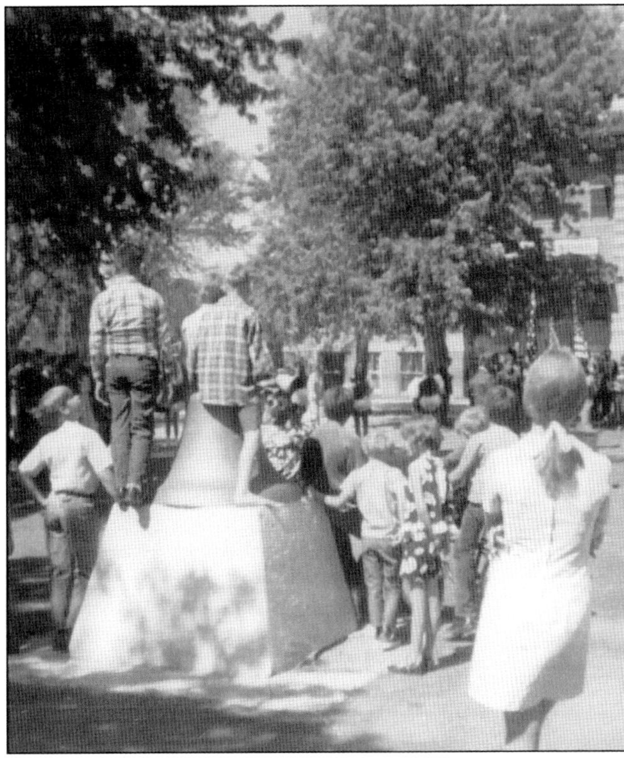

Carl Wiese rides his Morgan horse, Trooper, in the Fountain Fall Festival parade in about 1990. Wiese represents his hometown newspaper, the *Fountain Valley News*, which he cofounded with Fountain historian H. Kay Larson in 1958. Wiese was well thought of in his community and served his fellow citizens on numerous boards and committees. (FVN.)

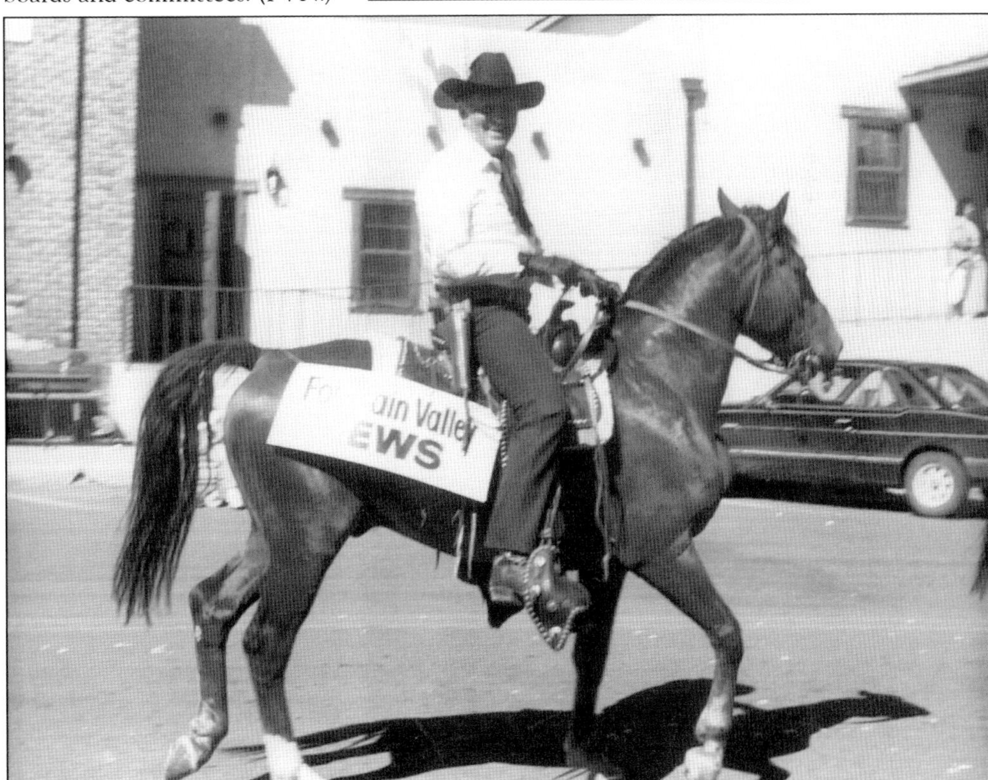

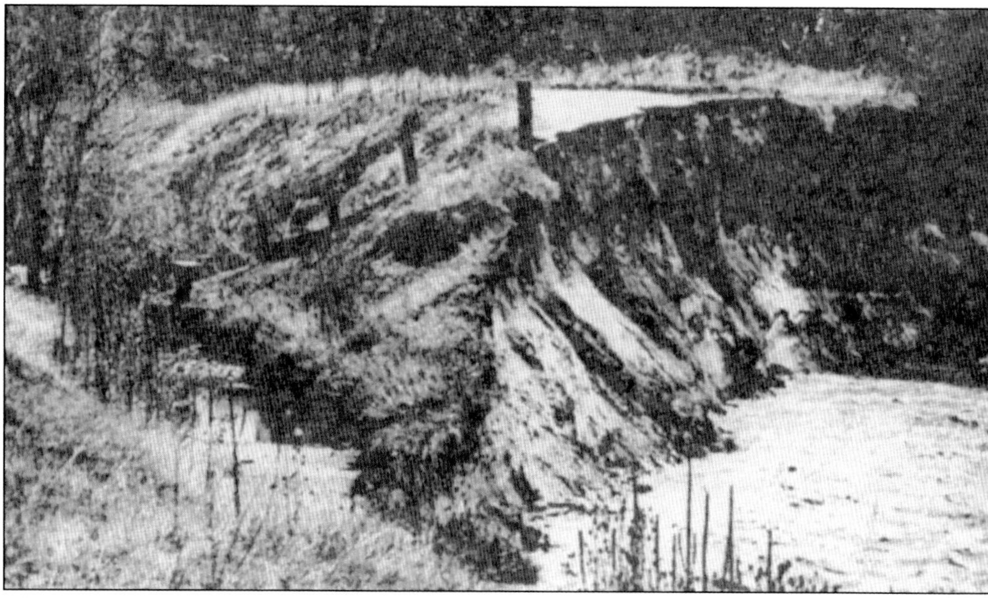

The 1999 flooding of Fountain Creek rendered this road impassible. Other memorable floods in the valley occurred in 1935 and 1965, with destruction of property and loss of lives. Fountain Creek and Jimmy Camp Creek (also known as Sand Creek) flow very quietly throughout most of the year, but heavy, seasonal rains cause the creeks to become raging torrents that churn away the banks, taking out trees and structures. (FVN.)

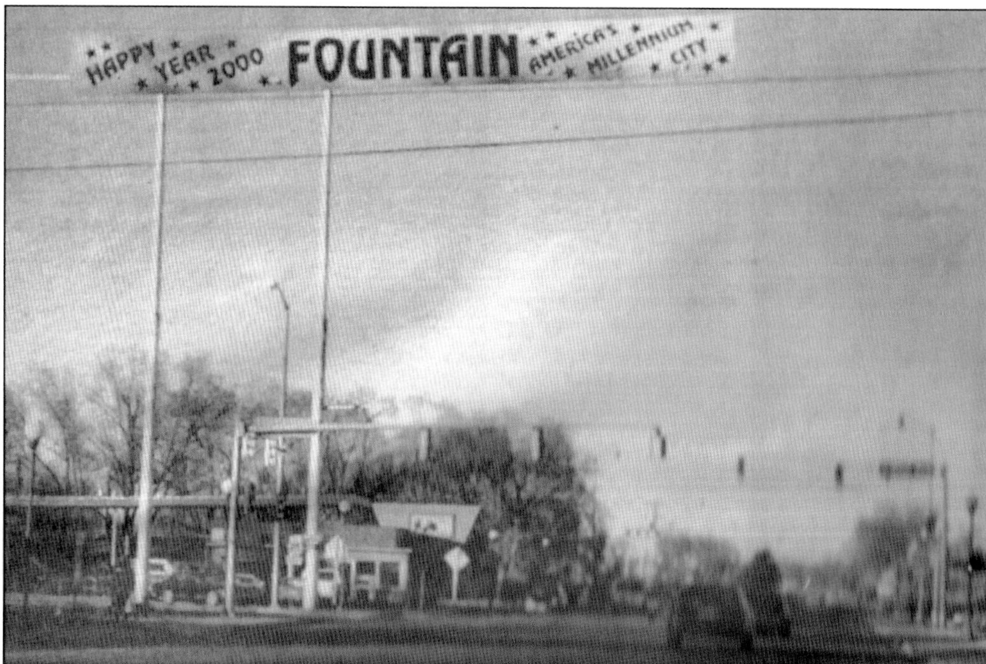

After interviewing many Fountain residents near the close of 1999, the *New York Times* magazine chose Fountain and neighboring Security-Widefield as the community that most matched the country as a whole with regards to population, growth, race, and income. Fountain was very pleased to be named America's Millennium City and raised this banner above the main thoroughfare. (FVN.)

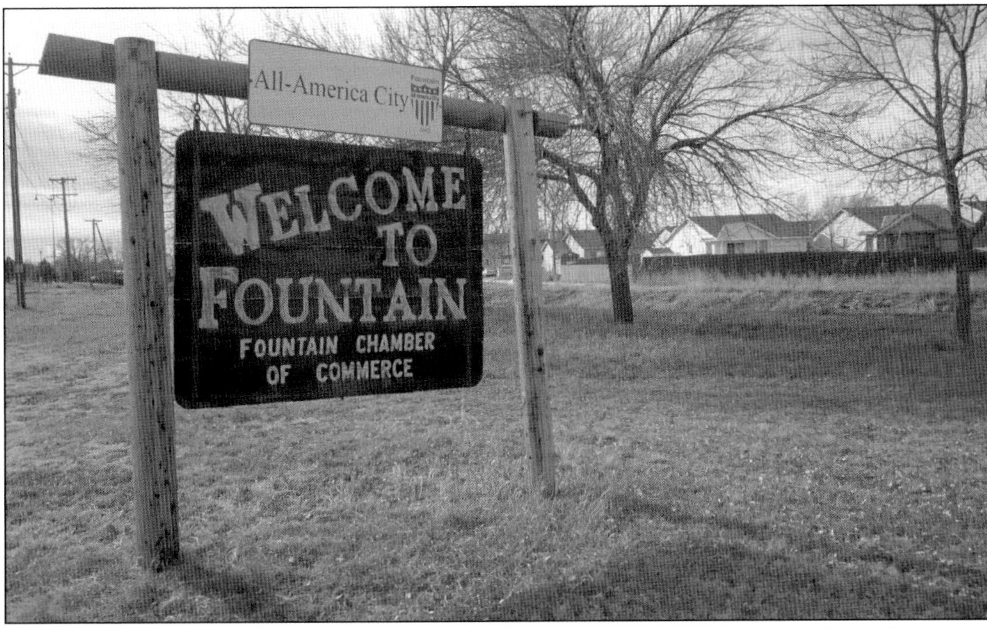

In 2002, Fountain was named one of the 10 best cities in the country at the 53rd annual award ceremony in Kansas City, when the National Civic League recognized civic excellence in "communities that best exemplify the spirit of citizen grassroots involvement and cross-sector collaborative problem solving." To compete for this award, Fountain sent a 45-member delegation consisting of youths, government officials, neighborhood activists, business leaders, and volunteers. (ATH.)

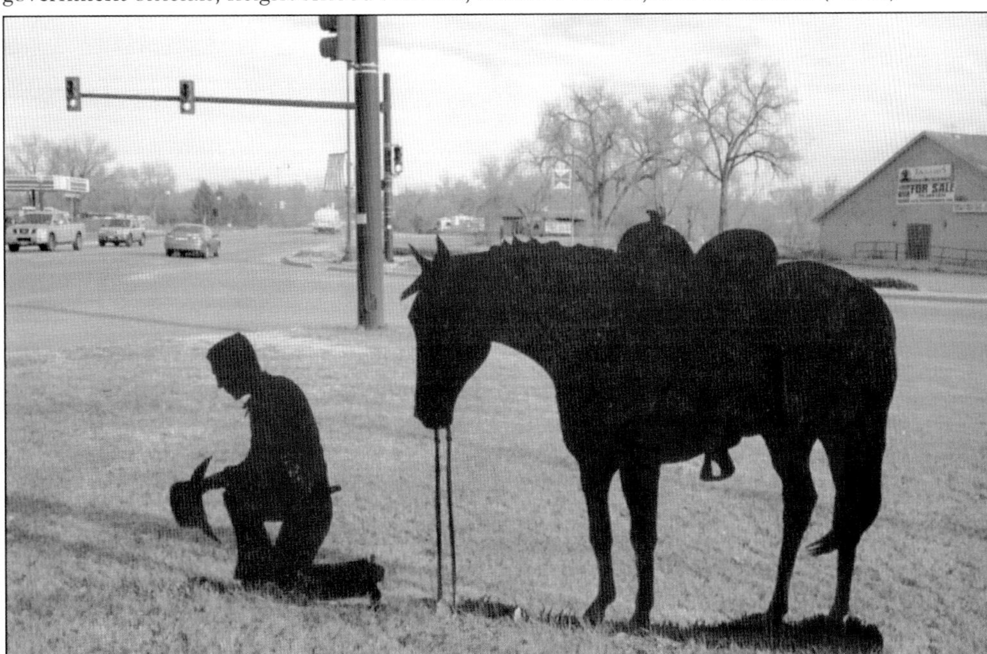

Anyone entering Fountain from South Santa Fe Avenue, also known as Highway 85, is met by this depiction of a praying cowboy. He reminds all residents and visitors that Fountain's heritage and legacy are rich in farming, ranching, and religious tradition. (ATH.)

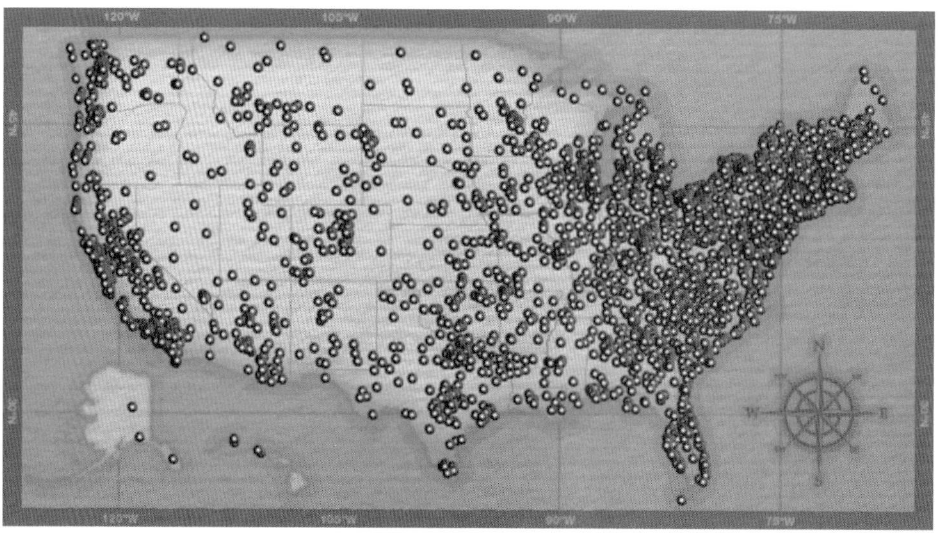